STATE, PRIVATE ENTERPRISE, AND ECONOMIC CHANGE IN EGYPT, 1918-1952

PRINCETON STUDIES ON THE NEAR EAST

STATE, PRIVATE ENTERPRISE, AND ECONOMIC CHANGE IN EGYPT, 1918-1952

ROBERT L. TIGNOR

PRINCETON UNIVERSITY PRESS
PRINCETON, NEW JERSEY

Library of Congress Cataloging in Publication Data
will be found on the last printed page of this book
ISBN 0-691-05416-9

This book has been composed in Linotron Baskerville

Clothbound editions of Princeton University Press books
are printed on acid-free paper, and binding materials
are chosen for strength and durability.
Paperbacks, while satisfactory for personal collections,
are not usually suitable for library rebinding.

Printed in the United States of America by
Princeton University Press
Princeton, New Jersey

TO LAURA, JEFFREY, AND SANDRA

CONTENTS

LIST OF TABLES

LIST OF FIGURES

PREFACE

Hundreds of millions of people live in poverty, most of them in Asia, Africa, and Latin America. The World Bank estimates that 800 million people live below a so-called poverty line, unable to provide themselves with adequate food, shelter, clothing, education, and medical attention. How these people and their societies are to improve the quality of their lives is problematic when they are not sure why they are poor. Are their problems a consequence of deficiencies within their own societies (educational, entrepreneurial, or political) and hence likely to be resolved by internal reforms? Or do they exist because of the strength and inhospitality of the international economic order, created in large measure by the industrialized societies of Western Europe and North America to favor their populations at the expense of the rest of the world? The experience of Egypt, a country with longstanding contacts with Europe and many modernizing phases, suggests answers to these questions. An intriguing chapter in the Egyptian story is the capitalist experiment carried out between 1918 and 1952, and that is the subject of this study.

My debts to others for their assistance during the research for and writing of this book are many. In particular, I want to mention those people whose interventions were timely and substantive. In order to deepen my knowledge of the bourgeoisie, I interviewed men and women, from foreign and Egyptian families, who were influential in this period. I learned much about the social life of the *haute* bourgeoisie and enjoyed unparalleled hospitality. I record my appreciation to all of them. Their names are listed in the last section of the bibliography.

A number of scholar-friends were kind enough to read

drafts and to make helpful suggestions. I would like to express my gratitude to Jerome Blum, L. Carl Brown, Charles Issawi, Arno J. Mayer, and Roger Owen. Each of them at one time or another read the entire manuscript. The many revisions which their comments necessitated had to be typed with speed and accuracy. That Helen Wright did, and I thank her as well.

Research cannot thrive without the assistance of scholarly institutions and organizations, and I availed myself of the help of many. I am grateful to numerous individuals associated with the Department of History, the Center of International Studies, and the Research Program in Development Studies at Princeton University. Abroad, I profited from affiliations with the American University in Cairo and the American Research Center in Egypt. The latter awarded me a fellowship for 1979, and the U. S. Department of Health, Education, and Welfare provided one for the academic year 1974–1975.

There is a final group without whose support little could have been achieved. A wife and three children saw their own plans interrupted more than they would have wanted. But their enjoyment of the adventure and their love of Egypt helped to sustain my enthusiasm for the work. I affectionately dedicate this book to my children.

A Note on Arabic Transliteration

I have used diacritical marks in transliterating Arabic only to represent the *ayn* as ' and the *hamza* as '.

Abbreviations

FEA   French Embassy Archives, Cairo
FO   Foreign Office
HCSP *House of Commons Sessional Papers*
PRO   Public Record Office, London
USNA   United States National Archives, Washington

STATE, PRIVATE ENTERPRISE,
AND ECONOMIC CHANGE
IN EGYPT, 1918-1952

INTRODUCTION

Perhaps the most consistent theme in the modern history of Egypt has been its relentless and often frustrating quest for modernity. Ever since the French troops of Napoleon revealed in a stark fashion the military weakness of the Mamluk forces, the rulers of Egypt, whether monarchs, landed aristocrats, or military leaders, have sought to overcome their alleged backwardness and to close the economic, material, and military gaps that separated them from the West.

The quest has taken many forms, from Muhammad ʿAli's forced modernization to Ismaʿil's imitative Westernization, Nasser's socialism (or state capitalism, if one prefers), and Sadat's *infitah* (open door) capitalism. Most of the modernizing campaigns in recent Egyptian history have been dominated by the state. However, between 1918 and 1952, Egyptian leaders endeavored to find sources of modernizing creativity other than the state (though even in this period the state continued to be important), and to use resources of private wealth (land and local industrial and commercial capital) to diversify the economy, create a vibrant and autonomous Egyptian capitalism, and fashion an independent middle class. This study assesses that effort.

In many ways, Egypt's interwar record serves as an instructive case study of capitalist development in the third world. To be sure, Egyptians did not draw up detailed economic blueprints or elaborate five-year plans, as many newly independent states did in the 1950s and 1960s. But the Egyptian approach to economic development was not very dissimilar, for example, from that of Kenya, the Ivory Coast, or Nigeria in the 1960s. In those countries, the elites who had achieved independence tried to effect economic transformation through the judicious use of foreign capital and foreign technical assistance, while at the same time encouraging the formation and growth of indigenous bourgeoisies. So did the Egyptians, and thus, the Egyptian experience, despite certain unique characteristics, can illuminate the possibilities and pitfalls that states are likely to face in utilizing such a method.

In many ways, Egypt was a decolonizing society during those years, though the pace of decolonization was in no way comparable to that which occurred in tropical Africa, for example, in the 1950s. Although not yet a sovereign state, the country had been gaining increased political autonomy since the end of World War I. In 1922, the British unilaterally proclaimed the country independent (although London reserved rights over defense, imperial communications, the Sudan, and foreign interests). The British encouraged the Egyptians to write a constitution and to develop parliamentary institutions. In 1936, an Anglo-Egyptian treaty allowed further measures of autonomy and paved the way for the abolition of the Capitulations, the special judicial and other privileges enjoyed by foreigners in Egypt. During this time, business and political leaders sought to loosen overseas economic controls by diversifying the economy and promoting indigenous industrial development.

Dependency theorists, as well as neo-Marxists, are scornful of the supposed independence of third-world countries and hold Western capitalism responsible for much of the backwardness of the third world. These critics contend that, while formal political independence was achieved, the economic ties of subordination and peripheralization remained unaltered. Indeed, it has been argued that formal colonialism was only a precursor—an "avatar"—of imperialism (or neocolonialism) and that the colonial period succeeded in binding the third world inextricably to the first as exporters of raw materials and importers of capital, technical assistance, and manufactures. Moreover, the argument runs, the elites created in the colonial period, compradors for Western capitalism, once in place sought to preserve the economic status quo, even though they were also anxious to gain a modicum of political power. Since the imperial powers had little to fear socially and economically from these elites and much to fear from their alienated and more radical but still weakly organized critics, they granted independence in the confidence that the main economic structures would not be fundamentally transformed.

The contention in this study, however, is that the local Egyptian elites—especially the emergent industrial and commercial bourgeoisie—were far from the parasitical groups so vividly described in Frantz Fanon's *Wretched of the Earth*. Though many of its members did spring from comprador backgrounds (as agents of metropolitan financial and trading firms), they often used their wealth and business expertise to forge new economic institutions, sometimes in conflict with the most solidly entrenched metropolitan bodies.

The main force for far-reaching economic change between 1918 and 1952 proved to be this local industrial and commercial bourgeoisie. Though this group never became large and its members never achieved great political power (largely because most of them were foreigners living in Egypt), they articulated a vision of a transformed Egyptian economy after World War I and then endeavored to implement a program to bring it into being.

The emergent bourgeoisie was composed of two fairly distinct elements. The predominant group was a foreign business elite residing in Egypt. Many of its leaders had been agents of large European financial and trading firms. The other wing was the native-born Egyptian business elite. Although the two segments shared a vision of an Egyptian economy independent of European control, their differences often outweighed their similarities and made cooperation difficult. Foreigners enjoyed extraordinary privileges in the form of the Capitulations and the Mixed Tribunals. These were resented by most Egyptians, especially Egyptian businessmen who felt that the privileges gave the foreign businessman an unfair advantage.

The two groups also tended to have different sources of capital accumulation. Foreign residents emerged from the comprador-metropolitan nexus and always endeavored to maintain close ties with overseas capital. Although some Egyptian entrepreneurs followed the same route to economic success (Ahmad 'Abbud being an outstanding example), the Egyptian elite mostly arose from the land. Some of the leading entrepreneurs had come from large landholding families themselves (Ahmad Farghali, Amin Yahya, the Lawzis, and 'Ali Islam) and had used agricultural profits to finance industrial and commercial experiments. Others—most notably Tal'at Harb—had commenced their business careers by seeking the favor and monetary support of landed magnates. Egyptian businessmen were likely to be caught up in nationalist enthusiasm and even to try to use nationalist sentiments to build support for their businesses. The foreigners, on the other hand, were fearful of radical nationalism, with its threats to their privileged status. Nor should the differences arising from nationality, way of life, and religion be ignored. The wealthy members of the foreign communities stressed their attachment to European culture and made little effort to hide their contempt for the Egyptian, Arab, and Muslim heritage of the country.

In the prevailing dependency paradigm, domestic third world bourgeoisies are seen as parasitical and weak, unable to establish independent bases for capital accumulation. Foreign residential business elites are usually described as appendages of more powerful metropolitan interests and hence both uninterested in and incapable of independent economic action. Samir Amin, for instance, contends that there is always in the colonial and neocolonial world that hidden and unseen actor, the great metropolitan bourgeoisie, which allows local business elites to move only into those areas of little interest to the metropole.[1]

Most accounts of the economic history of Egypt have

---

[1] Samir Amin, *Accumulation on a World Scale*, vol. 1, p. 177.

tended to focus on Egyptian entrepreneurs. Insofar as the foreign businessman has entered into the picture, he has been portrayed as removed from Egyptian society, living in privileged Europeanized enclaves (all of which was true) and serving the interests of overseas capital. In fact, however, although some of these foreign businessmen were compradors (as were some Egyptian businessmen), many others were forces for far-reaching structural social and economic change. Far from supporting the economic status quo, they worked aggressively for its alteration.

The time frame of this study is 1918 to 1952. Although the roots of the bourgeoisie can be traced to the decades before World War I, this group began to crystallize after the war. During the flurry of nationalist activities between 1918 and 1924, bourgeois ideologues articulated their vision of a transformed, industrialized Egyptian economy. New economic organizations, destined to spearhead change, also appeared, most notably the Egyptian Federation of Industries and Bank Misr.

The concluding date of 1952 is not so clear-cut. The Nasser military faction came to power in that year and brought an end to Egypt's parliamentary regime, but it did endeavor to reinvigorate the industrial bourgeoisie. Its patience, however, proved short-lived. Within three months of their assumption of power, the military leaders initiated a land reform, and while this measure was partly justified on the ground that it would facilitate the transfer of capital from the agrarian to the industrial sector, the assault on the sanctity of private property was a cause for alarm to industrial and commercial leaders. Very soon thereafter, the military turned against the industrial elite, nationalizing the assets of British and French nationals and Jews in the aftermath of the British-French-Israeli invasion of the country in 1956. Belgian holdings were nationalized in 1960, following the turmoil in the Congo. In the early 1960s, the military government dispossessed the Egyptian *grande* bourgeoisie, taking over almost all large-scale industrial and commercial concerns. Although 1952 may not have been decisive in some respects, it initiated a series of changes that undercut the power of the bourgeoisie.

The bourgeoisie did not spring full-blown into existence after the war, and its rise was a troubled one. During some periods its interests were in the ascendant (though these occasions were rare and usually occurred only when the interests of the bourgeoisie and the large landholders could be merged). But it struggled with larger, more solidly entrenched groups for attention. The emergence of the bourgeoisie is best seen in terms of shifting alliances and conflicts within the ruling elite. Besides the bourgeoisie, divided as it was into its two wings, there were four main groups that were directly involved in major political and economic questions and that as a consequence had decision-making powers. There was overlap between these groups, but they tended to represent somewhat different political and economic interests and to have different supporting constituencies (see figure 1). It was the bargaining among them that caused the story of Egypt to proceed along the route that it took.

In the period before World War I, three groups dominated: the British political and military establishment in Egypt; metropolitan capital; and the Egyptian landed oligarchy. Although some would portray the colonial rulers as the executive arm of metropolitan capitalism, in Egypt they had a much larger and more independent role to play. Egypt was of immeasurable strategic value to imperial Britain. The British political establishment in Egypt was eager to secure the tranquility of the Egyptian population lest national uprisings, like that which had occurred under Ahmad 'Urabi, jeopardize Britain's military and political hold. The political establishment was even willing to sacrifice the interests of metropolitan capital to these goals, and they did so on more than a few occasions.

Metropolitan capital was a particularly diverse and potentially fragmented group. Many different nationalities were represented. Its concerns in Egypt were centered on the receipt of interest payments on Egypt's large public

Figure I.1

The Egyptian Ruling Elite, 1918-1952

Dominant Elements	Constituent Groups	Supporting Elements in Egypt
British political-military establishment in Egypt	Embassy, British officials in the Egyptian government, and 12,000-man British army stationed in Egypt	
Metropolitan capital (finance, land, and foreign trade)	Belgian (Banque Belge Internationale en Égypte) French (Suez Canal Company, Sugar Company, Crédit Lyonnais, and Crédit Foncier Égyptien) British (National Bank of Egypt, Barclays Bank, DCO,* Anglo-Egyptian Oil Fields) Greek (Export-import families like Choremi, Benachi)	Local agents in Egypt drawn from foreign communities
Landed oligarchy	12,000 landowners with at least 50 feddans, but 2,000 big families	Smaller indebted peasants
Domestic bourgeoisie	Foreign elite (drawn overwhelmingly from local agents in #2) Egyptian elite (close ties with #3)	
National parties, mainly Wafd	Landed and professional classes (bureaucrats, educators)	Urban population

*Dominion, Commonwealth, and Overseas — the Barclays Bank enterprise for foreign operations.

debt and on banking, foreign trade, and land mortgaging and land development. Its members were also involved in large-scale construction projects for harnessing the Nile and accelerating the spread of perennial irrigation systems. Before World War I, metropolitan economic interests were administered from Europe. The leading conglomerates included Europe's big lending houses (Rothschild and others), the great European banks that had established branches in Egypt or had interests there (Crédit Lyonnais, the Ionian Bank, and the Comptoir Nationale d'Escompte), and the large European financial holding companies, like the Société Générale de Belgigue.

As these Egyptian financial and commercial interests grew, metropolitan capital came to depend on a local commercial elite, drawn primarily from persons of business talent in the expanding foreign communities. It also became common for the larger foreign firms, such as the Sugar Company, the Crédit Foncier Égyptien, and the National Bank of Egypt, to send out from Europe specially chosen managing directors. These persons often became the chief representatives of their country's financial interests in Egypt.

The third group consisted of the large landowners. The royal family must be included among them, since it was far and away the largest landowning unit in the country. Approximately 12,000 families, each owning fifty feddans or more (one feddan = 1.038 acres), possessed 40 percent of all of Egypt's cultivated area. In fact, most of the power of this group was wielded by an even smaller inner core, those who possessed estates of 200 feddans or more. There were less than 2,000 of the latter when Nasser carried out his first agrarian reform measure in 1952. They had exercised inordinate political power during the interwar years.

A new political group appeared after World War I, although its roots can be traced back to the 1890s and 1900s. This was the nationalists, as represented by Egypt's major populist party, the Wafd. The Wafd drew its support from landowners, professional classes, and educated urban dwellers. The other political parties which came into ex-

istence at the same time tended to represent much nar-
rower interests, such as the king, cliques of landed grandees, and perhaps in the 1940s the Egyptian bourgeoisie
(through the Sa'dist party).

Another element emerging in a very tenuous form after
World War I was a domestic bourgeoisie. Its members were
at first drawn overwhelmingly from the foreign populations, although there was even at that time an Egyptian
wing. Despite the fact that this fragment remained small
and was troubled by mistrust, and even some hostility, between its foreign and native-born wings, its influence in
decision-making circles was very strong. This was so because of the forceful way in which it first articulated a vision
of a transformed Egypt.

The impetus for change during these years tended to
come from the Egyptian-based groups. The landed oligarchs wanted to seize political control from the British.
While most of them confined their economic interests to
cultivation and the export of cotton, they backed programs,
like state purchasing of cotton and the role of Bank Misr
in the marketing and export of cotton, which increased
Egyptian participation in the country's agricultural, export-
oriented economy. The Wafd was narrowly focused on political issues throughout much of the period. It was preoccupied with realizing the goal of *al-Istiqlal al-Tamm* (complete independence), which most of its members interpreted
as the withdrawal of British troops from Egyptian soil and
the political unification of Egypt and the Sudan. It was only
in the late 1930s and then immediately after World War
II that its populist orientation and the rising social discontent caused the party to address socioeconomic questions
forcefully.

The domestic bourgeoisie, possessing the most dynamic
economic perspectives, endeavored to establish new industries and new financial and commercial institutions. They
created pressure groups and sought to bring about fundamental structural change in the Egyptian economy.

Although the metropolitan elements in the 1920s wanted

to return to the status quo ante bellum, they proved re-
markably flexible in adjusting to changing economic and
political realities. The British learned to coexist with the
Wafd and manipulated political power from behind the
scenes. They also redefined their priorities in Egypt, securing their political goals and being less aggressive in support of metropolitan financial demands.

Metropolitan financial groups were also resilient. They
retained a strong position in the Egyptian economy by
changing their interests there. Although their investments
diminished, they joined with local capitalists in the 1920s
and subsequently in joint stock industrial and commercial
ventures. The composition of their trade changed in response to the growth of local industries. By the late 1940s,
consumer nondurables had given way to consumer dura-
bles and capital goods. Moreover, there was a dramatic
change in Egypt's trading partners, as British trade and
investment declined and countries like Japan and Italy expanded their interest.

It had never been the intention of the Egyptian elite to
detach themselves from metropolitan capital. Rather, their
goal was to strike a different bargain, to reduce the authority of the export-import groups, and to broaden the
financial interests of banks beyond trade and cotton cultivation to industrialization and agricultural diversification.

To greatly oversimplify the narrative of the three decades, the nationalist fragment, as represented by the Wafd,
repulsed the Bristish plans for incorporating Egypt more
fully into the British empire and secured a measure of
political autonomy for the country. At the same time, the
nationalist fervor spilled over into the economic sphere,
causing new financial and industrial institutions to be created and new economic programs to gain considerable acceptance.

British politicians countered these triumphs. By conced-
ing some but not all of the political demands of the nationalists, they separated some conservative nationalist leaders
from the Wafd. Then, during the Stack crisis, they drove

the Wafd from power and installed minority governments. This reassertion of control had important implications for Egyptian economic development. The business elite looked to the state during these years to create conditions favorable to the growth of capitalism. In particular, its members called for state aid to nascent industries in the form of tariff protection and subsidies. But in the six years between 1924 and 1930, the government's effort to implement major development projects foundered for lack of ministerial stability and singleness of purpose.

The depression witnessed a renewal of economic initiatives. In the 1930s, Britain was much less interventionist, and the autocratic prime minister of Egypt, Isma'il Sidqi, merged the economic interests of the national bourgeoisie with those of the landed grandees. Tariff reform enabled the Egyptian government to impose duties which favored both industrialists and cultivators, at the expense of metropolitan trading firms as well as the Egyptian poor. Egypt's main industries expanded during the 1930s and most attained a secure place in the economy in this decade.

This alliance proved hard to sustain. It lacked the support of the Wafd. Further, the balancing of interests between the national bourgeoisie and the landed magnates was harder to maintain when the abolition of the Capitulations in 1937 enabled the Egyptian government to embark upon a major revision of its taxation system. Differences became even more pronounced after World War II, when the state sought to extract a greater amount of revenue from the population in order to modernize the army and to launch far-reaching social welfare programs for the by-now desperately poor masses. Although a considerable amount of industrial growth occurred during and after the war, the consensual vision began to break up. Leftist and rightist critics of the government became more insistent, and eventually the military stepped forward to restore order.

The state occupies a central place in this study. It does so for two reasons. In the first place, all of the elements of the ruling elite looked to the state to further their interests. Although the domestic bourgeoisie believed in private enterprise, they also thought that the state should assist the development of industry in its early stages. They also wanted the state to use its powers to rid the country of those international treaties and obligations which bound Egypt to Europe as an exporter of raw materials and an importer of manufactures. Secondly, it is at the governmental level (in parliamentary debates, ministerial programs, and party programs) that one can often see most sharply the aims and aspirations of different elite groups. The political arena, accordingly, serves as a prism for observing conflict and convergence within branches of Egypt's ruling element. In this respect, the state is regarded not as a prime mover of historical events but as a useful vantage point from which to observe the actions of all of the ruling segments.

CHAPTER 1

BACKGROUND

By the outbreak of the World War War I, Egypt had reached a crisis point in its economic development. Two problems were obvious. The first of these was that agricultural growth, the engine of economic change throughout the nineteenth century, had slowed markedly. In per capita terms, agricultural output had even begun to decline. In the second place, European capital, which had been fueling the agricultural engine, had assumed an overweening presence. Egyptians felt as if they were aliens in their own country, and the task of structural economic change was rendered especially difficult by this metropolitan presence.

Egypt had enjoyed steady, and sometimes spectacular, economic progress in the nineteenth century. Between 1821 and 1872–78, the volume of agricultural output rose twelve times and per capita agricultural production increased sixfold.[1] Thus, it was easy for Egyptians to believe that the same combination of hydraulic technology, substitution of perennial irrigation for the basin system, and extension of

[1] Patrick O'Brien, "The Long-Term Growth of Agricultural Productivity in Egypt," p. 180. Owen believes that net profits to cotton cultivators may have increased up to 200 percent between 1880 and 1910–1913. E.R.J. Owen, *Cotton and the Egyptian Economy*, p. 232. In this section on trade I have drawn extensively from the following materials: Bent Hansen and Edward Lucas, "A New Set of Foreign Trade Indices for Egypt"; Bent Hansen and Karim Nashashibi, *Foreign Trade Regimes and Economic Development: HCSP*, vol. 42 (1921), cmd. 1487, and vol. 51, cmd. 957; Egypt, Ministry of Finance, Statistical Department, *Annual Statement of the Foreign Trade of Egypt during 1919*; and Great Britain, Department of Overseas Trade, *Report on the Economy and Financial Conditions in Egypt for 1919*, by E. H. Mulock, *HCSP*, vol. 43 (1920), cmd. 843.

cotton cultivation would continue unabated into the twentieth century. Indeed, the conquest of the Sudan had opened up seemingly limitless possibilities for the further harnessing of the Nile and for the cultivation of cotton or new cash crops in parts of middle and upper Egypt where the basin system still existed.

But an agricultural slowdown had occurred, and it was even more real and dangerous than it was perceived to be. The economically sophisticated were aware of some disquieting facts. Crop yields had declined steadily between 1900 and 1914, reducing the revenues Egypt earned from the export of cotton. Intensive research into the problem suggested that the decline was the result of overwatering, faulty drainage, and overcultivation of cotton, but though the state planned extensive drainage construction programs and other efforts, none of the measures introduced before World War I had stemmed the decline.

Another problem, only dimly perceived at the time, was that the rural population had begun to outstrip increases in the cropped area. This important reversal of nineteenth-century trends occurred around the turn of the century.[2] It was accompanied by a rise in the landless rural population and an increase in rural lawlessness. Both of these developments were a worry to the elite.

It was also clear that future hydraulic projects, on which agricultural expansion would depend, would be more difficult and more costly to execute than earlier programs. With the first increase in the height of the Aswan Dam in 1912, British hydraulic engineers concluded (albeit in error) that the major irrigation works in Egypt had already been carried out. Henceforth, control of the Nile would require dams close to the confluence of the White and Blue Niles and vast construction schemes on Lake Tsana, the source of the Blue Nile, and Lake Victoria in Uganda.

[2] Bent Hansen, "Preliminary Report on an Attempt to Estimate National Product and Income for Egypt, ca 1880–1913," typescript (1974), pp. 3–4.

Although William Garstin, the chief irrigation expert under Lord Cromer, had made a tour of the Nile outside Egypt shortly after the conquest of the Sudan, little was yet known about the hydraulic and geological problems of these areas and the costs involved. Moreover, these programs would have to be undertaken outside of Egypt and would involve negotiations with other governments, although, except for Ethiopia, they were British-controlled ones. British and Egyptian opinion was sanguine, but there were well-founded fears about future difficulties in Nile River control.

Throughout the nineteenth century, the rulers of Egypt had been eager to develop export crops in addition to cotton, so that the country's trading economy would not depend entirely on a single commodity. Although sugar seemed to have great potential at one point, the country was not able to develop other exports.

Most Egyptians would not have believed that, as an economic historian commented later, "as far as agriculture is concerned Egypt may be said to have ended its period of rapid growth in 1914."[3] Overall agricultural decline had been masked by rising urban incomes up until 1907 and after that by an improvement in Egypt's terms of trade and a decline in its real factor payments abroad.[4] Yet by the outbreak of the war many were aware that the Egyptian population was expanding so rapidly that it would outdistance increases, likely to be achieved in the area under cultivation. Although the authors of the influential *Report on Commerce and Industry*, issued in 1918, anticipated a massive expansion of the cropped area from 9.9 million feddans to 15.4 million feddans by 1945, they also noted that the population would increase more rapidly. Thus, the amount of land available per person was expected to fall from 0.78 feddans to 0.77.[5] They believed that the only solution for rising man/land ratios was industrialization.

---

[3] Charles Issawi, "Egypt since 1800," p. 24.

[4] Hansen, "Preliminary Report," pp. 23 ff.

[5] Egypt, Commission du Commerce et de l'industrie, *Rapport*, p. 55.

We know now that the British expectations for increasing the supply of irrigation water available in Egypt, expanding the cropped and cultivated areas, and stemming the rise in man/land ratios were far too optimistic. Additionally, the rate of population growth was destined to rise beyond the predictions of most. The agrarian crisis facing Egypt in 1914 was more severe than most realized.

The second dilemma was more deeply emblazoned on the minds of people in Egypt. European economic power was pervasive. It was deeply resented, and even those Egyptians who believed that overseas capital had enhanced Egypt's prosperity in the nineteenth century were now anxious to liberate the country from its domination. By the outbreak of the war, foreign capitalists, mostly from the metropole, had invested close to £E200,000,000 in the country. Through banks, land mortgage companies, real estate firms, and stock exchanges, European capital was in a position to dictate Egyptian economic behavior. No doubt the foreigners took a very large proportion of Egyptian national income, though the amount is impossible to determine.

European economic predominance was most visibly manifested in foreign banks. Each of the European countries with economic interests in Egypt was represented by at least one bank, and these banks tended to organize and control the financial and commercial activities of their compatriots. Although Muhammad 'Ali, the Egyptian ruler from 1805 to 1848, had endeavored to create a purely Egyptian bank, the enterprise failed, and the field was left open to foreigners. The first banks were small-scale and preoccupied with lending to the khedive. They were succeeded, however, by larger, commercial banks, often branches of large European banking houses. Crédit Lyonnais and Crédit Nationale d'Escompte represented French capital. The British were at first represented by a number of banks, but in 1898, the National Bank of Egypt became the primary British-controlled banking institution in Egypt. Though a private commercial bank, with mainly British financing, the National Bank became the bank of issue in Egypt during World

War I. Belgian banking was in the hands of the Banque
Sino-Belge, which opened a branch in Cairo in 1912 and
one in Alexandria in 1914; also in 1914, its name was changed
to Banque Belge pour l'Étranger. Greek and Italian capital
also had banking outlets in Egypt. In 1880, French capital
created the Crédit Foncier Égyptien, a large, heavily capitalized land mortgage company. It lent long-term funds
to large landowners, using their land as surety. Subsequently, smaller, competitor land mortgage companies were
established. (See table 1.1).

Three major powers—Britain, France, and Belgium—
had massive investments in Egypt, and each in creating its
own economic empire there brought Egypt into the international economy in different ways. French money and
managerial talent were focused on a few heavily capitalized
firms; the entire economic complex looked to the Suez Canal
Company (390 million francs), the Crédit Foncier Égyptien
(690 million francs), and, at a much lower level of capitalization, the Sugar Company (84 million francs). An important area of French investment was public utility companies, where Lebon and Company exploited concessions
for supplying gas and electricity to Cairo, Alexandria, and
Port Said. In a detailed review of French investment in
Egypt in 1911, F. Charles-Roux estimated the French holdings of the Egyptian public debt at 1.25 billion francs and
the total French investment in the country, including smaller
companies and branches of large French firms, at close to
4 billion francs.[6]

French businessmen experienced great difficulty in
maintaining managerial control over French firms in Egypt.
French investment was widely dispersed, and small French
shareholders traditionally took little interest in the management of companies, so long as dividend payments continued to arrive. Hence, small groups of organized shareholders on the ground could gain control of companies,

[6] François Charles-Roux, "Le Capital Français en Égypte," *L'Égypte Contemporaine*, 8 (1911), 465–502.

Table 1.1.

Major Banks and Mortgage Companies
Operating in Egypt in 1914

Bank	Date of Founding	Subscribing Nation
Imperial Ottoman Bank	1864	Britain, France
Anglo-Egyptian Bank	1864	Britain
Crédit Lyonnais	1874	France
Banco di Roma	1880	Italy
Crédit Foncier Égyptien	1880	France
Land and Mortgage Company	1880	Britain
Cassa di Sconto e di Risparmio	1887	Italy
Comptoir Nationale d'Escompte de Paris	1889	France
Banque d'Athènes	1894	Greece
National Bank of Egypt	1898	Britain
Agricultural Bank of Egypt	1902	Britain
Caisse Hypothecaire d'Égypte	1903	Belgium, France
Land Bank of Egypt	1905	Britain, France
Ionian Bank	1907	Britain, Greece
Banque Sino-Belge	1912	Belgium

SOURCES: A. E. Crouchley, *Investment of Foreign Capital*, pp. 107-108, and 'Ali al-Jiritli, ''Tatawwur al-Nizam al-Masrifi fi Misr,'' pp. 229-232.

even though holding only a fraction of the shares themselves.

If one of the salient characteristics of French joint stock companies was looseness of control, Belgian companies were at the opposite end. Their Egyptian companies fit tightly into Belgian international capitalism. They were not so numerous as the British nor so heavily capitalized as the French.

They were specialized in electricity, public utilities, and railways. Overseas Belgian finance was dominated by a few large metropolitan banks, including the Société Générale de Belgique, the Banque de Bruxelles, and the Crédit Général Liegois, and by holding companies run by private bankers and men of affairs. One of the most powerful of these holding companies was the Société Générale des Chemins de Fer Économiques, which constructed railways in Western and Eastern Europe, Latin America, Southeast Asia, Africa, and China. Belgian companies had close ties with other European capitalist groups, especially French and Dutch banks, and intimate relations with King Leopold and other members of the Belgian royal family through that vast financial conglomerate, the Société Générale de Belgique.[7]

According to statistics compiled by George Paish in 1911, the amount of British capital invested in Egypt was £43,753,000, of which £29,709,000 was invested in joint stock companies.[8] Of the twenty-two British-run companies listed in Papasian's 1923 financial publication, sixteen were administered by boards made up of persons living in Great Britain; the other six were in the hands of local British entrepreneurs. This feature contrasts sharply with some of the French firms and many of the Greek and Jewish companies, which were managed by persons resident in Egypt. Also, one of the British firms—Anglo-Egyptian Oilfields—was an affiliate of a burgeoning multinational, Shell Oil.[9] The British economic empire in Egypt was to become more closely linked to multinationals in the interwar years than any other economic empire.

Foreign populations accompanied the movement of capital into nineteenth-century Egypt. Muhammad 'Ali and his successors interpreted the social, economic, and judicial

---

[7] See especially G. Kurgan-van Hentenryk, *Léopold II et les Groupes Financièrs Belges en Chine.*

[8] George Paish, "Great Britain's Capital Investment in Individual Colonial and Foreign Countries."

[9] Ed. Papasian, *L'Égypte Économique et Financière* (1923).

provisions of the Capitulations in a generous fashion, thereby allowing foreigners many privileges. The British occupation provided further impetus for foreign settlement in Egypt. Not only did the country continue to develop economically and to provide opportunities for persons with a knowledge of European languages and business practices, but its relative political stability and religious toleration contrasted with other parts of the Ottoman empire.

According to the census of 1882, Egypt's foreign population was 90,886. By 1917, that figure had risen to 205,949, or 1.62 percent of the total population, and it was to rise to 225,600 in 1927 (although the proportion in the total population at that time declined to 1.59 percent). In the census of 1917, the size of the leading foreign communities was estimated as follows:

Armenians	7,760
Syrians	7,728
British	24,354
French	21,270
Italians	41,198
Greeks	56,751

The foreigners lived overwhelmingly in the cities, and for the most part in wealthy residential areas. They constituted 8.1 percent of Cairo governorate, 19 percent of Alexandria, 19.8 percent of Port Said, 20 percent of Ismailia, and 13.8 percent of Suez. In the rural governorates, by contrast, nowhere did the foreign population constitute as much as 1 percent.[10] (See appendix tables A.1–A.5.)

There was scarcely an aspect of economic life untouched by overseas influence, and most of the economic decision-making powers in Egypt resided in foreign hands. Although on the surface commerce and industry appeared to be the domain of foreigners and agriculture that of Egyptians, even such a division would be misleading. To

---

[10] Egypt, Ministry of Finance, Statistical and Census Department, *Population Census of Egypt of 1917*.

be sure, Egyptians owned most of the land, but their land-holdings were mortgaged to foreign merchants, land banks, and export-import houses. Moreover, the marketing of Egypt's cash crop, cotton, on which the financial well-being of the country depended, was almost entirely in foreign hands. From the small moneylender to the Alexandria General Produce Association, the grand regulator of cotton merchandising, this essential activity was dominated by foreigners.

What is not clear is whether these arrangements, taken in toto, harmed or benefited Egyptians. One can put the questions in a very simple, even personal way. Was it an advantage or a disadvantage for Egypt that one of the persons attracted to the country was the Belgian entrepreneur, Baron Edouard Empain, the creator of the Paris Metro? Empain brought extraordinary technical and business skills to Egypt. But did his presence and those of others like him divert development into areas which made the country reliant on Europe and less able to determine its own economic directions? Did his presence make it difficult for Egyptians to gain financial, industrial, and commercial expertise? Did the European presence confine the Egyptian element to agrarian activities—to being underprivileged persons in their own country? Did a type of economy emerge which could not be transformed gradually but instead required revolution?

Prospects for Structural Change and Renewed Development

Egypt possessed certain advantages for renewed economic development in 1914. These advantages were a relatively prosperous population, a well-developed consumer market on which import-substitution industrialization could be based, a highly valued export commodity, and relatively easy access to foreign capital markets and technical and managerial talent. But against these factors must be weighed the smallness of the entrepreneurial pool, the nationalist stress on political rather than economic change, the public financial policies of the British, gaping educational deficiencies, a lack of savings, a disinterest in investments outside of agriculture and real estate, and the absolute paucity of industrial development. Some of these factors are worth further discussion.

Egypt's national income of roughly £E120,000,000 in 1913 (see table 1.2) reflected well on the prosperity of a country which in 1800 had shocked Napoleon's savants by its backwardness and poverty. The per capita income of £E10 was above that of India and even Japan, though it was only one-fifth that of Great Britain and one-eighth that of the United States.[11]

Much of the material prosperity of the country depended upon and was created by Egypt's robust foreign trade. The country's per capita trading average of £E5 ranked it well above many less developed countries and even put it on the same level as a number of European states (see tables 1.3 and 1.4). Cotton exports served Egypt well in the period before the outbreak of the war. Barter, income, and per capita income terms of trade all moved upward from the middle of the nineteenth century until around 1910. None of these measures of export buying power was to be exceeded until 1950–1951, when net barter and income terms of trade improved dramatically as a result of the Korean War.[12]

Although the British were Egypt's largest trading partner, they owed their lead to their manufacturing supremacy rather than to their political influence. Britain was Egypt's chief cotton buyer and supplied the country with most of its textiles, machinery, and coal. But Egyptians bought in the cheapest markets and sold in the dearest. They im-

[11] This paragraph is based on Charles Issawi, "Asymmetrical Development and Transport in Egypt, 1800–1914." Few estimates have been made of national income for this period. Issawi derived his figure from the work of Count Cressaty and the data compiled by the Egyptian Commission on Commerce and Industry.

[12] Hansen and Lucas, "Foreign Trade Indices," p. 18.

Table 1.2.

Estimates of Egyptian National Income, 1880-1922
(millions of £E per year)

	Hansen[a]	Issawi[b]	Lévi[c]
ca. 1880	39.1		
1894-98	67.6		
1899-1903	76.4		
1904-08	82.3		
1909-13	90.0		
1913		120	
1922			301

NOTE: These figures are not difficult to reconcile. Lévi's estimates have been criticized as being too high (James Baxter, "Notes on the Estimate of the National Income of Egypt for 1921-22," *L'Égypte Contemporaine*, 14 [1923], 405-427), but Egypt did experience a considerable rise in the cost of living between 1913 and the early 1920s, perhaps as much as 100 percent, and therefore Lévi's conclusion that per capita income was £E20 was not so far out of line with the prewar estimates.

[a]Bent Hansen, "Preliminary Report on an Attempt to Estimate National Product and Income," p. 29. Figures given in terms of 1913 prices.

[b]Charles Issawi, "Asymmetrical Development and Transport in Egypt, 1800-1914."

[c]I. G. Lévi, "L'Augmentation des Revenus de l'État: Possibilités et Moyens d'y parvenir," *L'Égypte Contemporaine*, 13 (1922), 596-624.

ported wheat flour and maize flour from the United States and Australia, silks from France, cotton yarn from British India, cotton hosiery from Brazil, and timber from Sweden. (See table A.6.)

Egypt's large trading volume had already given the country a potential for import-substitution industrialization. Its

Table 1.3.

Imports per Capita in Egypt, 1895-99 to 1913

	Tobacco		Coffee		Cotton Fabrics
	grams	milliemes	grams	milliemes	milliemes
1895-99	557	54	418	24	165
1900-04	650	58	527	20	231
1905-09	755	67	703	27	277
1910	713	99	557	25	290
1911	739	100	579	35	348
1912	750	101	596	41	291
1913	744	89	522	31	302

SOURCE: Egypt, Ministry of Finance, Statistical Department, *Annuaire Statistique*, 1922-23, p. 362.

Table 1.4.

Value of Foreign Trade in Ten Countries, 1912

Country	Dollars per Capita	Country	Dollars per Capita
Egypt	24.3	Mexico	15.4
India	4.3	Spain	21.3
Iran	10.3	Turkey	15.2
Italy	32.5	United Kingdom	125.3
Japan	12.6	United States	43.5

SOURCE: Issawi, "Asymmetrical Development and Transport," p. 384.

substantial imports included shoes, processed foods (flour, sugar, wines, beers, liquors, and vegetable oils), chemicals, metals and metal wares, and of course most important of all, textiles (see table A.7). In nearly all of these areas, except for metal wares, Egyptian industrialists had begun to make their first halting efforts at manufacturing local products, though the absence of a skilled labor force, their own lack of expertise, and the unresponsiveness of the British-controlled government of Egypt had placed obstacles in their path.

Egypt's economy was an open one; its customs duties were set by international treaty at 8 percent ad valorem, except for a 4 percent charge on coal, charcoal, mazout (fuel oil), and frozen meat. Tobacco carried a much heavier, revenue-earning tariff. There was also a 1 percent export tax and an 8 percent excise on certain local manufactures, put in place by Lord Cromer at the turn of the century, ostensibly because of his free-trading principles but in reality because of Britain's large trading interests in Egypt and Cromer's desire to prohibit the rise of indigenous, competitive manufacturing firms.

Although one can see Egypt's potential for industrial development in these trade statistics, the basis of the country's economic wealth continued to be agriculture. The country was still largely able to feed itself, and its exports were overwhelmingly cotton and cotton seed. In 1913, these two items constituted 90 percent of the value of Egypt's exports. The only other exports valued at more than £E100,000 were cigarettes, wood, eggs, onions, hides, rice, and oil cakes.[13]

Egyptian cultivators specialized in the cultivation and export of long-staple cotton (1⅛″ to 1½″). The country was responsible for approximately 40 percent of world production even as late as the middle of the twentieth century. It also had a virtual monopoly over the extra-long-staple (1½″ and over) market.[14] While Egyptian cotton enjoyed a premium over cotton produced in other countries because of the special uses to which long- and extra-long-staple cotton were put, its crop was not large enough to have a

[13] Egypt, Ministry of Finance, Statistical Department, *Annuaire Statistique*, 1914, pp. 284–288.

[14] National Bank of Egypt, *Economic Bulletin*, Vol. 5, No. 4 (1952), pp. 272 ff.

great influence over the world price, which was in large
part determined by the size of the American crop and world
demand. Nonetheless, one of the reasons that Egypt enjoyed continued economic growth until the outbreak of
World War I was that the premium paid on Egyptian long-
staple cotton, which had fluctuated between 10 and 20 percent before 1895, increased to 55 percent in that year and
averaged 40 percent thereafter.[15]

Finally, Egypt had ready access to foreign resources. Its
pleasant climate and the comfort of its two leading cities
had already attracted many skilled workers and artisans
during the nineteenth century—Greeks, Italians, Syrians,
and Armenians. Alexandria by 1914 was virtually a cosmopolitan city, at least in the minds of its European population. Wealthy international capitalists, like Edouard Empain, were fond of the country and spent much time there.
Empain built a huge palatial home for himself in the Cairo
suburb of Heliopolis and ordered that at his death his re-
mains be interred in the crypt of the cathedral there.

However, one of the reasons that Empain was compelled
to be in Egypt was to manage his Cairo Electric Railways
and Heliopolis Oasis Company. Local entrepreneurial and
managerial talent was very limited. Most of the joint stock
companies operating in Egypt were run by boards of directors based in Europe. In 1914, of the £100,152,000 invested in joint stock companies in Egypt, £92,039,000 was
in companies dominated by foreign capital, mostly drawn
from Europe.[16] Even in 1923, there were only twelve Egyptian directors in the eighty-seven joint stock companies listed
in a financial publication issued privately at that time. They
served on the boards of ten different firms; only three—
Muhammad Tal'at Harb, 'Abd al-Hamid, and Mahmud
Shakkur—had any business experience. Since eight of the
twelve had been or were Egyptian prime ministers or cab-

[15] Owen, *Cotton and the Egyptian Economy*, pp. 202 ff.
[16] A. E. Crouchley, *The Investment of Foreign Capital in Egyptian Companies and Public Debt*, p. 73.

inet members, it is logical to assume that they owed their corporate directorships to political position. They sat on the boards of large companies which enjoyed privileged concesions from the government and which were anxious to curry its favor—e.g., the National Bank of Egypt, the Banco di Roma per l'Egitto et il Levante, the Water Company of Cairo, the Electric Light and Power Company, and the Land Bank.[17]

Although a few pre–World War I nationalists stressed the importance of economic change—Tal'at Harb was one—most of the nationalists of this period were not interested in economic questions. Mustafa Kamil's message was singularly political. He was eager to win political independence from the British. The same emphasis on politics and a certain economic naiveté were to be prominent in the higher echelons of the Wafd when it was organized after the war.

Much of the infrastructure for economic transformation required thoroughgoing reformation. Public financing, long dominated by conservative British thinking, had been based on the notion that remunerative expenditures on hydraulics must be emphasized over "unremunerative" programs, such as education and public health. This approach had equipped the country with a vast hydraulic system and an advanced railway network, but it had left the country educationally impoverished. How, then, were the Egyptians to produce the entrepreneurial talent needed for industrialization or to find the skilled manpower so necessary for industrial expansion? Unless these problems were quickly and decisively addressed, Egypt would have to continue to rely on the ever-present foreigner.

Even as late as 1913, when British proconsuls had been subjected to two decades of carping criticism about their financial priorities, the state budget had changed little. (See table 1.5.) More than a quarter of state expenditure was still set aside for tribute and public debt payments, the

[17] Papasian, *L'Égypte Économique et Financière* (1923).

Table 1.5.

Main Expenditures in Egyptian State Budget, 1913

Expenditure Item	Percent of Total [a]
Tribute and public debt	26.0
Ministry of Public Works	15.8
Military	6.8
Administrative services and collection of taxes	6.1
Ministry of Justice	5.2
Ministry of the Interior	5.1
Ministry of Finance	3.3
Ministry of Public Instruction	3.3
Civil List	1.6
Total of these items	73.2

SOURCE: Egypt, Ministry of Finance, Statistical Department, *Annuaire Statistique*, 1914, pp. 410 ff.

[a] Total expenditures = £E17,659,961.

legacy of Isma'il's profligacy. There was little that any Egyptian administration could do about these expenditures. The next heaviest expenditure was for that favorite British item, the Ministry of Public Works, the lion's share of which went for hydraulics. Education, on the other hand, received a mere 3.3 percent.

Some of the results of this policy could be seen clearly in Egypt's educational deficiencies and the competitive educational edge which foreign communities residing in Egypt enjoyed (table 1.6). Besides showing the minuscule number of students enrolled in Westernized schools, the educational statistics also revealed that the literacy rate of for-

Table 1.6.

Students in Egyptian Schools, 1912-1913

School	Total	Egyptian	Foreign	Foreigners Percent as of Total
Preparatory	38,731	31,056	7,675	19.8
Primary	85,778	64,993	20,785	24.2
Secondary	9,697	6,793	2,904	29.9
Commercial	1,909	1,290	619	32.4
Superior	17,421	16,463	958	5.5
Normal	1,927	1,927	——	0.0
Professional	4,397	4,073	324	7.4
Agriculture	427	423	4	0.9
Special	2,069	1,559	510	24.6

SOURCE: Egypt Ministry of Finance, Statistical Department, *Annuaire Statistique*, 1914, pp. 65 ff.

NOTE: Enrollments in *kuttabs* (Muslim schools) not shown.

eigners was fourteen times greater than that of the Egyptian population. The fact that Egyptians predominated in the few postsecondary schools which the British allowed meant only that foreign families wisely sent their children overseas to acquire university training.

Although Egypt's agricultural and commercial sectors were relatively highly developed, the same was not true of its industry. Industry provided employment for 8 percent of the working population, compared with the 70 percent in agriculture (table 1.7). Hardly any large-scale, heavily capitalized, and technologically modern factories had secured a firm foothold in the Egyptian economy. Such large-scale industries as there were, and which were to become so important in the interwar period, hardly deserved that name before 1914. They tended to cluster in those areas where

Table 1.7.

Distribution of the Labor Force
by Economic Sector, 1907, 1917, and 1927

	Percentage of the Labor Force in Each Sector		
	1907	1917	1927
Agriculture	68.3	68.0	67.5
Mining	0.1	0.1	0.2
Manufacturing	8.2	8.4	8.1
Electricity, gas, and water	----	0.1	0.4
Construction	2.8	1.4	1.6
Trade and finance	4.7	7.5	8.7
Transport, and communication	2.9	3.5	3.7
Services	13.0	11.0	9.8

SOURCE: Samir Radwan, *Capital Formation in Egyptian Industry and Agriculture, 1882-1967*, p. 283.

Egypt already had a large consumer market—processed foods, building materials, and cigarettes—although they had not made much progress in the area where Egypt's consumer demands were most pronounced, namely textiles. (See table 1.8.)

The largest and the most heavily capitalized of the manufacturing firms in 1914 was the S. A. des Sucreries et de la Raffinerie, or the Sugar Company, the origins of which dated back to the era of Khedive Ismaʻil. Under his inspiration, sugar cultivation was expanded in Egypt, and the state, as well as a few wealthy landowners, founded small sugar processing workshops. Later, a large sugar refinery was built at Hawamdiya, just outside of Cairo. The modern sugar industry did not come of age, however, until French industrialists, persuaded that Egypt could become a great sugar cultivating and refining area, moved into the coun-

Table 1.8.

Industrial Firms with Total Capital of £E50,000
or More in 1911

Company	Total Capital (£E)[a]
S.A. des Sucreries et de la Raffinerie d'Égypte	1,341,534
Nestor Gianaclis	584,756
Associated Cotton Ginners	487,792
Egyptian Salt and Soda Company	485,347
United Egyptian Salt	292,500
S.A. Générale de Pressage et de Dépôt	195,000
Compagnie Frigorifique d'Égypte	180,000
Anglo-Egyptian Spinning and Weaving Company	146,250
Industrial Building Company of Egypt	146,250
S.A. des Tabacs et Cigarettes Matossian	146,250
S.A. des Brasseries d'Égypte	124,404
Cairo Sand Bricks Company	95,577
S.A. des Ciments d'Égypte	88,723
Salonica Cigarette Company	82,107
Kafr al-Zayat Cotton Ginning	78,000
Port Said Salt Association	78,000
S.A. des Presses Libres Égyptiennes	68,250
Rosetta and Alexandria Rice Mills	62,400
Crown Brewery of Alexandria	50,148
S.A. Egyptien des Presses Allemandes	50,000

SOURCE: Egypt, Ministry of Finance, Statistical Department, *Annuaire Statistique*, 1914, pp. 526-527.

[a]Includes common-stock shares and bonds.

try.[18] In 1891, the Raffinerie C. Say joined with a local firm, Suares Frères et Compagnie, to purchase a domain of 18,000 feddans in Minya and then opened a sugar processing factory at Shaykh Fadl. In 1893 they bought out the Hawamdiya refinery.[19] Then, in a relentless quest for market dominance, their Société de la Sucrerie Raffinerie d'Égypte effected a merger with the old khedivial firm in 1897. The resulting company had a virtual monopoly over the processing and refining of sugar in Egypt, although a number of small sugar workshops managed to remain in existence. In 1911, the sugar industry was said to employ about 20,000 workmen—15,655 in the Sugar Company itself and the rest in the 600 small workshops still operating.[20]

Despite the company's monopoly of internal production, its business success was far from assured before the war. Its sugar was expensive by world market standards, and yet as a result of faulty planning its productive capacity was greatly in excess of the small local market. Additionally, a financial challenge, organized by the powerful British financier, Ernest Cassel, saddled the company with large debt payments. In 1905, the company collapsed, and its managing director, Ernest Cronier, committed suicide.[21] The person who saved the company from liquidation and who was to prove a bulwark of Egyptian industrial development from that moment onward was Henri Naus, a Belgian sugar expert who had just come to Egypt from Java.

As might be expected, a great deal of Egypt's large-scale industry was devoted to the processing of Egypt's primary export, cotton. The ginning and pressing of cotton was carried out mainly by Greek merchant-industrialists. The leading figures had begun their careers in some form of

[18] Ernest Cronier, Ad. Del. de la Raffinerie C. Say to Marquis de Reverseaux, May 13, 1893, FEA, Box 232.

[19] French Consul to Hanotaux, May 23, 1895, FEA, Box 232.

[20] Pierre Arminjon, *La Situation Économique et Financière de l'Égypte*, p. 255.

[21] No. 31, French Consul to Rouvier, September 7, 1905, FEA, Box 234.

commerce, usually cotton marketing, and still maintained their commercial activities.

A powerful firm destined to play an important role in industry in the interwar period was the Egyptian Salt and Soda Company. Established with British money in 1899, it absorbed the Huilleries et Savonneries firm, which had been founded in 1890. It engaged in a wide variety of food processing activities—oil extracting, soap manufacture, butter preparation, and the making of oil cakes, glycerine, salt, and caustic soda. Its main large-scale competitors in 1914 were the Kafr al-Zayat Cotton Company, the Port Said Salt Association, and United Egyptian Salt.

Beneath these few large-scale firms was a small number of medium-sized firms. In the building trades industry, the Cairo Sand Bricks Company and the Société des Ciments d'Égypte manufactured cement and brick. An Italian industrialist, S. Sornaga, had opened a factory at al-Wadi in 1895 that specialized in bricks, cement, and pottery. Some medium-sized industries had been spawned by the investment of merchant capital. The two best examples are the cigarette and spirits industries. Egypt's cigarette manufacturing owed its origins to a nineteenth-century Ottoman decree restricting the production and sale of cigarettes to the state. Unable to ply their trade in Turkey or Syria, a number of Greek tobacco merchants emigrated to Egypt; in time they began to manufacture the cigarettes they were marketing. The leading figure, Nestor Gianaclis, was a tobacco merchant from Istanbul who first established himself at Suez in 1864. He moved to Cairo in 1869 and opened a factory there. Cigarette manufacturing was being done in small-scale shops: merchants with two to five workmen had cigarettes made on order for their clients. At first only a small export trade existed, but it expanded spectacularly when British army officers stationed in Egypt began to popularize Egyptian cigarettes outside the country. In response to a rising demand numerous Greek and Armenian firms were opened. By 1907, Cairo had at least thirty-seven cigarette workshops, employing 1,804 men and thirteen women. Despite the size of the foreign trade, which was valued at £E394,978 in 1913, the factories themselves remained small, little more than workshops. Many of the firms had no mechanical equipment at all.[22]

Mercantile capital was also channeled into an Egyptian spirits industry in the 1890s. Most of the entrepreneurial innovations were made by Greeks with an infusion of Belgian money. By the outbreak of the war, Egypt had wine, beer, and alcohol factories, many of which, like the Bolonachi wine factory at Alexandria and the Cozzika alcohol producers at Toura, had been founded by businessmen who originally had been importers and distributors of spirits.[23]

At first glance it is surprising that textile firms were so little represented in the large-scale manufacturing sector. Egypt's textile import trade would have seemed to offer an attractive opportunity for enterprising local businessmen. In 1899, two aspiring large-scale firms had in fact been created—Anglo-Egyptian Spinning and Weaving and the Egyptian Cotton Mills Company. But both of them faltered. The latter went into liquidation and the other sold off its assets to the Filature Nationale Égypte, which in 1914 was the only large-scale cotton textile firm in the country. At the time, it had 20,000 spindles and 560 looms and employed 800 to 900 workmen. But its output of 3,500,000 pounds of thread and 8 to 9 million yards of cloth was only a small fraction of Egypt's imports.[24] Also in existence, though still not heavily capitalized, was a modern silk factory at Damietta under 'Abd al-Fattah al-Lawzi.

The explanation most frequently offered for the delayed appearance of modern textile manufacturing was official

[22] Athanase G. Politis, L'Hellénisme et l'Égypte Moderne, vol. 2, pp. 329 ff.; and M. A. Sekaly, "La Culture du Tabac au Point de Vue de l'Économie Égyptienne," L'Égypte Contemporaine, 5 (1914), 345–376.

[23] Sahifa al-Tijara, 1 (1925), 2 ff.; Politis, L'Hellénisme, vol. 2, pp. 352 ff.; and M. P. Cozzika, "La Distillerie de Tourah," L'Égypte Contemporaine, 8 (1917), 44–49.

[24] Egypt, Commission du Commerce and de l'Industrie, Rapport, p. 145.

British opposition. No doubt this opposition was important, but equally influential was the persistence of small-scale textile workshops. Using a kind of cottage or putting-out system, local manufacturing was able to survive the influx of foreign textiles. Even in 1923, Egypt's 13,300 looms, largely hand looms, produced 22.5 million meters of textiles, and though this cotton piece-goods output was equal to only one-ninth of the country's imports, the local production of wool and silk piece goods and of cotton, wool, linen, and silk yarn was on a par with the volume of imports of these products. (See table 1.9).

Although many craft industries had been destroyed by European manufactures, textile artisans were not the only small-scale manufacturers who continued to thrive. Indeed, the line that divided the large-scale firms from the smaller ones was not clear-cut in 1914. A number of successful manufacturing enterprises had arisen from artisanal beginnings and continued to produce with primitive machinery or even without machines. It was not at all certain in 1914 that the leadership for industrial advances would come from the large-scale, heavily capitalized, but troubled firms rather than from the smaller, mercantile-industrial concerns.

Small-scale manufacturing enterprises were located throughout the country. Many of them catered to local and regional markets. Cairo and Alexandria predominated in metallurgy, leather making, carpentry, food processing, and construction activities, but the spinning, weaving, and dyeing of textiles were widely dispersed. More than half of the artisans engaged in the production of woolen textiles were located in the districts of Abu Tig, Sannuris, and Akhmin, while Minuf, Shibin al-Kum, and Qalyub had one-fifth of all the craftsmen working in cotton and silk. Damietta and al-Mahalla al-Kubra were large craft centers, noted for the excellence of their textiles. (See table 1.10.)

If industrial development was the hope for the future, the grounds for optimism could not be considered firm. The amount of investment in industry was certainly not

Table 1.9.

Egypt's Domestic Production and Imports of Textiles, 1922-1923

| | Number of Looms | Textiles Produced (square meters) | Yarn Spun (kg) | Imports | |
				Piece Goods (square meters)	Spun Yarn (kg)
Cotton	9,000	15,000,000	3,184,536	140,511,013	3,762,738
Wool	2,000	4,000,000	228,078	2,892,267	219,464
Linen	300	500,000	50,991	1,518,369	80,248
Silk	2,000	3,000,000	252,149	4,726,898	219,315
Total	13,300	22,500,000	3,715,754	149,648,547	4,281,765

SOURCES: Production, *Sahifa al-Tijara*, 1 (1924), 9; imports, Egypt, Ministry of Finance, Statistical Department, *Annuaire Statistique, 1922-1923*, pp. 328-345.

NOTE: The domestic production figures were compiled by inspectors sent out by the new Department of Commerce and Industry to gather information on local production.

Table 1.10.

Proportion of the Labor Force of Eleven Industries Located in Four Cities, 1907

	Percentage of the Labor Force Located in:			
	Cairo	Alexandria	Damietta	al-Mahalla al-Kubra
1. Textiles, total	6.2	1.0	2.6	4.7
Cotton and silk	8.3	0.8	4.6	9.2
Wool	0.5	0	0	0.3
Dying and printing	3.8	1.2	0.8	2.0
2. Skins and hides	23.1	25	1.0	1.3
3. Woodworking	15.8	4.9	1.9	2.2
4. Metals	33.4	13.0	1.2	1.5
5. Ceramics	2.9	1.1	0.1	2.1
6. Chemicals	25.0	11.7	38.8	0.7
7. Food processing	33.9	11.7	1.5	1.4
8. Footwear	29.5	10.8	2.4	0.6
9. Furniture	23.0	9.9	1.2	1.0
10. Building	33.9	13.5	3.2	1.1
11. Construction of apparatus and transport	11.6	9.9	0.9	2.2

SOURCE: Egypt, Ministry of Finance, Department of Statistics, *Population Census of Egypt*, 1907, pp. 163-284.

NOTE: In 1907, Cairo contained 5.8% of Egypt's total population, Alexandria 2.9%, Damietta 1%, and al-Mahalla al-Kubra 1.7%.

more than 1.6 percent of the gross domestic product and perhaps much less.[25] Egyptians had not cultivated the habit of saving, partly because of the availability of foreign funds. Moreover, industry, if it developed along the pre–World War I lines, would be in the hands of foreigners, some of them residing in Egypt and others based in Europe. The small number of really large-scale firms was almost entirely financed and managed by overseas groups.

Yet the economic situation was not as grim as this mechanical balance sheet of advantages and disadvantages suggests. Surprisingly enough, the great Egyptian speculative boom between 1899 and 1907 offered hope for industrial progress and entrepreneurial innovation. During that period, many new joint stock companies were created, as massive amounts of capital were invested in Egypt. Although the bulk of the capital was directed into those investment fields traditionally favored by foreign investors— land mortgage banks and urban and rural land development companies—the capital of industrial firms increased fourfold during the decade.[26] To be sure, some of these enterprises were bogus, created to take advantage of the speculative mania in Egypt at the time. Once the financial bubble burst, they went into liquidation. Nevertheless, of the eighteen manufacturing firms founded between 1899 and 1907, ten were still active in 1914. Their capital totaled £E1,732,000, and they included most of Egypt's important large-scale manufacturing industries, including the Egyptian Salt and Soda Company, the Brasseries des Pyramides, the Société Anonyme de Tabacs et Cigarettes Matossian, the Port Said Salt Association, the Société des Ciments d'Égypte, and the Associated Cotton Ginners. The darker side of the picture was the eight failed companies, whose capital had totaled £E737,000. Anglo-Egyptian Spinning and Weaving Company, Egyptian Cotton Mills, and the Egyp-

[25] Robert Mabro and Samir Radwan, *The Industrialization of Egypt, 1939–1973*, p. 21.

[26] Egypt, Ministry of Finance, Department of Statistics, *Statistique des Sociétés Anonymes par Actions* (1940), pp. 376–377.

tian Swiss Iron Works, however, represented industrial activities that were to be developed in the future.[27]

Perhaps the most significant harbinger of the future was the emergence of locally based boards of directors during this decade of vigorous economic activity. Although native-born Egyptian directors had barely appeared, the largest number of firms in 1907 were run by foreign businessmen drawn from different nationalities but residing in Egypt (see table 1.11). This development was not stable, however. A large number of these firms went into liquidation, and Egyptian joint stock company direction returned to its tradition of being organized along national lines and being dominated by businessmen residing overseas.

By the outbreak of the war, there was a mounting concern about the Egyptian economy. Although most Egyptian nationalists tended to focus their energies on the political arena and to be anxious to end the British occupation, they could not ignore the economic realities of an arrested agricultural growth, a weak industrial sector, and foreign economic dominance. It was clear that future economic prospects were not assured. This concern became even more pronounced as the war made more palpable Egypt's acute dependence on the rest of the world for its economic well-being. Cut off from European manufactures and European investment, and hard pressed during the first two years of the war to market its cotton crop, Egypt experienced grave economic shocks.

THE POLITICAL REVOLUTION OF 1919

'Political developments outpaced economic change immediately after World War I and even paved the way for the articulation of new economic ideas and the founding of new economic institutions. The outbreak of the war had seemed to offer to the British a unique opportunity to end

[27] The preceding data were drawn from Crouchley, *Investment of Foreign Capital*.

Table 1.11.

Joint Stock Company Management in 1907

Predominant Nationality of the Board of Directors	Number of Companies	Capitalization(£E)[a]
Egyptian	1	16,000
French	1	25,591,000
Italian	1	438,000
Syrian	2	390,000
Greek	7	4,760,149
Belgian	11	8,950,000
British	25	16,025,061
Jewish	8	2,149,784
Mixed nationality but predominantly residing in Egypt	54	20,039,459
Total	110	78,359,453

SOURCE: *Annuaire de la Finance Égyptienne, passim.*

NOTE: This privately compiled list does not include the Suez Canal Company. Total capitalization of the companies shown, together with the Suez Canal Company, is about £E10,000,000 less than Crouchley's figure, cited earlier in the text. The Egyptian Ministry of Finance reported 210 companies in 1907 with a total capitalization of £E102,177,532. Egypt, Ministry of Finance, *Joint Stock Companies*, p. 8.

[a]Includes common-stock shares and bonds.

the anomalies of their position in Egypt. British officials quickly separated Egypt from the Ottoman empire, proclaimed a protectorate over the country, and deposed their antagonist, Khedive 'Abbas, for the more compliant Sultan Husayn. These were but the first steps in an endeavor to incorporate Egypt into the British empire at the close of the war.

The British plans were stymied, however, by the rise of Egyptian nationalism and the creation of a populist party, the Wafd, in 1919. The nationalist outburst owed its force to the fact that virtually every segment of the Egyptian population had a grievance against the British. Landowners complained about the marketing of cotton. The educated and professional classes were alarmed at the loss of political power which seemed in the offing. The urban poor were hurt by the war-induced inflation, and the peasantry suffered from military recruitment and the loss of life and property during the war.

Unable to realize the goal of strengthening their political authority, the British sought to appease Egyptian nationalist feeling and to separate moderates from radicals. They hoped to achieve this end by redefining their interests and then negotiating a treaty with moderate Egyptian nationalists, in which they would concede a degree of political and social autonomy.

There was, however, one flaw in the British effort to find areas of compromise on which to build a treaty. In the enormous enthusiasm generated by the 1919 revolt, the overarching goal of the nationalists had been established as *al-Istiqlal al-Tamm*, complete independence. If the British proposals fell short of this goal, they were certain to be denounced by radical nationalist politicians like Sa'd Zaghlul. The major obstacle was the stationing of British troops on Egyptian soil. It is conceivable that moderate nationalists might have consented to an Anglo-Egyptian treaty which confined British forces to the Suez Canal zone. While certain individuals at the Foreign Office were willing to contemplate this attenuation of the British military presence, the War Office was not, and its view prevailed. The military establishment argued that troops stationed along the canal would be vulnerable to interdiction of food and water supplies and unable to intervene swiftly at the center of Egypt should difficulties arise. Whitehall maintained that England must be able to deploy military forces consonant with its responsibilities for protecting foreign interests in Egypt, maintaining imperial communications, and securing law and order throughout the country.[28]

Unable to find Egyptian politicians who were willing to sign a treaty and yet aware of the need for a restructuring of Anglo-Egyptian relations, the British finally proceeded to carry out their policy unilaterally. They hoped that even though Egyptian politicians were unwilling to sign a treaty, they would nonetheless form ministries and serve under a lightened form of British rule.[29] On February 28, 1922, the architect of the new policy, Lord Allenby, proclaimed an end to the protectorate, the abolition of martial law, and the independence of Egypt subject to reservations in four areas—defense, protection of foreign interests, imperial communications, and the Sudan—where Britain insisted on a right to interfere.

Following this declaration, ʿAbd al-Khaliq Tharwat formed an Egyptian ministry and created a committee to draw up a constitution for Egypt. The new constitution came into being, amidst great turmoil, in 1923. Elections were held for the new bicameral legislature, and in 1924 the Wafd, victorious party at the polls, assumed the reins of power under the prime ministership of Saʿd Zaghlul.

Allenby's declaration of February 1922 had conferred a modicum of political autonomy on Egypt. It is easy to belittle this limited freedom. The potential for its abridgment was enormous, the reserved points leaving the British high commissioner many justifications for intervention. The elaborate Egyptian constitution proved a cumbersome and unwieldy document. The exact powers of the king were not clear, and both Fuʾad and Faruq were able to manipulate ministries, block the ambitions of the Wafd, and keep a series of minority governments in power. Even so, Egyp-

[28] See "Military Policy in Egypt," Memorandum by the Secretary of State for War Respecting British Forces in Egypt, J. Murray, February 13, 1923, PRO FO 407/196.

[29] See No. 62, Allenby to Curzon, April 16, 1921, PRO FO 407/189, and No. 34 Tel., Allenby to Curzon, November 17, 1921, PRO FO 407/191.

tians enjoyed a measure of political leeway and were not entirely thwarted in their efforts to erect an autonomous political economy, even at times against the wishes and interests of the British.

The British proclamation of independence had been made with an eye to separating moderate and radical nationalists and bringing into existence political groupings through whom British control could be channeled. This objective was achieved. In the confused half decade from 1919 to 1924, the Wafd failed in its effort to become a political congress, an embodiment of the national will. The many cleavages within Egyptian society overwhelmed the enthusiasm of nationalism and anticolonialism. At the surface level, the leading politicians had differing views about the use of violence and the power of the leader, Zaghlul. They also argued that the party's leadership should be run democratically and hence its policies should be those favored by the majority of its executive committee. Zaghlul had a different perspective. Believing himself to be the veritable source of revolutionary and nationalist dynamism, he held that his own views should take precedence.[30]

At the deeper level other tensions were at work. Ethnicity divided the nationalist leaders. 'Adli Yakin, 'Abd al-Khaliq Tharwat, and Husayn Rushdi belonged to the old Turkish aristocracy, the large landed element whom Zaghlul and other Wafdists attacked, at least implicitly, when they sought to portray themselves as genuine and "pure" Egyptians.[31] There were also economic cleavages. Although many of the Wafdist leaders were large landowners, the party drew its support in the countryside from the medium-sized landowners. In the cities, it was supported by the urban middle classes, workers, and students. A much higher proportion of Wafdist members of the Chamber of Deputies in the 1920s came from urban occupations than was the case with

[30] Mahmud Abu al-Fath, *al-Mas'la al-Misriya wa-l-Wafd*, pp. 121–130, contains a good account of the appearance of divisions among the Wafdist leaders in Paris.

[31] Ahmad Qasim Judah, ed., *al-Makramiyat*, pp. 36 ff.

the minority parties, whose parliamentary members were drawn chiefly from the wealthy in the countryside.[32]

These diferences resulted in the creation of new political parties and endowed Egypt with a multiparty parliamentary government. The Watani party, which had been powerful before World War I, soon came back to prominence. In 1921 the Liberal Constitutional party was created, in opposition to the Wafd. Subsequently, other minority groups were established. Although the leadership of all of these parties was dominated by the large landed element, the Wafd throughout its history retained its ties to the people. It was the one and only populist organ among the established political groupings. As for the other parties, their ideological pronouncements notwithstanding, they tended to be coalitions of ambitious men, usually drawn from the landed and professional strata and lacking widespread support. They owed their tenure of power to British and royal manipulations.

Despite the fact that Egypt's political revolution of 1919 had fallen short of its goals, still by 1924 there had been subtle and even, in some cases, major shifts of political and economic power. These shifts were to become clear only as the implications of Egypt's new constitutional and parliamentary system revealed themselves during the interwar years.

In countless ways, British influence was safeguarded. There were many tangible arrangements for maintaining British power. The military garrison, which numbered 5,000 at the time of Cromer, was expanded to 12,000.[33] Admittedly because of local hostility to the repeated use of troops between 1919 and 1922, the British were weary of using the mailed fist. Even so, the very presence of the constabulary served to cow Egyptian nationalists.

The British had traditionally used the appointment of

[32] Marius Deeb, *Party Politics in Egypt*, p. 160.

[33] CP89, "The Garrison in Egypt," Memorandum by the Secretary of State for War, February 9, 1923, PRO FO 371/8960.

their own officials to high positions in the Egyptian government as a means of influence. This practice was modified after 1924, in response to Egyptian demands. Many European advisors were retired and their positions turned over to Egyptian civil servants. Moreover, the custom of placing high-ranking British advisors in the ministries of finance, justice, and public works—a custom which harked back to the end of Isma'il's reign—was terminated. Yet British officials continued to serve in the upper reaches of the bureaucracy. A Department of European Affairs was created in the Ministry of the Interior in 1924, with responsibility for protecting foreign interests. Under the vigorous leadership of Alexander Keown-Boyd, this bureau became a veritable British intelligence agency inside Egypt. It collected data on the Egyptian polity, economy, and society and relayed them to the British embassy for action.

Still, power had shifted noticeably in the direction of Egyptian autonomy and in favor of organized Egyptian groups. The political violence of 1919 was exploited by the landed magnates to enhance their authority. Equally benefited was the emergent commercial and industrial bourgeoisie, mostly foreign but resident in Egypt. Its members were anxious to create an independent capitalism. Their ambitions were articulated in various foreign and local chambers of commerce, the Egyptian Federation of Industries, and the Egyptian General Agricultural Syndicate, all of which were to be influential in fashioning Egypt's interwar political economy.

The political turmoil of the early 1920s moved the locus of power from the metropole to the periphery. To be sure, Britain's control over Egypt had been precarious at first, because of repeated promises of withdrawal. But with Cromer's skilled maneuvering, British authority had increased. Metropolitan sway had grown at the expense of local initiatives until, by 1900 at the latest, Egypt had become in all but juridical respects a colonial possession. The political settlements hammered out between 1922 and 1924 handed back some of the local authority lost in 1882 and paved the way for an increase in local economic initiatives. Not surprisingly, the nationalist successes were accompanied by economic changes which elevated Egyptian-based groups at the expense of metropolitan capital.

CHAPTER 2

NEW DIRECTIONS IN THE EGYPTIAN ECONOMY, 1918–1924

The political disturbances of the immediate postwar years were paralleled by an immense amount of economic reordering. New economic institutions, ideas, and leaders emerged. A domestic industrial and commercial bourgeoisie began to crystallize during these years.

Many factors underlay the new economic departures. Nationalism itself, though politically oriented, spilled over into the economic arena. Nationalist leaders called for the creation of new, autonomous economic institutions to support the hoped-for political independence. Radicals demanded a boycott of British goods and British financial and commercial institutions. Bank Misr, founded in 1920, became the quintessential expression of Egyptian economic nationalism.

The economic reordering also had wartime roots. Despite the many grievances it engendered, the war brought an unanticipated prosperity to some. Egypt enjoyed a huge, favorable trade balance of £E95 million for the period beginning in 1914 and ending in 1919. Landlords reduced their indebtedness to land mortgage companies by approximately £E15 million. Less encumbered with debt at the end of the war than they had been in many years, they were in a position to lend financial support to new economic activities.

The war also interrupted trading and investment ties between Egypt and Europe. The consequent sharp reduction in the real value of Egyptian imports provided opportunities for local manufacturers to increase their output (see table 2.1). Egyptian firms were kept busy producing

Table 2.1.

Egyptian Imports, Exports, and Cotton Production, 1913-1922

	All Imports	Consumer Goods Imports[a]	Exports[a]	Cotton Used in Local Workshops (000 qantars)[b]	Price of Cotton (£E per pound)[b]	Nominal Value of Cotton Crop Including Seed (£E000 Sold)[b]
1913	100	100	100	27	3.8	33,827
1914	79	77	86	47	2.4	18,537
1915	55	67	106	56	3.9	22,249
1916	61	77	83	63	7.6	42,843
1917	45	59	63	59	7.7	52,765
1918	54	81	73	57	7.4	39,459
1919	49	64	95	23	17.6	107,057
1920	86	107	59	49	6.9	47,429
1921	72	91	71	55	6.9	33,988
1922	77	88	93	71	6.1	46,334

[a]Adapted from tables in Bent Hansen and Edward Lucas, "A New Set of Foreign Trade Indices for Egypt"; data have been recalculated with 1913=100.

[b]Egypt, Ministry of Finance, Statistical Department, Annuaire Statistique, 1913-1922.

for the local population and for the large number of British and allied soldiers stationed in Egypt during the war.

Egypt's only large-scale textile firm, the Filature Nationale d'Égypte, was saved from bankruptcy by the war. Although textiles were not as freely available as they had been before 1914, their value as a proportion of total imports increased (see table 2.2). By 1918, the company's profits had risen to £E184,600, and the management was able to divide its stock three ways while still paying a dividend of £E1.17 per share.[1] Profits were thus three times the original value of a share, despite the facts that the firm's technical proficiency was not great and its product was simple coarse gray and colored textiles.[2]

The Sugar Company also took advantage of wartime conditions to increase its output, sales, and profits (see table 2.3). Its production nearly doubled between 1911–1912 and 1916–1917, and its profits rose 34-fold. Even while the company paid dividends of 42.5 percent on ordinary shares, it set aside amortization payments of over £E1,000,000 in 1915–1916 and again in 1916–1917.[3]

But in the years immediately after the war, nearly all of these wartime gains were threatened. The world price of cotton fell precipitously in 1920 and 1921, causing landlords to demand a more dynamic state role in the marketing of cotton. Trade with the metropole recommenced; Egypt's pent-up demand for European products was let loose with a fury in 1920. The real value of imports was nearly double what it had been in 1919. Textile imports rose in nominal value from £E18,845,787 in 1919 to £E34,441,258 in 1920. As Egypt's main textile supplier, Great Britain led the way by providing large quantities of sewing cotton, cotton piece goods, ready-made clothing, woolens, and mixed textiles. Japanese and Indian textile exporters also broke into the Egyptian market.

[1] *Le Bulletin Commercial*, June 16, 1918.

[2] Ibid., July 13, 1919.

[3] *Majalla Ghurfa al-Tijara al-Misriya*, 3 (April 1918), 140–44, and Note by Brunyate, August 1918, PRO FO 141/485.

Table 2.2.

Value of Egypt's Leading Imports, 1915-1923 (percentages)

	1915	1916	1917	1918	1919	1920	1921	1922	1923
Cereals, legumes, flour	8.2	4.7	4.7	2.7	4.8	13.0	20.8	9.0	9.9
Colonial products (sugar, coffee, etc.)	7.1	4.6	4.4	4.1	3.8	4.6	2.4	3.2	3.8
Wines, spirits, oils	8.6	9.9	9.6	9.3	9.0	5.8	6.9	6.5	6.4
Wood and coal	13.2	18.5	10.8	10.6	8.3	2.0	11.1	8.9	8.8
Chemicals, medicines, perfumes	6.7	4.0	4.8	3.7	7.1	5.4	4.3	6.8	5.5
Textiles	29.4	31.0	35.3	43.4	39.8	33.8	26.5	34.3	36.5

SOURCE: Egypt, Ministry of Finance, Statistical Department, *Annuaire Statistique*, 1920, pp. 180-181, and 1922-1923, pp. 348-349.

Table 2.3.

Sugar Production and Sales in Egypt,
1904-05 to 1921-22

	Sugar Production (tons)	Sugar Sales (metric tons)	Paid-Out Profits of Sugar Company (£E)
1904-05	45,734	89,424	
1905-06	64,684	47,484	
1906-07	42,195	61,934	
1907-08	25,541	57,455	
1908-09	34,844	62,969	
1909-10	55,338	67,091	
1910-11	49,403	64,839	
1911-12	54,960	77,208	13,854
1912-13	75,420	64,427	78,834
1913-14[a]			
1914-15	75,738	94,567	
1915-16	98,964	111,453	302,149
1916-17	101,678	110,978	468,349
1917-18	79,488	101,591	
1918-19	75,899	90,761	
1919-20	56,876	91,815	
1920-21	66,985	70,539	
1921-22	110,659	80,702	

SOURCE: Egypt, Ministry of Finance, Statistical Department, *Annuaire Statistique*, 1909 to 1922-1923.

[a]Figures not available for this year.

The Filature Nationale d'Égypte, the tobacco workshops, the new cement firms, the spirits manufacturers, and the food-processing factories, which had prospered during the war, were thrown on the defensive by the resumption of full-scale trading. Except for those firms involved in the ginning and pressing of cotton, most of the large-scale manufacturing companies saw their rate of profit shrink rapidly and were forced to reduce what were still precariously small reserve funds, built up largely during the war. The profit rate of the Egyptian Salt and Soda Company fell from 30 percent of nominal capital in 1919–1920 to nil by 1923–1924; that of the Filature Nationale d'Égypte went from 63 percent to nil during the same period (see table A.8).

Particularly vulnerable was the Sugar Company, which had to draw from its reserves to pay a profit in 1924–1925. Egypt's sugar yield of 80 tons per hectare compared unfavorably with 400 tons in Hawaii and 120 tons in Java.[4] But the firm was the most heavily capitalized manufacturing company in Egypt and had a strong management team, foreign financing, and a large Egyptian work force. More importantly, sugar was cultivated on the Upper Egyptian estates of some of the largest and most powerful landowners, including the royal family.

Thus, in the early 1920s the Egyptian manufacturing firms faltered much as they had in the decade before the outbreak of the war. The affected groups began to organize and to articulate views of a changed Egyptian economy. Large landowners created the General Egyptian Agricultural Syndicate, while the endangered local industrialists established the Egyptian Federation of Industries. The new economic ideas represented a vague strategy of economic development and were as important for Egypt's subsequent economic development as the concrete economic achievements of this period. Even the founders of Bank Misr realized that their vision of an industrialized and more au-

---

[4] Issawi, *Egypt at Mid-Century*, p. 119.

tonomous Egyptian economy depended on projecting their message into the far corners of the country.

The main economic ideas and institutions that appeared during these years had a common theme: the loosening of the bonds of control exercised by metropolitan interests. Although on the surface the programs appeared to be directed against the British, they were actually aimed at all European interests binding Egypt to Europe as a dependent export economy. The ideas extolled economic diversification and called for capitalist industrialization by the efforts of a rising bourgeoisie. The various elements of the vision were put forward by three factions within the ruling elite: the landed oligarchy, a native-born aspiring bourgeoisie, and a foreign residential business elite. These groups were bound together by a desire to distance themselves from metropolitan financial interests, but they were also separated from each other, though in blurred ways, by nationality and their position within the Egyptian economy.

REPORT OF THE COMMISSION ON COMMERCE AND INDUSTRY

The first and most striking statement of the new economic ideas was that put forward in the *Report* of the Commission on Commerce and Industry.[5] This body was constituted in 1916 with a view to proposing ways in which Egypt could foster local industrial and commercial growth in light of the interruptions of trade with Europe. Its report was published in 1918, and the work of the commission was influential at many levels.

The mixed composition of the commission revealed in the first place a hope that cooperation could be effected between the two groups most likely to favor industrial and commercial change—foreign residents and native-born Egyptians. The chairman was Isma'il Sidqi. He was ably assisted by important European personages working in

[5] Egypt, Commission du Commerce et de l'Industrie, *Rapport*.

Egypt: Sidney H. Wells, general director of technical, industrial, and commercial education in the Ministry of Education; J. I. Craig, controller of the Bureau of Statistics at the Ministry of Finance; Henri Naus, director of the Sugar Company; M. F. Bourgeois, director of the Gas Company at Alexandria; and M.C.W. Twelves, an attaché at the Ministry of France. The emerging Egyptian bourgeoisie was ably represented by Amin Yahya, an industrialist and merchant from Alexandria; the well-known Egyptian Jewish financier, Yusuf Aslan Qattawi; and Muhammad Tal'at Harb, at this juncture in his career an aspiring business leader.

The report of the commission struck important new themes. One of these was a concern for social stability. The commission called attention to Egypt's rapid population growth, which was taking place against a background of limited land and agricultural resources and incipient unemployment in the large cities. It warned that "there is here a situation especially in populous urban areas which concerns those who are in charge of the well being and tranquility of the public."[6] The members of the commission were worried about Egypt's capacity to generate employment for the increasing numbers who would gain access to higher education. This worry about social problems—even social revolution—was not confined to the commission. It appeared in many publications at this time. In 1918, for instance, the Egyptian Chamber of Commerce in Cairo published an article by Hasan Kamil al-Shishini, a professor of economics, discussing population expansion and increasing density on the land and pointing out the need for increased industrial productivity.[7]

Contending that Egypt's only solution lay in ending its heavy dependence on cotton, the commission called for agricultural diversification and the development of new export commodities less subject to the vagaries of world

[6] Ibid., p. 56
[7] *Majalla Ghurfa al-Tijara al-Misriya*, 3 (June 1918), 212–15.

prices. Its members believed that the country needed a more indigenous banking system and recommended the creation of an industrial development bank. Its proposals for industrialization were import substitution schemes of the purest kind: the creation or strengthening of industries like paper manufacturing, ceramics, glass, clothing, footwear, fertilizers, sugar, perservation of fruits and vegetables, tanning, soap, and oils, in which Egypt already had a substantial consumer market. The commission also asserted that, in order to succeed, this program of industrialization required state support. While it affirmed its faith in a local bourgeoisie as the main source of economic change, it also expected the state to enact protective tariffs, to create a favorble tax structure, to purchase locally produced commodities where prices were reasonably competitive, and to proffer state subsidies.

The chairman of the Commission on Commerce and Industry was Isma'il Sidqi, who became Egypt's most forceful capitalist spokesman in the postwar years. Born in 1875 into a well-known and established Egyptian family from Gharbiya, he was educated at the Collège des Frères in Egypt and worked for the Alexandria municipality in 1900, rising in government service until he reached the rank of a cabinet minister (Minister of Waqfs) in 1914. Sidqi was an optimist about Egyptian industrialization. He considered Egypt to be rich in natural resources—oil, manganese, and phosphate—and believed that the development of these resources could end the country's debilitating monoculture orientation.[8] Yet he also argued for gradual industrial growth, because of his fear of social disorder. Industrial development, he affirmed, must occur in proper sequences. A rapid and forced industrialization would be "une oeuvre néfaste." Proceeding slowly would ensure social stability.[9]

[8] Despatch from Walter A. Foote to the Secretary of State, May 17, 1922, USNA, Roll 21, 883.63/4.

[9] L'Égypte Industrielle, 7 (February-March 1931), 74.

Sidqi wanted Egyptian industries to be based on local raw materials tied to the agricultural sector.[10]

Sidqi strove to secure cooperation between the Egyptian and foreign wings of the emerging bourgeoisie. He believed that both elements could contribute to the implantation of an indigenous capitalism. In this vein, he agitated vehemently against the privileged, enclave position that foreigners enjoyed in Egypt. Contending that foreigners should not be favored over Egyptians, he pleaded with the foreign communities to renounce their capitulatory privileges and live in Egypt under the same laws and institutions as the Egyptian population.[11] Since his programs of economic development were likely to require substantial government expenditures, he looked forward to the state's being able to tax previously exempted sources of industrial, commercial, and professional wealth.[12] But the Capitulations forbade the levying of new taxes on foreigners without first securing the consent of their governments, and thus he was forced to plead with the foreign powers to renounce these privileges.

THE GENERAL EGYPTIAN AGRICULTURAL SYNDICATE

One of the first of the new economic pressure groups to form was the General Egyptian Agricultural Syndicate. It was established in early 1921 by landed grandees following the wild fluctuations in cotton prices which one of the Egyptian financial journals called "les debâcles." Its members favored greater Egyptian control over the economy and blamed foreign merchants and banks for the tumbling cotton prices in Egypt. In particular, it attacked the Alexandria General Produce Association—a small body representing large export houses, bankers, and merchants which dominated the marketing of cotton and other commodities. In

[10] *Sahifa al-Tijara*, 7 (September 1931), 181–84.

[11] *La Revue d'Égypte Économique et Financière*, 2 (October 21, 1928), 2–4.

[12] *Le Bulletin Commercial*, December 16, 1923; *L'Économiste Égyptien*, April 4, 1926; and *al-Siyasa al-Usbu'iya*, March 27, 1926.

the opinion of magnates like Yusuf Nahhas and 'Ali Manzalawi, this organization used its superior knowledge of
world market conditions to manipulate the Egyptian price
of cotton in order to favor the export houses and the banks
at the expense of cultivators.[13]

The General Egyptian Agricultural Syndicate elaborated
an extensive agricultural program for Egypt. The goal was
to give Egyptian cultivators and local merchants more influence over cotton marketing arrangements. The syndicate wanted to place cultivators directly in touch with European manufacturers, thereby bypassing the Alexandria
General Produce Association. They also argued against "on
call" cotton contracts, which they claimed enabled merchants to manipulate cotton prices to their advantage. They
demanded government representation on the committees
of the produce association and were eager to persuade the
state to purchase cotton when world prices fell.[14]

Although the syndicate claimed to represent the interests
of all Egyptian cultivators, the organization in fact was dominated by large cotton growers, especially those who had
begun to be involved in the merchandising of cotton and
who resented the dominance of foreign merchants. Among
the founders of the syndicate were Mustafa Mahir, 'Ali
Manzalawi, Moses Qattawi, Michel Lutfallah, Hasan Sa'id,
Mahmud Husayn, Abraham Adda, and Yusuf Nahhas, all
of whom were either landlords or merchants, or both.[15]

THE EGYPTIAN BOURGEOISIE

Although Sidqi championed cooperation between the native-born bourgeoisie and the foreign residents, it was natural that many of the institutions that arose in the furor
of the nationalists movement tended to be dominated by

[13] For information on Yusuf Nahhas, see Tel. No. 898, Allenby to Foreign Office, June 2, 1919, PRO FO 371/3717 f. 24930.

[14] Yusuf Nahhas, al-Qutn fi Khamsin 'Am, pp. 54–57.

[15] Le Bulletin Commercial, February 27, 1921, and No. 82, Allenby to
Curzon, April 25, 1921, PRO FO 407/189.

one group or the other. Among the elements working to diversify the economy and make it more indigenous were Egyptian merchants. Drawing their inspiration from foreign merchants who earlier had organized foreign chambers of commerce in Egypt, they formed Egyptian chambers. The first was established in Cairo in 1913. Soon after its creation, it began to issue a monthly bulletin espousing a nationalist and "Egyptian" point of view. It became a strong advocate of Egypt's need for economic independence as a precondition for political independence. Tal'at Harb was involved in its early activities. As vice president in 1918, he used the chamber's journal to spread his appeal for the creation of a national bank.[16]

The board of the Cairo chamber was composed of men of commerce, agriculture, and politics. It included such prominent figures as Yusuf Cicurel, head of the well-known Cicurel department store in Cairo; Yusuf Aslan Qattawi, a leading Jewish financier and person of political influence; and 'Abd al-Majid Rimali, a grain merchant and a person destined to play a leading role in the affairs of the chamber in the 1930s and 1940s. But the chamber also had a strong representation of Egypt's large landowning element, presumably those landowners who were beginning to invest in the commercial and financial sectors. Of the twenty-three board members in 1918, at least eight were from large landowning families, including Isma'il Barakat, Bushra Hanna, Thabit Thabit, and Hasan 'Abd al-Raziq.[17]

[16] *Majalla Ghurfa al-Tijara al-Misriya*, 3 (January 1918).

[17] It is extremely difficult to make definitive statements about which Egyptian merchants and industrialists belonged to large landowning families. I have had access to various lists of large landowners, from which I compiled an almost complete list of names of those who owned more than 200 feddans and were subject to the land reform law of 1952. These names are in Arabic. I also have seen an incomplete list of the names of grandees, mainly landed but also mercantile and industrial, compiled in the early 1920s for the palace. This list indicates the landholdings and other sources of wealth for each individual. The names are transliterated from Arabic according to the French style of that period. There are also various membership lists of the Egyptian Federation of Industries, the General Egyptian Agricultural Syndicate, the boards of directors of joint

The founding of the Egyptian Chamber of Commerce in Cairo stimulated the formation of other Egyptian chambers. By 1926, no fewer than twenty-three chambers existed in the provincial centers of Tanta, Zagazig, Minya, Mansura, Port Said, Benha, Damietta, Beni Suef, Aswan, Fayum, and Asyut.[18] A second powerful chamber was established in Alexandria. Though founded in 1922, it did not begin to issue a regular journal until 1938. Reflecting the more cosmopolitan and commercial orientation of the Alexandria elite, the chamber under its first president, Amin Yahya, was somewhat less caught up in the economic nationalism of the era and was thus more enthusiastic about joint foreign and Egyptian business ventures. The idea for founding a chamber in Alexandria originated with 'Abd al-Fattah Barkah. The chamber sprang up amidst the nationalist fervor after World War I and reflected the sentiments of this period. At the first formal meeting, on March 2, 1922, people talked about national sacrifice and Egypt's need for economic reform. Again, large landowners were well represented among the board members. Of the sixteen board members selected in 1922, at least five came from large landowning families.[19]

Unlike the foreign chambers of commerce on which they were modeled, the Egyptian chambers self-consciously and aggressively sought to represent native Egyptian interests. They were reluctant to accept foreigners as members, and they were opposed to allowing foreigners to influence policy formulation, for they had been founded in the belief that foreign businesses were not responsive to Egyptian

---

stock companies operating in Egypt, and chambers of commerce. Some of the lists are in Arabic, but most are transliterated according to the style of the organization or person doing the transliteration. In view of the resulting large margin for error, as well as the high proportion of extremely common Egyptian Muslim names (Muhammad, 'Ali, Ibrahim, 'Abd Allah, and so forth), the reader will understand why one cannot be certain about the identity of these families.

[18] al-Ghurfa al-Tijariya al-Misriya, *Taqrir*, 4 (1925–1926), 13–14.

[19] Ibid., 1 (1922–1923), 5.

interests and were prejudiced against Egyptian business-men.[20]

The most powerful organization of the Egyptian wing of the new domestic bourgeoisie was Bank Misr, which used the Arabic word for Egypt (Misr) in its name to stress its nationalist character. It owed its creation, on March 8, 1920, to a number of factors. First and foremost was its extraordinary founder, Tal'at Harb. Although he was from a modest family, Tal'at Harb had risen quickly in the business world.[21] After graduation from the Egyptian Law School, he had been employed in the government and then had served on the boards of several foreign firms, including the Kom Ombo Land Company, where he came to know leaders of the business community, including the Suares brothers, the Rolo family, and Yusuf Qattawi. He also sat on the board of the Crédit Foncier Égyptien,[22] and he was well connected before World War I with German banking leaders in Egypt. Equally important for his early financial training was his appointment as general manager of the large agricultural estates of the powerful landlord, 'Umar Sultan. This position afforded Harb entrée into the world of the large landlords—an advantage he was to exploit when he endeavored to raise funds for Bank Misr.

One of the reasons for the founding and early success of the bank was the growth of private deposit banking in Egypt during World War I. Banks had been central to the Egyptian economy since the latter half of the nineteenth century, but they had been established to facilitate trade between Egypt and Europe, not to attract the savings of private investors. Individuals with money preferred to hold their assets in gold or jewelry or to buy land. During the

[20] Ibid.

[21] Tal'at Harb, *Majmu'a Khutab Muhammad Tal'at Harb*, vol. 3, pp. 79–84, and interview with the grandson of Tal'at Harb, Samir Sami, in Cairo, June 24, 1979. On the early life and career of Tal'at Harb, one should consult Eric Davis, *Challenging Colonialism*.

[22] Hafiz Mahmud, Mustafa Kamil al-Falaki, and Mahmud Fathi 'Umar, *Tal'at Harb*, pp. 8–9.

war, however, private deposits rose rapidly. Part of the reason for this change was a growing familiarity with European banking practices. In 1901, Muhammad ʿAbduh issued a *fatwa* (a legal ruling) permitting the paying and receiving of interest on funds deposited in the post office's savings banks.[23] But the most important reason for the change was the declaration made at the outbreak of the war that the National Bank of Egypt's notes were legal tender and that these notes would not be exchanged for gold. As the note issue increased, so did the willingness of people to deposit their holdings of notes in commercial banks (see table 2.4).

Talʿat Harb's pleas for support for Bank Misr evoked only a limited response from well-to-do Egyptians. According to him, critical assistance was provided by Ahmad Midhat Yakin, a wealthy landlord with vast agricultural estates who was said to have made a profit of more than £E200,000 during the cotton boom of 1919–1920.[24] Although his contribution to the bank's capital was only £E500, his confidence in the future of the bank emboldened Harb to promulgate the charter. Nonetheless, the total subscribed was only £E80,000, an amount that Harb freely admitted was disappointingly small.[25] Using nationalist appeals, however, the bank quickly increased its capital to £E474,924 in 1924, £E720,000 in 1925, and £E1,000,000 in 1926.[26]

The first £E80,000 were subscribed by 124 shareholders. The largest contributors were ʿAbd al-ʿAzim al-Misri (£E1,000), ʿAli Ismaʿil (£E600), and six others at £E500 apiece: Yakin, Harb, Muhammad al-Shariʿi, ʿAbd al-Raziq

[23] Crouchley, *Investment of Foreign Capital*, p. 94.

[24] No. 277, Lloyd to Chamberlain, May 6, 1927, PRO FO 371/12388 f. 1353; Ilyas Zakhkhura, *Mira' al-ʿAsr fi Ta'rikh wa Rusum Akabir Rijal bi Misr*, pp. 149–150; and *al-Basir*, May 8, 1935.

[25] *al-Muqattam*, May 7, 1935.

[26] Bank Misr, *Taqrir*, 1925, p. 1. One of the powerful organs that backed the new bank and circulated its nationalist appeals was *al-Akhbar*. See especially the issue of March 18, 1920.

Table 2.4.

Volume of Banking Activities, 1913-1921 (£E000,000)

	Non-Government Deposits Held by the National Bank[a]	Total Deposits in National Bank and Anglo-Egyptian Bank[b]	Post Office Savings Accounts[c]	Savings Accounts of 5 Banks[c]	Value of National Bank Notes in Circulation[a]
1913	5.0		.6	.5	2.2
1914	4.4	6.5			7.5
1915	7.3		.5	.3	10.6
1916	10.0		.6	.4	19.3
1917	14.1		.7	.5	29.6
1918	17.2		.9	.8	44.5
1919	21.5		1.0	1.0	62.8
1920	19.4	35.5	1.1	.9	37.3
1921	12.8		1.3	.9	35.3

[a]*National Bank of Egypt, 1898-1948*, p. 122.

[b]Crouchley, *Investment of Foreign Capital*, p. 76.

[c]Egypt, Ministry of Finance, Statistical Department, *Annuaire Statistique, 1913-1921*. The five banks were Banque d'Athènes, La Cassa di Sconto e di Risparmio, La Banque d'Orient, Le Banco di Roma, and Banque Imperiale Ottomane.

al-Far, Muhammad Musa al-Fija'i, and the sons of Badawi al-Shayti.[27] A conscious effort was made to attract small investors, in order to broaden the base of capital accumulation. Tal'at Harb recruited his friends in the professions, business, and agriculture, and they in turn sought to involve their clients. 'Ali Islam, a landed magnate from Beni Suef, an entrepreneur in his own right and a founding subscriber to the bank, journeyed around his community calling upon people to purchase shares. Although many people were pessimistic about the bank's potential, they purchased shares all the same, perhaps considering them as their financial contribution to the nationalist cause.[28] The price of a share was £E4, but the bank's affiliated firm, Shirka al-Ta'awun al-Maliya, received payments of as little as £E1 and applied them to the purchase of a Bank Misr share.[29] This policy of appealing beyond the landed grandees for capital succeeded, at least to a limited extent. By 1931, the bank had 9,267 shareholders, who held an average of 27 shares or £E104 of the nominal value of the company's stock in that year (table 2.5). Tal'at Harb himself never owned more than 500 shares.[30]

Of the bank's 124 original shareholders, the majority came from the large landowning sector. Eighty-three were members of families who lost land in 1952 or who appeared as landed magnates on a list compiled in the palace in the early 1920s. Professional elements were rather sparsely included. Thirteen of the original subscribers bore the title of doctor (either physician or Ph.D.) and three identified themselves as lawyers. Five persons were shaykhs, which suggests that they were either heads of important tribal groups or religious leaders.[31]

[27] A list of the original subscribers may be found in Bank Misr, al-Yubil al-Dhahabi, pp. 153–154.

[28] Interview with 'Ali Islam, in Beni Suef, March 22, 1975.

[29] 'Abd al-Rahman al-Rafi'i, Niqabat al-Ta'awun al-Zira'iya, p. 165, and Bank Misr, al-Yubil, p. 54.

[30] Bank Misr, al-Yubil, p. 33, and Hossam M. Issa, Capitalisme et Sociétés Anonymes en Égypte, pp. 256–257.

[31] The data on the 124 were collected from the king's list of the early 1920s and from the list of families whose land was expropriated in 1952.

Table 2.5.

Shares and Shareholders of Bank Misr

	Number of Shares	Number of Shareholders	Number of Shares per Shareholder
1923	78,307	7,594	10
1924	118,731	7,608	16
1926	180,000	8,260	22
1931	250,000	9,267	27

SOURCE: Bank Misr, *al-Yubil al-Dhahabi, 1920-1970*, p. 33.

NOTE: All figures refer to the end of the year indicated.

Although the original shareholders were largely drawn from the agrarian sector, the board of directors of the bank reflected more of a business orientation. Of the ten original board members in 1920, five were men with business experience (Tal'at Harb, Fu'ad Sultan, Yusuf Aslan Qattawi, 'Abd al-Hamid al-Siyufi, and Yusuf Cicurel), one was a leading politician ('Ali Mahir), and six came from families with large landholdings (Fu'ad Sultan, 'Ali Mahir, 'Abd al-'Azim al-Misri, Iskandar Massiha, Ahmad Midhat Yakin, and 'Abbas Basyuni al-Khatib). The nine persons appointed to the board between 1920 and 1939 reflected the same blend of business interests, political position, and large landholdings. Three of the new appointees had considerable business experience ('Abd al-Fattah al-Lawzi, Ahmad 'Abd al-Wahhab, and 'Abd al-Hay Khalil), while three were influential in politics and five came from large landowning families.

There was an inherent tension in the bank's leadership right from the outset. The landlord group played a major role in founding the bank. Long before World War I, landlords had been eager to see a genuinely Egyptian bank created; such an institution, they believed, would compete with foreign merchants and banks in the marketing of cotton. No doubt the decline in the world price of cotton in 1920 and 1921 caused many wealthy landlords to back the bank in hopes that it would favor Egyptian cultivators in their dealings with European merchants and financiers.

But Tal'at Harb had already arrived at a different vision of the bank. Greatly impressed with German big banking firms, which he had studied during a pre–World War I tour of Europe, he envisioned Bank Misr as much more than a mere commercial bank specializing in export-import activities.[32] Rather, he saw it as a spearhead of fundamental economic change. He believed that the bank should attract Egyptian savings in order to create new commercial and industrial firms that would accelerate the diversification and industrialization of the Egyptian economy. In 1923, the bank established a special account (*hisab khass*) from its profits to be used to create affiliated Misr commercial and industrial firms.[33] The first efforts were small, but they were followed by much larger and ambitious schemes.

Even though the potential for conflict between the bank's long-range goals and the more circumscribed perspectives of the large landowners was great, in the first decade of the bank's existence its policies served the landlord-backers eminently well. The bank's early start was exceedingly shaky; its capitalization of only £E80,000 a cause of great concern. Moreover, it had to compete in a country which already had a plethora of banks. Where indeed would this new firm make a niche for itself? Its only chance at this stage was to stress its purely Egyptian national origins and to make a powerful appeal to Egypt's one indigenous wealthy element—the landed grandees. This the bank did by becoming heavily involved in all phases of cotton export. Thus, it seemed to fulfill the goals of the landlords. In 1924, it established a ginning and pressing company, and in 1930 it created a company for the export of cotton. It also en-

---

[32] Tal'at Harb, "Taqrir 'an Sina'a wa-l-Tijara al-Almaniya," June 12, 1916, in Harb, *Majmu'a Khutab*, vol. 1, pp. 14 ff.

[33] This procedure was described in Bank Misr, *Taqrir*, 1932, pp. 14 ff.

tered the cotton marketing competition aggressively by making a large number of loans to cultivators. Between 1924 and 1926, the bank moved from seventh place to first in the financing of the cotton trade.[34] It played a particularly active role in support of landed interests during the cotton marketing crisis of 1926. At a time when the Banque Belge was dissolving its cotton department and other foreign houses were absorbing heavy financial losses and curtailing their cotton loans, Bank Misr won the gratitude of Egyptian landowners by holding cotton in its storage facilities until the prices at Alexandria improved.[35]

But nationalist appeals and an alliance with large cultivators had troublesome consequences. The nationalism of the bank was much resented by metropolitan banking groups in Egypt, who were upset when favored customers looked to this upstart. In 1920 and 1921, for instance, the deposits and capital of Bank Misr grew rapidly, while the number of depositors and the amounts deposited in many other banks were shrinking (table 2.6). The National Bank of Egypt, aspiring to be a central bank holding the deposits of the government, was alarmed when funds belonging to municipal governments were transferred to Bank Misr.

Foreign firms portrayed Bank Misr as xenophobic and castigated it for reckless banking practices. Although the criticisms were exaggerated, the bank clearly had adopted bold financial policies that were not common among the Egyptian commercial banks of that period. In order to make a place for itself, it tied up a great deal of its working capital in advances and failed to secure a comfortable margin of liquidity. Although foreign commercial banks in Egypt also made substantial advances to cultivators and merchants, their risks were much less great because of the backing of parent firms. Thus, long before Tal'at Harb became involved in underwriting large-scale industrial firms, he had

---

[34] Bank Misr, *Taqrir*, 1926, p. 13, and Bank Misr, *al-Yubil*, pp. 232 ff.
[35] *L'Économiste Égyptien*, November 7, 1926.

Table 2.6.

Volume of Activity of Bank Misr and Other Banks, 1920-1927

	Capital of Bank Misr (£E)[a]	Deposits of Bank Misr (£E)[a]	Deposits in National Bank (£E)[b]	Number of Deposits in Post Office Savings Bank[c]	Amounts Held in Post Office Savings Banks (£E)[c]
1918			27,955,400	211,970	909,820
1919			36,191,100	224,760	1,016,400
1920	175,108	200,960	16,804,600	222,200	1,140,300
1921	200,528	405,406	13,577,400	93,360	1,268,130
1922	269,184	981,218	20,931,200	86,040	1,378,500
1923	313,228	1,769,356	26,237,500	114,803	1,594,844
1924	484,924	2,623,953	35,350,600	133,192	1,750,667
1925	750,000	3,189,919	39,678,300	144,013	1,809,889
1926	750,000	4,424,707	36,234,000	155,963	1,867,015
1927	1,000,000	5,517,817	33,764,200	165,343	2,038,836

[a]Bank Misr, al-Yubil, pp. 171-172.

[b]National Bank of Egypt, 1898-1948, p. 122.

[c]Egypt, Ministry of Finance, Statistical Department, Annuaire Statistique, 1918-1927.

already acquired the habit of stretching the bank's resources to dangerous limits.

The contrast between the fiscal policies of the National Bank of Egypt and those of Bank Misr was striking.[36] The two banks were not strictly comparable. The National Bank was a bank of issue and the primary, though not exclusive, holder of government accounts. However, both were private, shareholder-owned commercial banks, and unlike the other banks in Egypt, neither had a parent firm whose financial support could be expected in times of trouble. The National Bank pursued conservative policies and maintained considerable financial liquidity. It had large holdings in government securities, which were much easier to realize than loans on merchandise and securities. Proportionately more of its liabilities were held in reserves, and as the primary deposit bank for the Egyptian and Sudanese governments, its liabilities were less likely to be exposed to bank depositors' runs. Bank Misr, on the other hand, had a high proportion of its assets tied up in loans, smaller reserve funds, and a large number of small depositors who during a financial panic might be expected to make a run on the bank (table 2.7).

In the 1920s, Bank Misr represented the most strikingly nationalist, even antiforeign, wing of the domestic bourgeoisie in Egypt. At its inception, Tal'at Harb described it as "a bank pure in its Egyptianness."[37] Its official language was Arabic, for its founder wanted to demonstrate that Arabic could be a language of finance. No less significantly, he barred foreigners from being shareholders or directors in the bank.[38] Thus nationalism was much more

[36] This point was made in *La Revue d'Égypte Économique et Financière*, 1 (April 14, 1927), 17–19.

[37] See Tal'at Harb's speech on the fifteenth anniversary of the bank, as contained in an anniversary scrapbook compiled by the bank and located presently in the library of the Tal'at Harb Club in Cairo. *'Id Bank Misr*, pp. 4 ff.

[38] The charter of the bank may be found in Bank Misr, *al-Yubil*, pp. 155 ff.

Table 2.7.

Uses of Assets and Liabilities of Bank Misr and National Bank of Egypt, 1920-1930

	Advances as % of Total Assets		Reserves as % of Total Liabilities		Deposits of Bank Misr as % of Total Liabilities	Government Accounts as % of Liabilities of National Bank
	Bank Misr	National Bank	Bank Misr	National Bank		
1920	45	33	0.0	7.4	53	11
1921	58	42	0.0	10.8	65	12
1922	66	29	0.1	8.2	76	35
1923	53	30	0.6		80	
1924	63	20	0.9		80	
1925	71	17	3.2		74	
1926	67	26	2.9		79	
1927	68	30	4.5	6.6	77	41
1928	66	31	4.0	6.4	80	46
1929	70	31	4.0	6.7	80	47
1930	68	27	4.3	9.7	80	20

SOURCES: Bank Misr, al-Yubil, 170-171; National Bank of Egypt, 1898-1948, pp. 121-122; National Bank of Egypt, Bilan de l'Exercice, 1928-1930.

than an ideological façade or a cynical device for winning financial support. Though Harb was friendly with a number of foreign businessmen and worked closely with several of the foreign residentials, he was an ardent patriot and a devout Muslim, suspicious of foreigners and the goals of foreign capital. In his pre–World War I writings, he had characterized European capitalism as exploitative and had stressed the need for Egyptians to preserve the essentials of their Arabic-Muslim civilization from the Western onslaught.

Other Egyptian entrepreneurs appeared at this time, though none was so dazzling as Tal'at Harb. Muhammad Farghali was head of the Farghali Cotton and Investment Company, which had been founded in 1865 by his grandfather, an Alexandrian cotton merchant. Amin Yahya was in charge of an emerging and subsequently far-flung business empire based in Alexandria and enjoying the support of foreign residential capitalists.[39] 'Ali Islam and the Lawzis were smaller, regionally based entrepreneurs, who used landed wealth to establish textile plants.[40] These leaders, all of whom were to be important within the native-born Egyptian bourgeoisie in the interwar period, ran family businesses that had been created by channeling profits made in land and commerce to industry.

THE FOREIGN RESIDENTIAL BOURGEOISIE

The Egyptian Federation of Industries was founded in 1922 primarily to represent the foreign residential business community of Egypt. It reflected the interests of foreign industrialists who had established or strengthened their firms during World War I and after the war were threat-

[39] Arnold Wright, ed., *Twentieth Century Impressions of Egypt*, p. 439.

[40] There are numerous accounts of the Lawzi textile plant in Damietta. I am indebted, however, to Ahmad al-Lawzi for the information he gave me in an interview on November 15, 1974, in Cairo. Other valuable sources of information were 'Ali Islam, whom I interviewed in Beni Suef, March 22–23, 1975, and *L'Égypte Industrielle*, 13 (May 15, 1937).

ened by a renewed influx of European manufactures. Leading spokesmen conceived the federation as a government pressure group and an agency to facilitate cooperation among industrialists in Egypt.

The founders of the federation had established themselves in Egypt long before the war. S. Sornaga, an Italian ceramics industrialist resident in Egypt, was one of its first presidents. He was the owner of a modern factory on the outskirts of Cairo. Henri Naus, Belgian head of the Egyptian Sugar Company, was equally influential and also a later president of the federation.[41] Members of the leading Greek business family, the Salvagos, were also involved.

Although the Egyptian Federation of Industries came into being as a natural, almost inevitable, response to changed economic conditions resulting from the end of the war, it is doubtful if it would have become a powerful organization had it not been for the organizational and intellectual vitality of I. G. Lévi, one of the most articulate and knowledgeable proponents of Egyptian capitalism of his generation. Born in Istanbul in 1878 and a graduate of the University of Naples in law, political science, and Oriental languages, Lévi came to Cairo in 1903. He worked first as a lawyer, then as attaché at the Italian embassy in Cairo and as director-general of the Egyptian Bureau of Statistics. Although other persons received the credit, Lévi was the real moving force behind the federation and served for many years as its secretary-general. He was responsible for bringing out its influential journal, *L'Égypte Industrielle*, first published in 1925. He was also secretary-general of the Egyptian Society for Political Economy, Statistics, and Legislation, which published *L'Égypte Contemporaine*, an important organ of capitalist opinion.[42]

The Egyptian Federation of Industries was another institution putting forward capitalist ideas. In many ways its

---

[41] On Naus, see especially *Majalla Ghurfa al-Iskandarrya*, 3 (October 1938), and *L'Informateur*, September 28, 1938.

[42] *Annuaire des Juifs d'Égypte et du Proche Orient* (1942), p. 254.

notions were not radically different from those espoused by Tal'at Harb at Bank Misr, except that it emphasized the contribution that foreign residential business leaders could make to Egyptian economic development. Both the federation and Harb were strong advocates of cartelization and economic planning. Because the internal market was narrow and shallow, the federation urged industrialists to agree on a rational division of markets. It fostered the creation of numerous industrial chambers and eventually itself became a federation of these associations.[43]

What worried the Egyptian Federation of Industries, however, was the chasm that separated Egyptians and foreigners. The federation tried to reduce this antagonism through its official actions and publications. To counter nationalist sensitivities toward foreign capital, the leaders of the federation argued that the nationality of an enterprise was not nearly so important as its contributions to national well-being.[44] At the same time, the federation welcomed Egyptian businessmen into its midst. In the 1930s, it established a special committee composed of such influential Egyptian businessmen as Isma'il Sidqi, Ahmad 'Abbud, Tal'at Harb, Fikri Abaza, 'Abd al-Majid al-Rimali, and Sayyid al-Lawzi.[45] But these efforts were never completely successful. Foreign residents remained more prominent in industry and commerce then Egyptians. Aware of their own small numbers and feeling discriminated against, Egyptian businessmen were inclined to create their own national enterprises.

DIVERGENT AIMS

The turbulent years immediately following the close of World War I witnessed repeated challenges to British political authority and metropolitan financial dominance. Many

[43] L'Égypte Industrielle, 1 (1928), 29.
[44] Ibid., 6 (March 1930), 47–64, and 9 (March 15, 1933), 26.
[45] Ibid., 11 (November 1, 1935), 3.

promising new organizations resulted from the political
outbursts and the economic rethinking. Most of the persons
concerned with Egyptian economic diversification were enthusiastic about Egypt's prospects for generating economic
growth and changing the prevailing economic structure,
especially in light of the increased political autonomy won
by the Wafd between 1922 and 1924.

Four groups played crucial roles in mounting the challenge to metropolitan predominance. The Wafd contested
Britain's sway in Egypt, while the landed magnates, the
small native-born Egyptian bourgeoisie, and the foreign
residential business elite urged greater Egyptian control
over the economy. These groups were united in wanting
to enhance Egyptian autonomy, but they achieved only an
uneasy alliance. The Wafd, with its populist orientations,
made its appeal to the urban and rural masses. The landed
magnates wanted to create independent commercial and
financial institutions, largely to aid them in exporting cotton and developing the agricultural sector. The Egyptian
and foreign residential business leaders were anxious to
implant a more diversified and autocentric capitalism in
Egypt. Foreigners resident in Egypt feared the more radical
expression of Egyptian nationalism.

At this juncture, Egypt's domestic bourgeoisie was a tiny
group, not fully differentiated from the elements from which
it sprang (figure 2.1). The division of its two rather separate, though not completely distinct, wings was based not
so much on economic activities, since both segments were
eager to develop Egypt's potential for import substitution
industrialization based on food processing and textiles. Instead, the separation stemmed from ideology, source of
capital formation, and management.

The native-born business group, represented mainly by
Tal'at Harb at Bank Misr, was caught up in the nationalist
euphoria of those years and hopeful of creating purely
"Egyptian" capitalist institutions. It was suspicious of the
foreign presence and resentful of the privileges accorded
foreigners through the Mixed Tribunals, Capitulations, and

Old Groups

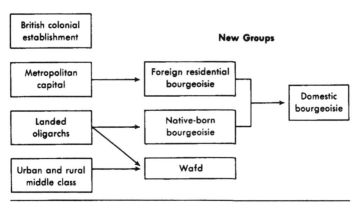

Figure 2.1 Origin and Evolution of the Ruling Elites in the 1920s

British military and political predominance. Egyptian capitalists sought their capital from the Egyptian population,
especially, at this stage, from the landed class. They wanted
to confine the direction of Egyptian companies to Egyptian
nationals.

Although the foreign residential wing of the bourgeoisie
was also interested in raising capital from the landed class,
their companies already had a great deal of overseas capital
and their management tended to be drawn from foreign
business leaders permanently domiciled in Egypt or sent
to Egypt from the metropole. The two most heavily capitalized manufacturing firms—the Egyptian Sugar Company and the Egyptian Salt and Soda Company—drew their
capital largely from France and Britain, respectively and
were run by a team of foreign businessmen from Europe
and Egypt. The foreign wing of the domestic bourgeoisie
was not as suspicious of metropolitan capital as were native-
born businessmen. But they were strongly opposed to allowing metropolitan financial and trading interests to return Egypt to its pre–World War I status as a purely
agricultural, export-oriented country.

Although the actual economic achievements of these

postwar years were modest, the opportunities for economic change looked exceedingly bright. Despite the restoration of Egypt's old trading ties with Europe, an indigenous bourgeoisie, some foreigners resident in Egypt, and some native-born Egyptians had created new institutions, the purpose of which was to diversify the economy and achieve local control over it.

CHAPTER 3

HIGH HOPES DASHED, 1924–1929

The various economic visions put forward in the years after World War I all accorded an important role to the state. The proponents of a private enterprise system in Egypt—whether they were large landowners or members of the domestic bourgeoisie—expected the state to continue to discharge its traditional responsibilities for education, public health, hydraulics, and state railways. If anything, they expected the government to be more vigorous in education and public health than the British had permitted it to be before the war. But these groups also realized that private enterprise could not prosper in Egypt unless state power was used to loosen the international bonds that tied Egypt to Europe as an open, agricultural, export economy. The main elements of the Egyptian domestic elite were eager to see Egypt capture more of the profits of its export trade and supply more of its internal market with local manufactures. What stood in the way of these advances was a variety of European controls over the economy, including the marketing of cotton, tariffs fixed at 8 percent ad valorem by international treaties, and the Capitulations.

While all the groups looked to the state to refashion the political economy, they had very different ideas about just what it should do. The landlords wanted greater governmental control over the marketing of cotton. They demanded the ending of the Capitulations, since their abolition would permit the introduction of new taxes and a reduction of the land tax. They were not enthusiastic about tariff protection, however, for they benefited from an open economy in which they were able to sell cotton in the dearest market and buy imports cheaply.

The domestic bourgeoisie placed its greatest hopes on tariff reform. Behind tariff barriers, local manufacturing could flourish. But they were sharply divided over the Capitulations. The foreign residents defended them on the grounds that they attracted foreign capital to the country; the Egyptians contended that the Capitulations and the Mixed Tribunals gave foreigners unfair economic and political advantages.

Attention was thus focused on the political arena in 1924. The Wafd, led by a respected, even charismatic, leader, Sa'd Zaghlul, scored a stunning electoral triumph. Could the Wafd use the legitimacy it had achieved in its nationalist struggles with the British to reorder the political economy and to set in motion a process of economic growth based on local initiatives and domestic capital accumulation? Its mandate for reform was clear and unchallenged. The international economy was also prospering; Egyptian cotton commanded high prices on the world market. With such profits, it was not unrealistic to hope that the wealth accruing to landlords and merchants might be invested in-industrial ventures. Already pressure groups, like the Egyptian Federation of Industries, and joint stock companies, like the Filature Nationale d'Égypte, the Sugar Company, and Bank Misr, were broadcasting their appeals for investment and championing the case of industrialization.

THE WAFDIST MINISTRY OF 1924

If the Wafdist ministry of 1924 was not the most important government of Egypt's parliamentary era (perhaps that distinction belongs to the last Wafdist government), it was certainly the most promising. Coming to power, as it did, following the nationalist outbursts of the early 1920s, it inevitably aroused the hopes of nearly every segment of Egyptian society. The landed magnates and the commercial

and industrial elite expected active support for their interests, confident that their positions in the upper echelons of
the party would ensure their control of Wafdist policies.
But organized labor also looked for some improvement in
its material conditions; its leaders readied plans for strikes
and the occupation of factories in order to achieve their
demands. A small group of communists demanded the recognition of labor unions and their own right to exist. The
student population, so potent a force during the era of
confrontation politics, expected the Wafdist government to
use its newly found power to extend the boundaries of
Egypt's political and economic autonomy.[1]

No doubt it was naive of these groups to place so many
hopes on the shoulders of a party whose main support came
from the urban population and medium landowners and
whose populist nationalism often had an antiforeign and
antiwealth emphasis. Nevertheless, in the half decade prior
to coming to power, the Wafdists had put forward a rich
and highly diverse, not to say contradictory, set of economic
visions, though they were all within a capitalist framework.
The most radical of the Wafdists—usually those who insisted on no political concessions to the British—had on
occasion been advocates of uncompromising economic nationalism. In 1922, at the height of anti-British tensions,
Hamid al-Basil and others signed a petition calling on Egyptians to have nothing to do with the British and to boycott
British goods and commercial institutions.[2] This perspective, however, was a minority one.

Most Wafdists, including their leader, Zaghlul, were accommodationist and believed that foreigners had made
contributions to Egyptian economic development and would
continue to do so. In a 1919 speech, Zaghlul declared that

---

[1] No. 991, Loraine to Henderson, December 7, 1929, PRO FO 371/
1385. Also see Sulayman Muhammad al-Nukhayli, Ta'rikh al-Haraka al-
'Ummaliya fi Misr.

[2] Annual Report for 1922, Allenby, pp. 17–18, PRO FO 371/10060,
and Tel. No. 28, Allenby to Curzon, January 23, 1922, PRO FO 371/
7730.

he even favored retaining the Capitulations, though in a modified form, since they attracted foreign capital and talent.[3] Zaghlul was a political, as distinct from an economic, nationalist. He thought the struggle for political independence should take precedence over economic concerns. Thus, he was opposed to the boycott campaigns, and in various campaign speeches made in 1923, he cautioned that the burdensome economic legacy of colonialism would require a long time to throw off. He added that his role was to instill a new spirit of unity in the country rather than forge a complete economic and political break with Europe.[4]

Egypt's first election was held at the end of 1923 and resulted in a smashing electoral success for the Wafd. Despite the fact that the Wafd won only 50 percent of the total votes cast, it obtained 179 seats in the new parliament to 32 for its opponents. All of the leading figures of the Liberal Constitutional party were defeated except for Muhammad Mahmud ʿAbd al-Raziq. Ismaʿil Sidqi was rejected in favor of a lowly cook.[5]

The electoral triumph of the Wafd was such a total and stunning one that it could easily have emboldened Zaghlul to assume a less cautious stance toward British colonial power and European financial dominance. Nonetheless, the Wafd's tenure of power was short; the British ousted Zaghlul before a year had elapsed. But even while in office his government did not demonstrate clear economic vision. Egypt's interwar economy started off on the wrong foot.

Like so many newly independent or decolonizing regimes, the Wafd opted not to challenge well-entrenched and vital metropolitan financial and political interests. Although the Wafd opened conversations on the abolition of the Capitulations, tariff autonomy, and the creation of new taxes, these discussion were initiated quietly and were expected to take a long time. The reasons for caution were

[3] Ahmad Shafiq, *Hawliyat Misr al-Siyasiya*, vol. 1, pp. 205 ff.
[4] *Le Bulletin Commercial*, October 14, 1923.
[5] No. 54, Kerr to Curzon, January 19, 1924, PRO FO 371/10019.

compelling. The party needed a breathing space to consolidate authority and restore unity in the ranks. It feared
the enthusiasms which its coming to power had generated,
especially among organized labor, which the Wafd wanted
to dominate without making major concessions. The nationalist struggles of the early 1920s had taken their toll
on many Wafdists, who, while unwilling to renounce the
ultimate goal of complete independence, by now had a
keener appreciation of the powers still at the disposal of
the British and metropolitan capital.

But the party had other reasons for wishing to pursue
pragmatic goals at first—reasons which it fully expected to
disappear after it had been in power longer. The party
assumed office in 1924 hardly prepared to govern. It had
expended nearly all of its energies in organizing the nationalist struggle and in running a slate of candidates. Recognizing its lack of preparation for office and believing that
it would have a long tenure in office, the Wafd chose simply
to administer and learn in its first year, expecting to elaborate more comprehensive and even radical economic programs once it had grown accustomed to the halls of power.

The first indication that Zaghlul would be conciliatory to
overseas interests came in his cabinet nominees. The Wafd-
ist-led rebellion of 1919 was represented in the ministry by
Fath Allah Barakat and al-Nahhas, both of whom had been
exiled; Marqas Hanna and Wasif Ghali, who had originally
been condemned to death by a British tribunal; Najib al-
Gharbali, who had been exiled and imprisoned; and Hasan
Habib. But in an effort to create a ministry of all talents,
Zaghlul—much to the dismay of many of his followers—
also included a number of non-Wafdists.[6] Their presence
annoyed many Wafdists, who believed these men to be too
closely aligned with the old Turkish aristocracy. In truth,
Zaghlul did not have unfettered control over the selection
of his cabinet. The king had a say in the inclusion of six
of the ministers and expressly forbade the nomination of

---

[6] Mustafa Amin, *al-Kitab al-Mamnu'*, vol. 1, p. 262.

'Ali Shamsi.[7] The British made it known that they were profoundly opposed to the inclusion of Ahmad Mahir and Mahmud Fahmi al-Nuqrashi, contending that these two persons had played a decisive role in the assassinations campaign directed against their officials.

Wafdist pragmatism was clearly manifested in early programmatic statements. Although the speech from the throne enunciated long-range goals, the Wafdist ministry elected to be general and noncontroversial. Zaghlul stressed a commitment to the constitution and a need to maintain unity. In the social and economic arenas, he spoke in favor of the extension of education and health care, extolled economic improvement, and emphasized the building up of the reserve fund, land reclamation, and a fairer distribution of tax burdens. He promised to curb the expansion of the bureaucracy.[8] But the speech contained no call for action against overseas financial interests, and to the dismay of radical nationalists it was silent on Britain's continuing political presence in Egypt. The economic themes of the speech were unexceptionable, even uninspiring, aspirations, which any of the leading politicians would have been expected to offer.

The new ministry had come to power so late in the fiscal year and so unprepared for its financial responsibilities that it was unable to draw up a full budget. In the budget report submitted to parliament, the ministry stressed the need for cautious and careful fiscal planning. The government hoped to build up a large reserve fund and to reform the system of taxation before undertaking major programs of transportation development, industrialization, public health, and free mass education. Under some attack in parliament, the ministry did give a glimpse of its future priorities. It promised to diffuse elementary education throughout the country, predicting that educational spending would rise from

[7] 'Abd al-Khaliq Muhammad Lashin, *Sa'd Zaghlul*, p. 358.

[8] Ibid., p. 370; Égypte, Chambre des Députés, *Comptes Rendus*, vol. 1 (March 15, 1924) pp. 2–3, and vol. 1 (June 7, 1924), pp. 389–408.

£E4,500,000 to £E10,000,000 in a span of ten years. But once again its spokesmen sounded a note of caution, arguing that the state must first devise new and "appropriate means for increasing budgetary receipts while not suppressing or reducing the existing resources" before these projects could be realized.[9]

One of the problems that faces virtually every newly independent government is how much of the old economic order to accept. In asking for delay before developing its economic policies, the Zaghlul government in effect accepted those economic accords which governed Euro-Egyptian relations. Although the government chose not to challenge vested metropolitan interests on major issues (tariffs, Capitulations, and taxation), it did seek accommodation on two smaller matters. Here its experience would demonstrate just how intransigent and powerful the metropole could be. The two questions were Law No. 28 of 1923 and payments on the Ottoman loans.

Law No. 28 of 1923, which had been negotiated by the Yahya Ibrahim ministry, accorded generous termination and pension payments to those foreign officials whose service with the Egyptian government was being ended because of the country's independence. Nationalists asserted that the law saddled the Egyptian government with heavy pension payments at a time when the state needed funds for many other purposes. They also pointed out that the law had been negotiated by an unrepresentative and manifestly unpopular ministry. The left wing of the Wafd exhorted Zaghlul to repudiate the agreement. Zaghlul was openly critical of the law, and in private discussions he tried to persuade the British government to pay some of the expenses. But he did not renounce the agreement.[10]

Although yielding on Law No. 28, Zaghlul was adamant

[9] "Rapport de la Commission des Finances sur le Projet du Budget de l'État pour l'Exercice, 1924–25," Chambre des Députés, *Comptes Rendus*, vol. 1 (June 7, 1924), p. 415.

[10] Tel. No. 92, Allenby to MacDonald, March 16, 1924, PRO FO 407/198.

that the Egyptian government had no obligation to continue making payments on the Ottoman loans. Zaghlul's difficulties and those of his successors on this issue illustrate how difficult it was for Egypt, enmeshed as it was in the network of international capitalism, to break these ties. In 1854, 1855, 1871, and 1877, the Ottoman empire had negotiated four loans from European banking houses. They were guaranteed by Egyptian tribute payments to the Ottomans. Subsequently, these four loans were consolidated into three—1855, 1891, and 1894—the service of which absorbed virtually all of Egypt's tribute payments.[11]

Zaghlul refused to continue these payments on the grounds that, as the Ottoman state had ceased to exist at the end of World War I, Egypt was no longer obligated to pay tribute. The response from European bondholders was immediate and angry. The Rothschild banking houses in London and Paris had issued the loans and handled the payments, and they mobilized powerful European financial groups against the Egyptian government. They were able to rally the British Committee of the Stock Exchange, the Council of Foreign Bondholders, the British Insurance Association, and various other leading financial houses interested in these loan payments.

Though the legal position of the bondholders in general was not strong, their case for the payment of the 1855 loan was particularly weak. That loan had never received Egyptian consent; furthermore, when it was originally contracted, the Ottomans had made provision for a sinking fund through which the debt would have been extinguished by 1900. The law officers of the Foreign Office, after a thorough ransacking of their archives and those of the Egyptian Ministry of Finance, concluded in a confidential and unpublished note that the Egyptian case for nonpayment was a powerful one.[12]

[11] "The Ottoman Loans Secured on the Egyptian Tribute," Note by Maurice Amos, October 12, 1916, PRO FO 371/8981.

[12] Memorandum by Merwyn Talbot, March 4, 1925, PRO FO 371/10893.

Yet, using the leverage they had over the British and Egyptian governments and manipulating Egypt's international institutions, most notably the Mixed Tribunals, the foreign financial interests were ultimately able to extract generous concessions from the Egyptian government. When Zaghlul and his successors refused to make payments, the Rothschild firms brought a case against the Egyptian government in the Mixed Tribunals, where a majority of judges upheld their right to payment. As the same time, they worked closely with the British Foreign Office, even on occasion being allowed access to secret documents belonging to the Foreign Office and the Egyptian Ministry of Finance so as to enable them to make a more persuasive case before the courts. For five years, negotiations were carried on. The Egyptian government placed payment funds in a suspense account pending resolution of the dispute. Finally, in 1929, a comprehensive settlement was reached. The Egyptian ministry of Muhammad Mahmud agreed to turn over to Rothschild a first payment of £630,600 and to make sixteen periodic payments of £90,000 each. In all, Egypt paid close to £2,000,000 to settle a loan the proceeds of which had never been expended in the country. The reason the British were able to compel Egyptian payment was that they refused to release Egypt's share of the German reparations until the government had concluded a settlement with Rothschild.[13]

Toward the end of Zaghlul's first year in power, his ministry began to move to the left, giving some evidence that had the Wafd remained in power it might have made a vigorous assault on the international controls over the Egyptian economy. The failure of the treaty negotiations with the British removed one of the incentives for pursuing accommodationist policies. Additionally, Zaghlul had felt the force of sometimes vicious parliamentary and press criticism for compromising Egyptian autonomy. He was anxious to retain his mantle as nationalist scion. The move

[13] F. W. Leith Ross to Patrick, March 18, 1929, PRO FO 371/13864.

to the left, if this was what was intended, began with a cabinet reshuffle. Ahmad Mahir was appointed minister of education and Fath Allah Barakat was moved from the Ministry of Agriculture to the Ministry of the Interior. Mahmud Fahmi al-Nuqrashi and 'Abd al-Rahman Rida were appointed as undersecretaries in the Interior and Foreign Affairs ministries.

These men were loyal Wafdists. Some of them were hated by the British and the palace. Their earlier appointment to office had been interdicted. Mahir and Nuqrashi were a vital part of the populist wing of the party. They had close ties to the students. Rida was an expert on labor matters.[14] Zaghlul followed these changes by refusing to retain the post of judicial advisor and by refusing to pay retiring European officials the termination allowances due them under Law No. 28.[15] He also encouraged a rapid Egyptianization of the Railway Administration and threatened no longer to seek the advice of the London Consulting Office of Engineers when placing foreign bids. But before the Wafd could make clear its policies, it was forced out of office.

That the Wafd did not have a second year of rule was fundamentally the responsibility of the British. The murder of Lee Stack, sirdar of the Egyptian army and governor general of the Sudan, by Egyptian assassins brought Zaghlul's ministry to an end. In point of fact, British officials in Egypt and London had been waiting for a pretext to reassert British power. The resumption of power by the Conservative party in Great Britain led Foreign Office officials to seek an opportunity to intervene in Egyptian politics. The British were facing a campaign of assassination and intimidation in the Sudan, and they felt that their officials in Egypt were subject to harassment. The new foreign secretary, Austen Chamberlain, telegraphed to Allenby on November 10, 1924, that the British might have to use force

[14] Lashin, Sa'd Zaghlul, p. 413.
[15] George Ambrose Lloyd, Egypt since Cromer, vol. 2, pp. 82 ff.

to curb recalcitrant Egyptian leaders. "It is therefore necessary to select as the subject of our representations one which public opinion at home and in the dominions will recognize as an essential imperial interest."[16]

The assassination of Stack was just such an issue, and Allenby exploited it with a vengeance far exceeding even the expectations of the Foreign Office. As the murder of Stack was part of a wave of terror in the Sudan, it brought forth a British demand that Egyptian army officers and soldiers be withdrawn from the Sudan and an independent Sudanese defense force be established. This demand was a harsh one, for it severed an important link between Egypt and the Sudan. It was deeply wounding to Egyptian *amour propre*. But it was only one of a series of draconian demands. As Allenby indicated to Chamberlain, "We must not fail to use fully this opportunity to bring Egypt to her senses, to assert our power to harm her, and to stigmatize the regime of the present government."[17] Accordingly, Allenby also insisted that Egypt draft a letter of apology, punish the assailants, remit a large payment to Stack's widow, and place no limitation on the area of land to be irrigated in the Gezira section of the Sudan. Unwilling to agree to such an extraordinary range of demands, the Zaghlul ministry resigned. Zaghlul was succeeded by a ministry headed by Ahmad Ziwar, who, fearing an even greater British incursion on the country's autonomy, accepted the ultimatum.

The Stack assassination, the British ultimatum, and the Zaghlul resignation were formative events in the early years of this newly, albeit quasi-, independent country. They removed the Wafd from power before the party had even had time to formulate, let alone implement, any economic goals. Zaghlul was never again to lead the government. Although the Wafd was returned as the majority party following the 1926 elections and Zaghlul contemplated as-

[16] Tel. No. 209, Chamberlain to Allenby, November 10, 1924, PRO FO 371/10043.

[17] No. 380, Allenby to Chamberlain, November 21, 1924, PRO FO 371/10043.

suming the premiership for a second time, the British had decided to interdict his assumption of office. Lord Lloyd drafted a declaration which he was prepared to read to Zaghlul and which forbade his acceptance of office. The pretext was to be Britain's responsibility for protecting foreign interests.[18] In the 1924 crisis the British had demonstrated to Egypt their capacity to intimidate, and the lesson was not lost on subsequent governments.

These events demonstrated that the physical presence of British troops in Egypt (stationed in Cairo) made a difference in the Egyptian experiment in neocolonial rule. The British were able to obstruct, if not crush, radical and anti-British tendencies, as they did when they ousted the Wafd from power in its first year of parliamentary rule. Although similar sharp and decisive British interventions did not occur frequently (the next important instance came in 1942), the threat was ever present. During tense moments the British often sent a warship to Alexandria. They were ready to invoke contingency plans for occupying the Alexandria customs offices should a ministry prove resistant to their demands.

Thus, the ten-month period of Wafdist rule had a decisive and formative influence on the interwar Egyptian political economy. It produced a preliminary definition to the limits of Egyptian initiative. When the Wafd came to power, it was operating in the uncharted waters of independence, a new constitution, a new parliament, and new elections. Just what the Wafd would be able to do to reorder the international accords that bound Egypt to Europe was unclear. Although it did not choose to challenge these arrangements in any fundamental way, Allenby's intervention showed a British willingness to use power when vital interests were at stake. To be sure, the triggering mechanism was political violence in the Sudan and challenges to the British military posture (traditionally Britain's most vital interest in Egypt), but future Egyptian ministers could

[18] No. 49, Lloyd to Chamberlain, June 2, 1926, PRO FO 407/202.

hardly conclude that they had a free hand to alter traditional economic arrangements.

SUCCESSOR REGIMES

The Wafd's dismissal from power ushered in a period of ministerial instability until Isma'il Sidqi was appointed prime minister in 1930. The one government which undertook energetic social and economic reform policies was that of Muhammad Mahmud (1928–1929). After proroguing parliament for a three-year period on the ground that parliament was a Wafdist tyranny, the Mahmud ministry elaborated an ambitious economic program. Its schemes represented what many in the Egyptian political elite believed that governments could and should do domestically to support development. The lion's share of government expenditure was intended for hydraulic projects. Perhaps in an effort to curry the favor of landed magnates and urban dwellers against the anticipated opposition of students and rural dwellers to the prorogation of parliament, the Mahmud ministry proposed to dry up marshy areas, distribute potable water to the villages, improve workers' housing, and distribute state lands.[19] It also drew up a scheme of taxation reform designed to increase state revenues and enhance the interventionist capacity of the state. Although its proposal to introduce petrol, municipality, and stamp taxes was extremely modest and had the support of British officials at the Foreign Office, it was immediately opposed by leading foreign businessmen in Egypt.[20] Henri Naus and M. E. Miriel, head of the Crédit Foncier Égyptien and a director of the Suez Canal Company, intervened with their embassies against the tax, prompting Foreign Office officials to express astonishment at the obstinacy and narrow

[19] *La Revue d'Égypte Économique et Financière*, 2 (September 23, 1928), 2–3.
[20] Lloyd to R. Lindsay, April 21, 1929, PRO FO 371/13842.

egoism of the foreign commercial community in Egypt.[21] Like so many other ambitious governments, the Mahmud ministry was able to implement only a fraction of its plans.

One of the fundamental reasons that Egyptian governments achieved little in the 1920s was that they were inexperienced in economic and fiscal planning. The annual budget was framed hastily and unrealistically. Year after year, important developmental projects were written into the budget but not carried out; large surpluses accumulated while new works failed to be put into effect. The Ministry of Finance found itself with little control over the budget. Many departments, notably Irrigation, Education, Railways, and State Buildings, submitted their budgets three months late or more, leaving the Finance Ministry only a few weeks to put the final, overall budget in shape. Moreover, departmental budgets were put forward without the benefit of detailed criticism. As one observer noted, "the result is a whole window-full of dummies, schemes which their authors have not the slightest notion how to carry out."[22] The excess of receipts over expenditures in 1925–1926 was £E5,370,000, of which £E2,080,000 was underexpenditure on ongoing projects and £E1,020,000 was unexpended on new works.[23] In 1926–1927, the underexpenditure on new works was 41 percent of the new works budget; in 1927–1928, it was 30 percent.

HYDRAULIC PROJECTS AND AGRICULTURAL DEVELOPMENT

In all the proposals for encouraging economic development in Egypt, agriculture was intended to occupy a major role. A reinvigorated and diversified agrarian sector

[21] Tel. No. 41, Foreign Office to Lloyd, May 1, 1929, PRO FO 371/13842.

[22] No. 556, Lloyd to Henderson, June 19, 1929, PRO FO 371/13870, and No. 641, Henderson to Chamberlain, November 2, 1927, PRO FO 371/12378.

[23] Egypt, Ministry of Finance, *Final Account for the Year 1925–26*, pp. v–vii, and ibid., *1924–25*, pp. v–vii.

was supposed to yield surpluses which could be invested in industries. During the occupation, the British had expended vast sums on large-scale hydraulic projects and had come to believe that control of the Nile was the most efficacious way to promote economic development. The British and the Egyptian regimes continued to emphasize irrigation works after the war, but hydraulic plans were then much harder to realize. In the changed political climate of a partially independent polity, Egypt's agricultural development got off to an unpropitious start, as a result of faulty hydraulic projections, nationalist sensitivities, and political squabbling.

As World War I drew to a close, British hydraulic engineers began to put forward ambitious new plans for regulating the Nile waters. These plans had originated in the period just after the conquest of the Sudan (1898), when the then head of the Ministry of Public Works, William Garstin, made a hydrological investigation of the Nile basin and formulated proposals for harnessing the river's waters. He suggested dams across the Blue and White Niles and forecast the cultivation of upwards of two million feddans of cotton at Gezira in the Sudan. Just prior to the outbreak of the war, a small Gezira irrigation project was begun.[24]

The head of Egypt's Ministry of Public Works at the conclusion of the war was Malcolm MacDonald, a talented construction engineer but not an expert on hydraulics. MacDonald had been elevated into this position by Lord Kitchener because of his reputation for getting things done. MacDonald quickly put forth an exciting and grandiose series of plans for Nile development. Entitled *Nile Control* and published in 1920, this program estimated that Egypt's potentially cultivable area was approximately 7,300,000 feddans (200,000 feddans of which had to be subtracted because they needed to be set aside for fishing). Of this total, 4,800,000 feddans were in the delta and 2,500,000

[24] Egypt, Ministry of Public Works, *Annual Report*, 1914–1915, pp. 3–13.

in Upper Egypt. Three million feddans in Lower Egypt were already under cultivation, as were 2,200,000 feddans in Upper Egypt. Thus, MacDonald concluded that 1,900,000 feddans could be brought into cultivation provided more irrigation water was available. Another 1,200,000 feddans could be converted from the basin to the perennial system by the provision of additional waters.[25]

Arguing that Egypt must move promptly to expand its supply of water because of a "rapidly increasing population which has about doubled itself in the last forty years," MacDonald described a thirty-five-year plan to reclaim waste land at a rate of 60,000 feddans per year and to change from basin to perennial irrigation at a rate of 40,000 feddans per year.[26] The additional waters were to be made available to Egypt, and also to the Sudan, by means of five substantial hydraulic projects: a barrage at Nag Hammadi, designed to secure summer water for parts of Upper Egypt; a dam across the Blue Nile at Sennar, for the Gezira area in the Sudan; a dam across the White Nile at Gebel Awlia, to increase the summer water supply for Egypt generally; a reservoir at Lake Albert; and a channel in the Sudd region, to assure that the Lake Albert waters reached the main channels of the Nile. MacDonald recommended that work commence at once on the first three projects.

Appendix XI to the report contained another important recommendation. It argued against a second heightening of the Aswan dam on the grounds that the gates of the dam would have to be closed earlier than previously in order to retain a large quantity of water. In doing so, flood water laden with silt would be stopped behind the dam, resulting in silt precipitation at the base of the dam and the dam's eventual obliteration.[27] All but one of MacDonald's proposals anticipated the construction of large-scale and expensive Nile control works outside of Egypt, a

[25] Egypt, Ministry of Public Works, *Nile Control Works* (1919), p. 1.
[26] Egypt, Ministry of Public Works, *Nile Control*, vol. 1, p. 1.
[27] Ibid., appendix XI, pp. 259–262.

fact that was worrisome to Egyptian nationalists, who were suspicious of British intentions.

No sooner had this document been published than a storm of criticisms descended upon it. The first complaints came from an unexpected quarter—British hydraulic engineers themselves, some of whom were opposed to MacDonald's entire vision. Their reservations were put forward by M. R. Kennedy and William Willcocks, the latter an erratic and headstrong hydraulic official but one of the world's leading authorities on the Nile. These two men made numerous criticisms, ranging from criminal charges (MacDonald had falsified and concealed information on the Nile flow) to frivolous and mystical assertions (the Nile had shown its approval of the Aswan dam by sending four low Nile floods while construction was underway and had manifested its displeasure with the Gebel Awlia project by sending a series of high floods). But the crux of their argument was that Egyptian interests were being sacrificed to Sudanese irrigation needs. They proposed instead a second heightening of the Aswan dam, a much reduced reservoir at Gebel Awlia, and a dam or series of dams in the Sudd area.[28]

Even without the prodding of these experts, Egyptian nationalists would certainly have objected to MacDonald's plans. The British could hardly have picked a worse moment to suggest a vast program of hydraulic works located outside Egypt. National sensitivities were high, and nationalist leaders were bound to suspect British motivations. Indeed, the nationalists were suspicious, as was Kennedy, that the British intended to use hydraulic works located in the Upper Nile area to bring any Egyptian government to its knees. They were also concerned that the development of Gezira as a cotton cultivating area would result in stiff competition with Egypt.[29]

[28] See William Willcocks, *The Nile Projects* and *The Sudd Reservoir*.

[29] Memorandum on Political Aspects of Egyptian Irrigation Scandals by M. R. Kennedy, contained in No. 573, Allenby to Curzon, November 22, 1919, PRO FO 371/3710 f. 736.

The Wafd was drawn into this controversy from the outset. Zaghlul in Paris wrote to ʿAbd al-Rahman Fahmi warning that the British irrigation program was inimical to Egypt.[30] The nationalist organ, al-Akhbar, reported the debate over MacDonald's scheme and claimed that British policy was designed to separate Egypt from the Sudan.[31] The Nile control works became emotive nationalist issues.[32] Various Egyptian ministers were physically threatened for supporting the plans, and for a brief period in 1920 the minister of public works, Ismaʿil Sirri, resigned. Sirri withdrew his resignation only after extracting an assurance that the British would limit the amount of land irrigated in Gezira to 300,000 feddans, only 100,000 feddans of which were to be planted in cotton.[33]

As if these difficulties were not serious enough, the British experts were dismayed to discover that MacDonald's financial estimates, prepared in haste, were as little as half the revised estimates.[34] These miscalculations called into question the entire scheme, and the government suspended work in 1921.[35] A major problem was that the revised costs at the Blue Nile dam could not be met if Gezira irrigation was limited to 300,000 feddans. But the prospect of increasing the irrigated area at Gezira, and thereby increasing the amount of water taken by the Sudan from the Nile, was a sore point with Egyptian nationalists. It also brought to the fore a problem thus far not squarely faced, the division of Nile irrigation waters between Egypt and the Sudan.

This problem had existed before Egypt's parliamentary and electoral system had been established. But once par-

[30] Amin, al-Kitab al-Mamnuʿ, vol. 1, p. 160.

[31] al-Akhbar, February 23, 1920.

[32] Tel. No. 147, Allenby to Curzon, February 18, 1920, PRO FO 371/3695.

[33] Shafiq, Hawliyat, vol. 1, part 1, p. 684.

[34] Tel. No. 227, Allenby to Curzon, April 11, 1921, PRO FO 371/6318, and No. 336, Allenby to Curzon, April 25, 1921, PRO FO 371/6318.

[35] Tel. No. 384, Allenby to Curzon, June 5, 1921, PRO FO 371/6311.

liament was in place, nationalist sensitivities had a forum for expression, and implementation became more difficult. Although the Sennar dam and Nile waters division problems were eventually resolved, the Gebel Awlia project remained a focus of discontent. A regular political pattern emerged. Demands for construction would be put forward by various minority Egyptian governments—the Ziwar ministry in 1925, the Mahmud ministry in 1928, and the Sidqi ministry in 1932—and criticized by Wafdists, who, when they returned to power (in 1926 and 1930) would call a halt to the construction effort. As the debate raged, plans for a second heightening of the Aswan dam were revived. A new technical commission found the MacDonald report to be in error and declared that the dam could be safely heightened.[36] A second heightening was completed in the early 1930s.[37]

Although leading Wafdists had devoutly hoped that the heightened Aswan dam would satisfy Egypt's ever-increasing demand for additional water, that was not to be the case. As the ministry of Muhammad Mahmud had asserted, Egypt's irrigation needs required both the Aswan dam and the Gebel Awlia.[38] Under the minority ministry of Isma'il Sidqi, the Gebel Awlia dam was completed, in the face of bitter nationalist complaints.[39] The reservoir behind the dam was filled for the first time in the summer of 1937 and increased the water supply available for Upper Egypt.[40]

[36] Egypt, Ministry of Public Works, *Annual Report*, 1926–1927, vol. 2, p. 205.

[37] Construction at Aswan did not proceed smoothly. The original engineering firm of Norton Griffiths went bankrupt, and its work had to be completed by Topham, Jones, and Railton. See especially *La Revue d'Égypte Économique et Financière*, 3 (March 15, 1931).

[38] *La Revue d'Égypte Économique et Financière*, 2 (September 30, 1928), 2–3, and 7 (October 14, 1928), 12. But al-Nahhas objected. See No. 815, Hoare to Cushendun, November 3, 1928, PRO FO 371/13138, and *La Revue d'Égypte Économique et Financière*, 2 (November 18, 1928), 8–9.

[39] No. 83, Loraine to Simon, January 20, 1933, PRO FO 371/16105.

[40] Great Britian, Department of Trade, *Report on the Economic and Commercial Conditions in Egypt*, May 1937, by G. H. Selous, p. 127.

British hydraulic planning in this period was far below the standards established before World War I, when Scott-Moncrieff and Garstin headed the Irrigation Department and completed the Aswan dam in four years. Nevertheless, after the heightening of the Aswan dam and the completion of the Gebel Awlia dam, the amount of available water was tripled. Unfortunately, these developments did not materialize until just before the outbreak of World War II and did not contribute greatly to interwar agricultural growth.

Before World War I, delays in hydraulic construction would have been disastrous to Egyptian agricultural growth, since the provision of extra irrigation water was essential to the expansion of the cultivated and cropped areas. In the 1920s, however, other factors played a major role in the growth in the value of agricultural output, which occurred at somewhat less than 2.5 percent a year. Fertilizers became important in stemming the decline in crop yields. The question of drainage finally received the attention it deserved, and drainage canals were built after a period of long neglect. A slight increase in the cropped area was realized, largely as the result of more cultivation of cotton rather than a spread of perennial irrigation.[41] (See table 3.1.)

Sluggish Industrialization

Since Egyptian ministries proved unable to alter the international obligations tying Egypt to Europe, private entrepreneurs could hardly be expected to bring about far-reaching economic change. Metropolitan trading and financial interests, which had reimposed themselves in Egypt following the hiatus of war, enjoyed a period of extraordinary success. With Egyptian cotton obtaining high prices, Egyptian consumers spent freely on European manufactures. The real value of imports into Egypt rose in the 1920s and reached levels not to be attained again until the 1950s.

[41] See the discussion in Alan Richards, *Egypt's Agricultural Development, 1800-1980*, pp. 142–167.

Table 3.1.

Aspects of Agricultural Development, 1920-1929

	Index of Total Agricultural Production[a]	Index of Cultivated Area, Major Field Crops[a]	Index of Yield, Major Field Crops[a]	Drainage Canals[b] (kilometers)	Fertilizer Imports[b] (metric tons)
1920	100	100	100	6,364	120,246
1921	97	95	99	6,558	43,744
1922	106	104	101	6,523	118,207
1923	109	101	107	6,756	101,755
1924	112	102	110	6,786	179,087
1925	118	106	113	6,678	258,306
1926	120	106	113	7,030	243,073
1927	118	105	112	7,088	225,421
1928	125.	107	117	7,369	275,370
1929	130	112	120	7,453	327,863

[a]Adapted from tables in Bent Hansen and Michael Wattleworth, "Agricultural Output and Consumption of Basic Foods, 1886/87-1967/68," pp. 465 and 468.

[b]Egypt, Ministry of Finance, Statistical Department, *Annuaire Statistique*, 1920-1929.

Table 3.2.

Egyptian Imports and Exports, 1924-1929

	Real Value of All Imports	Real Value of Consumer- Goods Imports	Real Value of Exports
1924	100	100	100
1925	119	117	88
1926	112	107	88
1927	111	108	98
1928	116	119	101
1929	131	132	102

SOURCE: Adapted from tables in Hansen and Lucas, "Foreign Trade Indices"; data have been recalculated with 1924 = 100.

The composition of these imports was very much as it had been before the war, with textiles and machinery constituting nearly half the total value. (See tables 3.2 and 3.3.)

Under these conditions, most Egyptian industries were unable to expand. The country did become largely self-sufficient in flour milling and soap manufacture, local artisans produced ten times as many shoes as were imported, and tanners and leather workers sold as many leather pieces as the country imported (see table 3.4). But these products were all produced by small-scale artisans, and the finished goods were of a distinctly inferior nature. As for large-scale establishments, the only firms that had a large share of the market at this stage were the Sugar Company and a Belgian-Swiss cement conglomerate. The latter manufactured about half of all the cement used in Egypt. Even these two heavily capitalized firms had not yet achieved financial security. The Sugar Company paid high dividends until 1927, but only by continuing to draw down its reserves. Like other

Table 3.3.

Value of Egypt's Leading Imports, 1925-1929
(percentages)

	1925	1926	1927	1928	1929
Cereals, flour, agricultural products	12.2	11.4	8.7	7.5	9.0
Colonial products (sugar, coffee, etc.)	5.4	5.6	5.4	5.9	5.8
Wines, spirits, oils	6.1	7.3	7.6	7.5	7.1
Wood and coal	8.3	8.3	8.7	8.2	7.7
Chemicals, medicines, perfumes	7.2	7.2	7.3	7.7	7.6
Textiles	30.9	26.0	28.6	29.6	28.7
Metals and metalware	14.6	16.7	17.0	17.3	17.5

SOURCE: Egypt, Ministry of Finance, Statistical Department, *Annuaire Statistique*, 1929-1930, pp. 510-513.

manufacturing firms, it tried to use high dividend payments as a way of maintaining financial visibility as the year of tariff reform approached. Indeed, the only vibrant industrial firms in the late 1920s, as measured by the size of reserves and the profit rate on shares, were the cotton ginning and pressing companies. (See table A.9.) But of course they had achieved their prominent position well before World War I.

The Bank Misr companies were not any more successful than the others, in spite of their commitment to industrialization. Although the bank founded eight companies between 1922 and 1929 (five of which were industrial companies), their total capitalization was small (see table 3.5). Indeed the only heavily capitalized industrial Misr firm was to be the Spinning and Weaving Company, which did not commence production until the 1930s.

The Misr companies established in the 1920s relied on

Table 3.4.

Domestic Production and Imports of Selected Products,
1925 or 1929

	Domestic Production	Imports
1925		
Flour (metric tons)	2,482,419	202,980
Tanned hides (number)	250,000	266,000
Leather footwear (pairs)	6,500,000	624,397
1929[a]		
Soap (metric tons)	37,980	9,500
Textiles (square meters)		348,396,442
Traditional production	30,000,000	----
Filature Nationale[b]	5,500,000	----
Sugar (metric tons)		
Refined	108,952	53,072
Molasses	56,922	10
Cement (tons)	245,000	60,000
Cottonseed oil (tons)	64,202	0

SOURCE: Report prepared by the Egyptian Department of
Commerce and Industry, submitted to the British Board of
Trade and published in Great Britain, Board of Trade, *United
Kingdom Trade Mission to Egypt*, pp. 51-56.

[a]In many respects, 1929 was an exceptional year. The
real value of Egyptian imports was the highest ever recorded.
Much of the increased activity was due to the impending
tariff reform and the desire of local manufacturers to import
goods before the new higher duties went into effect.

[b]The Filature Nationale d'Égypte was the only major
modern textile factory in Egypt at this time. It had 60,000
spindles and 800 power looms and consumed 60,000 qantars
of cotton per year. The Misr Spinning and Weaving Company
in al-Mahalla al-Kubra had 12,000 spindles and 480 power
looms and expected to use 12,000 qantars of cotton per year.

Table 3.5.

Number and Capitalization of Companies Founded
between 1919 and 1929

	All Companies	Bank Misr Companies	
		Number of Amount	Percentage
Number founded	145	9[a]	6
Total nominal capital (£E)	12,011,000	1,580,000	13

SOURCES: Crouchley, *Investment of Foreign Capital*, p. 104, and Bank Misr, *al-Yubil*, p. 191.

[a]Including Bank Misr itself.

a small group of wealthy supporters for their start. In 1927, the bank created four industrial companies: the Misr Company for Silk Weaving (capitalization, £E10,000); the Misr Fisheries Company (£E20,000); the Misr Linen Company (£E10,000); and the Misr Spinning and Weaving Company (£E300,000). More than half the capital of the three smaller companies was provided by the bank and the Misr Company for Transport. The remaining capital (£E17,200) came from ten individuals, all of whom were powerful patrons of the Misr economic empire: Tal'at Harb, Midhat Yakin, Fu'ad Sultan, four members of the Lawzi family, Mahmud Bahnis, Sayyid Khashaba, and Yusuf Cicurel. With the exception of the Jewish merchant Circurel, all of these individuals had substantial landholdings, although the Lawzis and Tal'at Harb were also individuals of genuine business acumen.

The Misr Spinning and Weaving Company was meant to be a substantial textile firm, as indicated by its large capitalization. Indeed, it was destined to become the biggest firm in Egypt. In this case, the bank's leaders made a concerted effort to raise capital from a larger group of investors. The bank and its affiliated companies still provided £E145,000, or slightly less than the usual 50 to 60 percent of financing. Thirty-four individuals furnished the rest of the backing. The two Badrawi-'Ashur brothers were by far the leading contributors, subscribing over £E100,000. And well they could be, for aside from the royal family they were the largest landowning family in Egypt. The other investors took much smaller shares. The only ones investing more than £E1,000 were Midhat Yakin (£E10,000), Tal'at Harb (£E5,000), Fu'ad Sultan (£E5,000), Muhammad Sha'rawi (£E4,000), 'Abd al-'Aziz Radwan (£E2,500), Muhammad Mahmud Khalil (£E7,000), Sadiq Qallini (£E2,000), Muhammad Bayumi Mabram (£E1,200), and Ahmad Abu Sayf Radi (£E2,000). The original subscribers were drawn overwhelmingly from the large landowning element, as one might have anticipated, since the company was likely to be an important consumer of Egyptian cotton. Of the thirty-four private shareholders, at least twenty-five were from large landowning families.

Perhaps the most imaginative development proposal put forward during these years was contained in a report issued in 1929 by the research staff of Bank Misr, projecting a ten-year development plan and calling for the establishment of a government-run industrial development bank. The report recommended the creation of a permanent economic organization, composed of industrialists, financiers, thinkers, and government notables, to scrutinize industrial projects. This organization would bring in experts to make reports on Egyptian industrial potential and would then select those areas where major efforts should be made. Emphasizing import substitution industrialization and delineating industrialization prospects in textiles, ready-made clothing, chemicals, mining, cement, leather, and glassware, the report stressed that Egypt should produce at this stage only what it could consume. Industries should be carefully established to ensure their long-term efficiency.

While applauding the state for beginning to lend money

for worthy industrial projects, the Bank Misr report stated that state loans had so far been small (usually only about £E1,000) and short term (up to only five years). What was needed was a major investment effort through an industrial credit bank. The report contended that the most important task for industrial growth was aggregating capital and making it available to the captains of industry. Thus far, Bank Misr had played such a role, but as a general, commercial bank, with short-term liquidity concerns, it could not be as powerful an agent of industrial growth as the country needed. Moreover, the report invoked the specter of social turmoil, citing statistics to demonstrate that the population was outstripping agricultural resources. People were flocking into the cities in search of employment, creating a serious social problem. Only industrialization could solve the population problem.[42]

The report was largely neglected, however. It was debated in the higher echelons of the government, but in a cursory fashion. The depression intervened and turned the government's attention from forward-looking industrial projects to agricultural recovery. As a consequence, Bank Misr continued its role as the main source of industrial investment capital, despite the difficulties inherent in being both a general commercial bank and an industrial bank. Not until after the war did the state create an industrial bank.

The five years preceding the onset of the depression were disheartening ones. Although they commenced on the high note of a new parliament, a triumphant and consensual political party, and a cluster of new economic organizations (all dedicated to effecting structural economic changes), very little of lasting value was achieved. The Wafd was ousted from power in less than a year. Major hydraulic plans failed to engender a working consensus, and with the export-import economy booming once again, the efforts of

[42] Bank Misr, *Insha' al-Sina'at al-Ahliya.*

local entrepreneurs, including the Misr group, to initiate industrial development came to little. Except for the façade of parliamentary democracy and the existence of new economic pressure groups, Egypt in 1929 was not markedly changed from its appearance in 1914.

CHAPTER 4

THE DEPRESSION, 1930–1935

In the first half decade of political autonomy (1924–1929), the Egyptian elite had been unable to realize many of the goals set by the economic nationalists after World War I. But in the next half decade, a conjuncture of forces enabled the elite to renew the drive for economic flexibility and industrialization. Behind many of the changes was a decision by the British to adopt a stance of "neutrality" toward the Egyptian political scene. Translated into action by its chief British architects in Egypt, this policy allowed Egypt's prime minister, Isma'il Sidqi, to reform the constitution and to govern in an autocratic fashion. Sidqi was the political leader most committed to achieving the economic goals of the post–World War I period. He was an advocate of a balanced economic approach, believing that industrial and agricultural progress would be mutually reinforcing.

Several other factors contributed to the changed economic orientations of these years. The depression burst the bubble of agricultural prosperity and caused landlords and merchants in Egypt to consider economic alternatives to agriculture, land purchases, and cotton export. In February 1930, Egypt gained tariff autonomy. The government immediately inaugurated a new set of customs duties that protected the nascent industries of the domestic bourgeoisie and created privileged markets in which large landowners sold their agricultural produce to Egypt's growing urban population. In this fashion, an alliance was struck between the agrarian and industrial wings of the ruling elite. But this alliance was consummated at the expense of certain metropolitan financial and trading groups, especially those manufacturers who now faced competition from Egyptian textile and food processing industries. It was also forged at the expense of the Egyptian consumer, who had to pay higher prices for many essentials (clothing, sugar, bread, kerosene, and so forth). Since these policies were enacted by the manifestly unpopular Sidqi government, with scant attention to segments other than the landed oligarchs and the domestic bourgeoisie, they antagonized the Wafd.

The alliance was fragile, and it began to disintegrate in 1934 and 1935. The *coup de grâce* came when the British saw an opportunity to negotiate a treaty with the Wafd, and therefore once again intervened in the political process, encouraging the ruling elite to permit elections at the end of 1935.

Sidqi owed his elevation to office and his relative longevity as prime minister to a number of factors. He enjoyed the support of King Fu'ad and the British. As a way to undercut the Wafd and enhance royal authority, Fu'ad helped to engineer Sidqi's coup. But since Fu'ad was interested in his own political aggrandizement, he never assisted Sidqi's efforts to solidify political power. Rather, in 1933 Fu'ad happily rid himself of his by-then unpopular prime minister, and for two years he governed through cabinets which were no more than fronts for royal influence.

Among the British, Sidqi's most energetic backer was Alexander Keown-Boyd, head of the European Department of the Egyptian Ministry of the Interior. He was able to persuade the British high commissioner, Percy Loraine, and the British Foreign Office that Wafdist power and popularity had been exaggerated and that a strong and purposeful leader, like Sidqi, could win the support of the landed elite, the crucial social group in Egypt. Keown-Boyd claimed that the formula for successful minority rule lay in "personal and family influence and a strong government."[1]

A further source of Sidqi's support was the Egyptian

[1] No. 558, Loraine to Simon, June 17, 1932, PRO FO 371/16108.

business community, mainly though not exclusively foreign. As a former president of the Egyptian Federation of Industries and director of no fewer than eleven joint stock companies, Sidqi was a champion of Egyptian industrialization; as prime minister, he sought to favor the elements promoting it. Sidqi's ministers had close ties to local business, notably Hafiz 'Afifi, Tawfiq Duss, 'Ali Mahir, and 'Abd al-Fattah Yahya. Among the senators whom Sidqi appointed were such staunch advocates of Egyptian industrialization as Yusuf Qattawi, Isma'il Sirri, Tal'at Harb, and Ahmad 'Abbud.[2]

Seeking to enhance his authority and that of the palace, Sidqi introduced a new constitution in 1930. It differed from the 1923 constitution in enlarging royal prerogatives and ministerial independence. The constitution was described as a gift of the crown rather than a right of the nation. Franchise requirements were tightened, and elections were to be held in two stages. Sidqi justified these electoral changes on the grounds that the new constitution was better suited to the agrarian and peasant nature of the country. The two-tiered voting procedures were designed to break Wafdist control of the ballot box.[3]

The Foreign Office was suspicious of Loraine's policy of neutrality. Their worry was that an unpopular Sidqi government might provoke urban disorders, leading Egypt back to the confrontation politics of 1919 and 1920. By the time that Lampson replaced Loraine as high commissioner, the British and Fu'ad had tired of the prime minister. Hence, when Sidqi suffered a stroke in the summer of 1932, Fu'ad began to undermine his authority. Eventually, in September 1933, Sidqi was replaced by 'Abd al-Fattah Yahya, and

[2] No. 138, Loraine to Henderson, June 17, 1931, PRO FO 407/213. Muhammad Husayn Haykal leveled a stinging attack on the Sidqi ministry and its business ties in his pamphlet al-Siyasa al-Misriya wa-l-Inqilab al-Dusturi.

[3] See especially Haykal, al-Siyasa al-Misriya, and 'Abd al-Rahman al-Rafi'i, Fi A'qab al-Thawra al-Misriya, vol. 2, pp. 110 ff.

for the next two years the palace was the dominant force in Egyptian politics.[4]

TARIFF REFORM

In the 1930s, the main instrument for refashioning the Egyptian economy and forging an alliance between economic groups was tariff reform. Although Egyptian ministers had endeavored to persuade European states to alter the tariff structure in the previous decade, they were unsuccessful. Hence, the government had to wait until the treaty with Italy expired in February 1930 before bringing into existence a new set of customs duties.

The Sidqi government did not have a completely free hand in revising the tariffs. Customs duties constituted the single most important source of state revenue, and the state thus had to balance its desire to protect local economic interests by enacting prohibitively high tariffs with its need to collect revenues through a lower scale of duties. Even after the abolition of the Capitulations of 1937 made possible reforms in Egypt's taxation system, tariffs still remained the chief revenue source. They were not raised to prohibitive levels until the 1950s.[5]

Another difficulty that Sidqi faced was opposition from the Western powers. The British and French Chambers of Commerce in Egypt were quick to express their unhappiness. While the French worried that high tariffs would be levied on the luxury commodities in which their trade was specialized,[6] the British made their appeal on humanitarian and populist grounds, arguing that tariffs on textiles and foodstuffs would injure the poorer classes of Egypt.[7]

[4] No. 18, Campbell to Simon, September 1, 1933, PRO FO 407/217.

[5] Mabro and Radwan, *Industrialization of Egypt*, p. 47.

[6] "La Réforme Douanière Égyptienne," *Bulletin de la Chambre de Commerce Française*, 38 (1929), 1–6.

[7] "The Proposed New Customs Law and Tariff: Note Presented by the Chamber to the Egyptian Government," *Monthly Journal of the British Chamber of Commerce of Egypt*, 17, (1930), 1–9.

A further problem was that most of the specific recommendations for tariff rates had been prepared before the depression caused world commodity prices to collapse. Many duties were not as high or as protective as the Egyptian government had intended, and during the 1930s the government was compelled to make many adjustments.

The architect of the tariff reform was I. G. Lévi, secretary-general of the Egyptian Federation of Industries. The new tariff structure bore the stamp of his desire to forge an alliance of industrialists and landowners which was bound to be at the expense of the nonowning, poorer segments of the population, especially the urban work force. Lévi's proposals were consciously designed to appeal to the common interests of import-substituting industrialists and export-oriented cotton cultivators. Just as German politicians erected a grain and steel amalgam in the late nineteenth century, so Lévi and others aspired to a textiles and cotton alliance in Egypt in the 1930s.

Lévi had his greatest success in mobilizing the aspiring industrialist group. He was able to employ the Egyptian Federation of Industries in rallying support for the cause of tariff reform. He held open meetings to discuss tariffs, sent out questionnaires to members asking for information on the raw materials each industrialist used and the extent of foreign competition, and then drafted a fifty-page report which included a complete tariff reform proposal.[8]

Nor did Lévi neglect the agricultural side. Well aware of the predominant power of the large landowners, he sought to accommodate their interests as well. The agriculturalists were less well prepared for tariff reform. Lévi himself admitted that the Ministry of Agriculture, the Royal Society of Agriculture, and the General Egyptian Agricultural Syndicate had not organized around this issue.[9] Seeking to defuse discontent from these quarters, Lévi worked with another agricultural pressure group, l'Union des Agricul-

[8] *L'Égypte Industrielle*, 2 (1926), 59.
[9] *Bulletin de l'Union des Agriculteurs*, 28 (1930), 7–14.

teurs, which represented European land companies and expatriate landowners. In many statements, Lévi argued for the compatibility of agrarian and industrial interests and contended that "Egyptian industry considers and must never cease to consider the prosperity of agriculture and the well being of the workers of the land as an essential condition of its own prosperity."[10] To this end, he spoke for a reduction in the duties on fertilizers, agricultural machinery, and fuel and an increase in the duties on wheat and flour.[11]

The new Egyptian tariff system of 1930 was three-tiered. Nominal or reduced duties were enacted for items of first necessity, a middle range for half-finished and finished products, and high rates for all other imports. A major effort was made to restrict the import of wheat flour and to give Egypt's two large-scale textile firms (Misr Spinning and Weaving Company and the Filature Nationale d'É-gypte) an opportunity to expand. In 1932, the tariff on wheat and flour imports was doubled, and duties on cotton textiles were raised steadily throughout the 1930s.

Although Lévi said that the tariff reform in 1930 was "very timid" and did not afford real protection to nascent industries, perhaps he was unduly harsh.[12] The new tariffs assisted industrial growth and helped cultivators to find an important market for their cereals at a time when cotton prices were tumbling. The tariff reform brought changes in Egyptian imports, reducing the value of imported food-stuffs and increasing the importation of machines and various types of raw materials, mainly those used in Egyptian industries. By 1939, textile imports, which had accounted for 40 percent of the value of all Egyptian imports in 1920, had declined to 16.5 percent. Egyptian industrialization had been given an important boost. (See table 4.1.)

[10] "Lettre Ouverte à MM. les Experts Douaniers," ibid., 26 (1928), 1.
[11] Bulletin de l'Union des Agriculteurs, 27 (1929), 1.
[12] L. Gaddi and I. G. Lévi, "Observations Générales sur le Nouveau Tariff Douanier," L'Égypte Contemporaine, 23 (February-March 1932), pp. 217, 232.

Table 4.1.

Proportional Value of Major Imports, 1930-1939

	Percentage of Total Value (£E) of Imports Represented by Each Category in:									
	1930	1931	1932	1933	1934	1935	1936	1937	1938	1939
Foodstuffs	11.7	13.1	10.8	7.0	7.5	7.3	7.0	6.3	6.7	6.2
Processed foods, including spirits and tobacco	8.5	6.0	5.9	5.3	4.9	5.0	5.8	4.7	6.2	6.7
Chemicals and pharmaceuticals	9.8	10.2	11.1	12.4	12.7	13.1	13.6	13.5	13.1	13.5
Textiles	26.2	24.7	27.7	29.9	28.0	25.1	24.1	23.2	19.1	16.5
Metals, metalware, and machines	13.0	15.3	15.8	15.8	15.1	15.6	16.3	17.0	17.7	18.6

SOURCE: Egypt, Ministry of Finance, Statistical Department, *Annuaire Statistique*, 1930-1931 to 1939-1940.

The Defense of Agrarian Interests

If agricultural profits were to be invested in industry and commerce, as Sidqi believed they must be, then the severe shocks of the depression would have to be withstood, if not moderated. Sidqi devoted much of his energy to trying to salvage a battered agricultural sector from the storms of the depression. In defending the interests of the landlords, the Egyptian prime minister often found himself ranged against important metropolitan interests based in Egypt, notably the land banks and the foreign commercial banks.

Colonial and dependent territories were quickly and severely buffeted by the Great Depression of the 1930s. Cotton exporters like Egypt were hard hit, for not only was cotton the most valuable agricultural commodity in international trade (constituting a robust 11.3 percent of the total value of world agricultural exports in 1929), but the demand for it was relatively elastic.[13] Hence, there was a steep price decline in the 1930s.[14] Egyptian exports suffered a 60 to 65 percent drop in value between 1928–1929 and 1932–1933. By August 1931, the Liverpool price of Egyptian cotton was one-third what it had been in August 1929. This proved to be the low point. The value of Egyptian cotton exports fell from a high of £E57,443,000 in 1924 to £E12,816,000 in 1932, and even as late as 1939 their value had recovered to only half of what it had been in the first half of the 1920s.[15]

In developing a response to the difficulties posed by the depression, Sidqi was ably assisted by Ahmad 'Abd al-Wahhab, whom Sidqi appointed as under secretary of state for finance. 'Abd al-Wahhab was Sidqi's equal in economic matters and served in the Ministry of Finance, sometimes

[13] Charles R. Kindleberger, *The World in Depression, 1929–1939*, p. 87.

[14] International Institute of Agriculture, *World Cotton Production and Trade*, p. 211.

[15] Material in this paragraph was compiled from Egypt, Ministry of Finance, Statistical Department, *Annuaire Statistique*.

as the minister himself, until the Wafd returned to power in 1936.[16]

'Abd al-Wahhab's first assignment was to develop a cotton policy. He was expected to answer a number of questions that were being posed by cultivators and economists at the time. Should the state restrict the cultivation of cotton in hopes of driving up the world price of Egyptian cotton? Should it encourage the cultivation of other crops? His report of 1930, a remarkable document, laid out the main lines of the Egyptian cotton policy which was pursued during the 1930s.[17]

'Abd al-Wahhab was convinced that Egypt's cotton exports were too small for Cairo to be able to influence world prices through reductions in cotton acreages or the holding back of its exports. In his view, the main determinant of world prices was the American cotton harvest, which accounted for approximately half of the world cotton trade.[18] 'Abd al-Wahhab urged, therefore, that barring international agreements to reduce cotton cultivation, Egypt should maintain its cotton acreages. This was the policy followed during the 1930s, except in 1931–1932. It proved to be extremely successful. By maintaining a high level of cotton exports, Egypt's export earnings suffered much less than those of other cotton-exporting countries.[19]

Although this policy afforded some relief to cultivators, it did not keep them from making their perennial demand that the state purchase cotton at prices above the world market price. But the government's financial powers were limited. Although politicians boasted of the size of the gov-

[16] On Ahmad 'Abd al-Wahhab, consult *Majalla Ghurfa al-Iskandariya*, 3 (May 1938), 25–26, and Zaki Muhammad Mujahid, *al-A'lam al-Sharqiya*, vol. 1, p. 56.

[17] The report, in three parts, can be found in *Sahifa al-Tijara*, 6 (1930).

[18] These views were corroborated by a subsequent study: Mahmoud el-Darwish, "Note on the Movement of Prices of Egyptian Cotton," *L'Égypte Contemporaine*, 32 (1931), 641–644.

[19] International Institute of Agriculture, *World Cotton Production and Trade*, p. 236.

ernment reserve fund (£E40,000,000 in 1930) and regarded it as a protection against harsh economic times, in
reality it was of little long-run help. Much of it had already
been committed early in the depression. By the end of
1930, the state had expended close to £E19,000,000 from
the reserve for the purchase of cotton and, responding to
nationalist appeals, it had used another £E9,000,000 to acquire Egyptian public debt coupons, which it could not
dispose of without driving down their price and radically
depreciating the reserve fund.[20] The reserve fund in effect
was window dressing, tied up in loans, advances, and Egyptian government securities.[21] By 1932, it had been reduced
from £E40,000,000 to £E32,624,000, of which £E15,187,000
was on loan (£E8,711,000 in cotton), £E9,358,000 was invested in the Egyptian debt, and £E6,786,400 remained in
British securities.[22] The state could do little to cushion the
impact of declining world prices through cotton purchases.
Furthermore, the state was also precluded by international
understandings from reducing the level of the land tax as
a way of affording relief to the cultivators, and hence the
impact of taxation on cultivators increased markedly during the 1930s (table 4.2).

   The one area where the state did seek accommodation
was in the burden of indebtedness facing Egyptian cultivators. Funds had been borrowed in the 1920s, when plum-
meting world prices were not anticipated; as a result, landlords found themselves hard pressed to meet interest and
principal payments. Here cultivators and the state con-
fronted some of the most heavily capitalized and well-entrenched overseas interests at work in the Egyptian economy. The most active lender to the Egyptian farmer was
the Crédit Foncier Égyptien—the largest and most powerful of the land mortgage companies and indeed the most

[20] *La Revue d'Égypte Économique et Financière*, 4 (December 4, 1930).

[21] Charles Issawi, *Egypt: An Economic and Social Analysis*, p. 144.

[22] *Report of the Parliamentary Finance Committee on the Budget for 1932–
1933, Annales de la Chambre des Députés*, 5th Legislature, 2nd Session, July
5, 1932, p. 284.

Table 4.2.

Rural Taxes and Value of Cotton Harvest,
1919 to 1938-1939

	(1)	(2)	(3)	(4)
			Value of Cotton Harvest[a]	$\frac{1+2}{3}$
	Land Tax (£E)	Ghaffir Tax (£E)	(£E)	(%)
1919	5,123,513	1,048,656	107,057,000	5.8
1920	5,138,071	1,240,099	47,429,000	13.4
1921	5,176,695	1,402,985	33,977,000	19.4
1922	5,183,774	1,481,750	46,883,000	14.2
1923	5,189,041	1,361,041	58,170,000	11.3
1924-25	5,200,299	1,366,953	64,996,000	10.1
1925-26	5,219,917	1,300,648	54,508,000	12.0
1926-27	5,200,847	1,395,653	38,041,000	17.3
1927-28	5,452,335	1,370,958	41,357,000	16.5
1928-29	5,213,620	1,156,078	47,718,000	13.3
1929-30	5,128,060	1,317,979	40,025,000	16.1
1930-31	5,007,422	1,396,704	23,323,000	27.5
1931-32	4,938,836	1,497,990	15,753,000	40.9
1932-33	5,208,114	1,397,051	14,756,000	44.8
1933-34	5,603,476	1,269,158	22,072,000	31.1
1934-35	4,996,768	1,218,542	23,413,000	26.5
1935-36	5,242,915	1,191,457	27,349,000	23.5
1936-37	4,987,619	609,239	31,393,000	17.8
1937-38	5,023,877	255,571	27,220,000	19.4
1938-39	5,199,747	262,289	21,220,000	25.7

SOURCE: Egypt, Ministry of Finance, Statistical Department, *Annuaire Statistique*, 1919 to 1938-1939.

[a]Includes cotton and cottonseed.

heavily capitalized joint stock company in Egypt. Not only did it enjoy support in the highest echelons of French society, but its many small French shareholders brooked no interruption or reduction in their customary dividend and interest payments. The land mortgage firms could not be expected to be conciliatory toward Egyptian borrowers or to share Sidqi's vision of transforming the Egyptian economy by channeling capital out of agriculture.

Controversy swirled about the amount of the indebtedness and the difficulties of repayment. The land mortgage companies claimed that rural indebtedness was still relatively light and that landlords could repay if they stopped expecting help from the government. Elie Politi, editor in chief of the influential *L'Informateur*, asserted in 1932 that total rural indebtedness was approximately £E35,000,000, or £E8 per feddan, a manageable burden.[23] But another economic journal, *L'Économiste Égyptien*, objected. It pointed out that two-thirds of the landholders owned plots of less than five feddans and were not included in this figure of £E35,000,000. Estates of five feddans or less could not be expropriated because of the Kitchener five-feddan law of 1911, and hence they did not qualify for loans from the land mortgage companies. The journal estimated that the average debt on a feddan of mortgaged land was £E50— probably much closer to the truth.[24] According to data published by the Crédit Foncier Égyptien in 1934, the average debt was £E31.19 per feddan, roughly 75 percent of the sale price of land in 1935.[25] By the mortgage standards of the 1920s and 1930s, this was heavy indebtedness.[26]

The only recourse available to mortgage banks for failure to meet regular debt payments, other than allowing arrears

[23] *L'Informateur*, November 25, 1932.

[24] *L'Économiste Égyptien*, December 11, 1932. The landlord perspective may be found in *al-Fallah al-Iqtisadi*, especially vol. 1, no. 5.

[25] See the annual report of the Crédit Foncier for 1934 in *L'Informateur*, January 25, 1934.

[26] Memorandum by G. H. Selous, "Mortgage Debts of Egypt," April 2, 1935, PRO FO 141/638.

to accumulate at a higher rate of interest, was expropriation of estates and forced sales. Quite a lot of land expropriation did occur during the 1930s. By the end of 1931, forced sales had begun to take place in a substantial way. Between August 20 and November 9, 1931, the Mixed Tribunals of Cairo, Alexandria, and Mansura heard 1,007 cases of forced sales on properties of less than thirty feddans and 422 cases on properties of more than thirty feddans. The total amount of land involved was 70,627 feddans.[27] Between 1931 and 1939, no less than 188,418 feddans, worth £E6,166,689, were expropriated because of failure to pay debt charges (table 4.3).

Forced sale on a large scale was an unhappy prospect

Table 4.3.

Agricultural Land Expropriated
for Reasons of Debt, 1931-1939

	Area (feddans)	Value (£E)
1931	34,911	825,722
1932	26,471	1,256,063
1933	15,982	535,956
1934	14,970	446,400
1935	42,982	685,918
1936	18,397	831,655
1937	15,502	798,177
1938	6,643	293,701
1939	12,560	493,097
Total	188,418	6,166,689

SOURCE: Egypt, Ministry of Finance, Statistical Department, *Annuaire Statistique*, 1931-1932 to 1939-1940.

[27] *L'Informateur*, November 25, 1932.

for the land banks, however, and this fact gave the government and landed magnates considerable leverage. The money the banks would realize in a declining land sale market might not cover the principal on the debt. Additionally, the land banks were not prepared to hold and work the land of their bankrupt clients while awaiting a rise in land values. Thus, both the land mortgage companies and the hard-pressed landowners were eager to reach some accommodation. As was so often the case, they looked to the state for assistance.

The state did not fail to respond. In 1930, it used £E7,200,000 of its reserve fund to purchase 1,540,000 qantars of cotton, and it advanced £E2,250,000 to cultivators.[28] These steps were mere palliatives, however. In the same year and with financial backing from most of the major commercial and land banks in Egypt, the government created a new agricultural bank, the Crédit Agricole. This bank was given £E1,000,000 to help cultivators acquire seed and fertilizer.[29] Although ostensibly intended to assist small and medium holders, the Crédit Agricole did not distinguish between them and larger owners. A Foreign Office official concluded that the Crédit's real purpose was to prevent land sales and maintain the price of land.[30]

Other devices were also employed. In 1931, the state gave the Société Foncière d'Égypte a sum of £E100,000 to purchase lands being sold below market value. Again, it would seem that the overarching aim was to maintain the price of land.[31] In 1932, the state allowed an £E850,000 reduction in two types of rural taxes—£E750,000 in the provincial council tax and £E100,000 in the land tax.[32]

The major attack on rural indebtedness, however, did

[28] Foreign Office Minute, by Murray, May 11, 1930, PRO FO 371/14647.
[29] L'Informateur, July 1, 1932, and Sahifa al-Tijara 7 (August 1931), 1140.
[30] No. 777, Hoare to Henderson, August 22, 1931, and Note by J. Keon, No. 778, Hoare to Henderson, August 22, 1931, PRO FO 371/15428.
[31] La Revue d'Égypte Économique et Financière, 5 (December 5, 1931), 6, and L'Économiste Égyptien, December 13, 1931.
[32] L'Informateur, February 5, 1932.

not come until 1933, when Law No. 7 was enacted. This compromise agreement involved mortgage companies, debtors, and the government. It called for concessions on all sides. Because of the law's complexity, it is difficult to estimate which of the parties made the greatest sacrifices. Rural debtors argued that the land companies should reduce interest rates and write off arrears because of the unanticipated downturn in the economy and the sheer impossibility of making the payments. The companies, on the other hand, argued that they must honor shareholder and bondholder obligations, pointing out that bondholders were guaranteed a fixed rate of return. They added a further word of caution: Their shareholders and bondholders were insisting upon payment in gold, and should payments have to be made in gold, the value of which had risen when Britain and Egypt went off the gold standard in September 1931, the companies' financial plight would become desperate.

The law extracted concessions from the mortgage companies at some expense to the state. Applied to Egypt's three main mortgage banks—the Crédit Foncier Égyptien, the Land Bank of Egypt, and the Land Mortgage Company of Egypt—the law consolidated the principal and the interest on both principal and arrears of all three companies. It stipulated that the newly consolidated debts of the Crédit Foncier Égyptien and the Mortgage Company of Egypt would be payable in thirty annuities and those of the Land Bank of Egypt in thirty-five annuities. Interest rates were reduced. The Crédit Foncier Égyptien received a 6.5 percent interest rate for the first five years and 7 percent for the remaining twenty-five. The Land Mortgage Company of Egypt received 6.5 percent over the entire period, and the Land Bank 6.5 percent for ten years and 7 percent for the remaining twenty-five. In return for agreeing to interest reductions and a longer repayment period, the three establishments obtained government Treasury bonds to cover two-thirds of the arrears in annuities for the years 1929 to 1932. The Treasury bonds were quickly subscribed by the public and paid 4 and 4.5 percent interest. By turning over the proceeds of these bonds (£E4,000,000) to the mortgage companies, the government helped the banks overcome a severe liquidity crisis.[33]

Further reductions in mortgage interest rates occurred in 1935 and 1936. In 1935, the state agreed to forgo the interest due it from the mortgage companies for 1933, 1934, and 1935, a sum of approximately £E450,000.[34] The mortgage companies also allowed further reductions in interest rates in 1936.

When one considers the financial power of these mortgage firms, it is at first sight surprising that the Egyptian government was able to extract the concessions it did. But in fact, their position was transformed in the 1930s, and the change marked an important structural alteration in the Egyptian economy. In 1914, the land mortgage banks had been the heart of Egypt's open, cotton-exporting economy. Their capitalization of £E54,568,521 constituted 47 percent of the capital of all joint stock companies. Even in 1929, they still represented 41 percent of the capital invested in Egyptian joint stock companies. But the depression hit them hard; most were shaken to their foundations, and they lost much of their preeminence. To be sure, they paid a healthy 10 percent return on capital between 1928 and 1939, and their reserves were 111 percent of capital. But they did so mainly by reducing their capital from the £E45,000,000 of 1929 to £E22,000,000 by the outbreak of the war. While company profits remained high in proportion to capital, the total amount of profits paid to shareholders declined steeply during the 1930s.[35]

These aggregated land mortgage statistics are somewhat misleading, however; they reflect mainly the experience of

[33] *L'Économiste Égyptien*, December 11, 1932, and Jean G. Economides, "Le Problème de l'Endettement Rural en Égypte," *L'Égypte Contemporaine*, 43 (1952), 35–65.

[34] *L'Informateur*, April 19, 1935.

[35] Charles Issawi and Felix Rosenfeld, "Company Profits in Egypt, 1929–1939," *L'Égypte Contemporaine*, 32 (1941), 679–686.

the largest, most heavily capitalized, and politically most influential firm, the Crédit Foncier Égyptien. Crédit Foncier was able to maintain its reserves throughout the depression, and it paid a steady dividend of 12 percent of nominal capital. Yet its battle with the depression was not as successful as the figures imply. In 1933, the British ambassador in Egypt, Percy Loraine, cautioned that if Crédit Foncier had to pay its bondholders in gold, its liabilities would increase by £E7,000,000 and the company would be driven into bankrupty.[36] French diplomats and influential French business leaders were unwilling to allow this result, for the company enjoyed backing from the Crédit Foncier de France, the Banque de France, the Société Générale, and the Crédit Lyonnais.[37]

The financial situation for the other two major land mortgage companies was less happy. The Land Bank of Egypt had prospered in the late 1920s; in 1928, its reserves were 37.5 percent of its nominal capital, and it paid a 97 percent dividend. But it was unable to pay dividends in 1932, 1933, 1935, 1938, and 1939, largely because it experienced great difficulties collecting annuities.[38] In 1933, for instance, it realized only 40 percent of the annuity payments owed to it.[39] Although it was able to retain relatively substantial reserves, these were set aside for the possible gold payments demanded by its shareholders.

The third major firm, the Land Mortgage Company of Egypt, found its financial position even more precarious. It had the misfortune to be the chief land mortgage company in some of the most severely depressed regions in Egypt; in the 1930s, its operations were gradually absorbed

[36] No. 197, Loraine to Simon, February 25, 1933, PRO FO 311/17011.

[37] See especially No. 220, Gaillard to the Ministry of Foreign Affairs, December 28, 1931, FEA Box 225.

[38] Egypt, Ministry of Finance, Department of Statistics, *Statistique des Sociétés Anonymes par Actions*.

[39] Annual Report of the Land Bank of Egypt, 1932–1933, in *L'Informateur*, April 5, 1933.

into those of the Agricultural Bank, and both firms went into liquidation in 1936.

Egyptian agricultural growth slowed during the decade of the 1930s, but the value of agricultural production was able to grow at an annual rate of approximately 1.5 percent even under the adverse conditions of the depression—an indication that the government's efforts to defend the agrarian sector were not completely fruitless. Wahhab's determination to maintain a high level of cotton production in the face of declining world prices had proved to be a wise one. Although the terms of trade turned against Egypt in the early 1930s, they improved again in the mid-1930s. The reservation of the local grain market to Egyptian cultivators helped farmers, and so did the reduction in interest payments to the mortgage banks. Nevertheless, cultivators were outraged that the land tax could not be adjusted and that industrial and commercial wealth was largely untaxed because of the Capitulations.

INDUSTRIALIZATION

The second ingredient in Sidqi's economic vision was industrial growth. Sidqi's hope that tariffs would spur industrial expansion proved realistic. Heightened duties coupled with a general contraction in world trade resulted in a marked decline during the 1930s in the real value of Egyptian imports, particularly consumer goods. (See table 4.4.)

Although Egyptian industries grew during the 1930s, their progress was clearly hampered by the contraction of the Egyptian economy as a result of the depression. Egypt's gross domestic product, for instance, declined 2.5 percent per annum between 1929 and 1935.[40] Nevertheless, the amount of capital invested in industrial joint stock companies rose. In 1930, less than 9 percent of the total cap-

[40] Robert Mabro and Patrick O'Brien, "Structural Changes in the Egyptian Economy," p. 412.

Table 4.4

Egyptian Imports and Exports, 1929-1939

	Real Value of All Imports	Real Value of Consumer-Goods Imports	Real Value of Exports
1929	100	100	100
1930	91	88	80
1931	70	65	92
1932	63	59	90
1933	65	57	98
1934	75	61	100
1935	85	67	106
1936	80	60	95
1937	83	59	112
1938	82	56	96
1939	70	46	109

SOURCE: Adapted from Hansen and Lucas, "Foreign Trade Indices"; data have been recalculated with 1929 = 100.

italization of all joint stock companies operating in Egypt was located in industrial firms; by the outbreak of the war, that proportion had risen to 17 percent (table 4.5).

An increasing proportion of the capital invested in Egypt was held in Egypt, though much of it was held by the companies themselves. How much of the remaining capital belonged to foreigners resident in Egypt or native-born Egyptians is impossible to tell.[41] Indicative of changing investment habits, however, was the growth in bank deposits. Despite the sharp downturn in the world economy, the amount of money invested in savings accounts or placed

[41] Crouchley, *Investment of Foreign Capital*, p. 94.

Table 4.5

Capitalization of Industrial Joint Stock Companies
in Egypt, 1930-1939

	Total Capitalization of Industrial Companies[a]	
	Value[a] (£E)	Percentage of Capitalization of All Companies
1930	9,722,300	8.8
1931	10,071,685	8.7
1932	10,099,825	8.7
1933	10,132,813	9.1
1934	10,871,259	9.7
1935	11,638,140	11.5
1936	12,617,267	12.9
1937	13,041,039	14.8
1938	13,905,403	16.0
1939	14,686,823	16.9

SOURCE: Egypt, Ministry of Finance, Department of Statistics, *Statistique des Sociétés Anonymes*, 1940, p. 380.

[a]Includes stocks and bonds.

in bank deposits rose steadily during the 1930s (table 4.6). What is impossible to know is what proportion of these moneys came from Egyptian cultivators, as Sidqi hoped, and what proportion came from the small but wealthy and economically sophisticated foreign residential communities.

For the most part, the leading industrial firms did well financially during the 1930s, though not spectacularly so. It might be said that it was at this time that the large-scale,

Table 4.6.

Volume of Banking Activities, 1929-1938

	Post Office Savings (£E)	Number of Active Post Office Accounts	Savings in Banks (£E)	Number of Savings Accounts in Banks	Deposits in 7 Commercial Banks[a] (£E)
1929	2,271,504	175,242	1,746,890	27,441	29,212,000
1930	2,323,396	203,788	1,900,396	31,742	29,475,000
1931	2,418,786	208,700	1,806,756	30,839	32,881,000
1932	2,947,708	249,746	2,169,228	34,400	33,374,000
1933	4,476,803	276,825	2,503,970	33,335	32,484,000
1934	5,620,097	313,905	2,685,063	33,434	36,484,000
1935	6,462,358	345,964	2,589,765	31,680	38,513,000
1936	7,927,762	380,999	3,120,002	32,636	
1937	8,742,813	416,779	3,462,839	33,555	
1938	9,342,473	446,583	3,619,969	34,556	

SOURCE: Egypt, Ministry of Finance, Statistical Department, *Annuaire Statistique.*

[a]The seven banks were the National Bank of Egypt, Bank Misr, the Commercial Bank of Egypt, Banque de Commerce, Banco Italiano-Egiziano, Banco Commercia Italiano, and Banque Belge Internationale en Égypte.

heavily capitalized firms finally established their predominance over the smaller shops. As we have seen, even as late as 1929 the smaller workshops were still responsible for a high proportion of Egypt's domestic manufacturing. But they began to lose out to the large firms during the depression. By the outbreak of the war, these large manufacturers were in a much less precarious position than they had been before tariff reform and the depression.

As one might have expected, given the decline in the value of world trade, the cotton ginning and pressing companies all showed declining profit rates. But they had enjoyed extraordinarily high profit margins in the 1920s and had amassed substantial reserves; their financial position in 1939 was therefore not a cause for alarm.

The other main Egyptian industrial firms tended to concentrate in food processing, construction, and textiles. For the first time, leading textile manufacturers, cement producers, the Sugar Company, and spirits manufacturers were able to pay out regular dividends and begin to build up reserve funds. Still, their financial positions were very far from being secure. Their reserves were a mere fraction of working capital. In order to maintain the attractiveness of their stock, they felt obliged to offer dividend payments of 6 percent or higher—a practice that rendered it difficult to build up the reserve capital needed to withstand financial crises. (See table A.10.)

The improved financial situation of the industrial firms was reflected in an increase in their output and a corresponding reduction in Egypt's reliance on imported consumer commodities. Tariff protection and governmental assistance played a role here. Egyptian millers took over the flour market, for example. Although much of the market continued to be supplied by small establishments, a number of larger factories emerged, the most powerful being the Grands Moulins d'Égypte. The local spirits industry also expanded.

At the heart of Egypt's expanding manufacturing sector were three firms, each of which began to forge ahead under

tariff protection and various forms of government assistance. These were the Filature Nationale d'Égypte, the Misr
Spinning and Weaving Company, and the Sugar Company.
Their combined capitalization of slightly more than
£E5,000,000 represented nearly 40 percent of all of the
capital invested in Egyptian industrial joint stock companies
in 1937. All three firms were run by men from Egypt's
industrial elite. The president of the board of the Filature
was Michel C. Salvago, leader of the Greek business community in Egypt. The managing director was Linus Gasche,
a well-respected textile expert with long years of service in
Egypt. Other board members, like H. E. Barker, A. I. Lowe,
and J. Rolo, were among the most distinguished foreigners
resident in Egypt. The Misr Spinning and Weaving Company was directed by Tal'at Harb; not only was it the primary manufacturing enterprise of the Misr industrial complex, but it also spawned other successful Misr textile
enterprises—most notably the Misr Silk Spinning and
Weaving Company (1935), the Misr Spinning and Fine
Weaving Company at Kafr al-Dawar (1938), Bradford Dyers
(1938), and the Misr Rayon Company (1946). The Sugar
Company was directed by Henri Naus, president of the
Egyptian Federation of Industries, and later by Ahmad
'Abbud.

The three firms were heavily capitalized by Egyptian
standards of the 1930s. The Filature tripled its capital at
the end of World War I, from £E50,000 to £E150,000, and
then expanded its capital to £E500,000 in 1936. Misr Spinning and Weaving was founded in 1927 with a capital of
£E300,000 but expanded its operations and capital to nearly
£E2,000,000 in 1937. The Sugar Company's capital was
£E2,500,000 throughout the 1930s.

All three companies were capital intensive and employed
modern machine equipment. The Sugar Company's refining plant had been imported from France, Belgium, and
Germany between 1900 and 1920. It was of a high standard
at that time, but it was not replaced until after World War
II, by which time it was in a bad state of repair. Both the

Filature and the Misr Spinning Company purchased their spindles and looms in Europe. Some of the early equipment was sold to them by firms going out of business or modernizing their plant. Later, as these two firms prospered, they bought more modern equipment. In 1933, the Misr Spinning and Weaving Company purchased a large quantity of British textile factory equipment. The Misr Company had a much larger plant than the Filature. It started with 12,000 spindles and 484 looms, powered by three diesel engines of 4,500 horsepower each, and it expanded rapidly thereafter.

Egypt's textile firms were primarily involved in the manufacture of cotton piece goods, although a few firms specialized in wool, silk, linen, and rayon piece goods. Even fewer of the modern industries were involved in the manufacture of apparel, an activity which remained largely in the hands of artisans working in small workshops. The cotton piece goods produced in Egypt, at first of a poor quality, had a thick weave and were plain whites and yellows. With the passage of time, Egyptian weaving and dyeing became more expert, but the quality of the finished Egyptian product was not as fine as that of European and Asian imports.

Though modern, the Egyptian textile plants operated with many disadvantages. The 1916 ordinance prohibiting the importation of cotton compelled firms to employ the more expensive domestic cotton. Their technical capabilities were limited, and for most of the decade their finished product was a relatively unattractive cloth, not whitened or dyed and with a thick thread.[42] Although their spokesmen argued that Egyptian textiles were sturdier than the cheaper Japanese, Indian, and Italian goods, in fact textiles from these countries threatened to undermine Egyptian textile development.[43]

Egyptian textile operatives looked to the state for help.

[42] Harb, *Majmu'a Khutab*, vol. 3, pp. 36 ff.
[43] Ibid., pp. 138–144.

The state increased textile tariffs steadily throughout the 1930s and reserved an increasing portion of the local market to domestic producers.[44] (See table 4.7.) Between 1930 and 1937, for example, Misr Sinning and Weaving and the Filature Nationale increased their production of cotton piece goods from 6,000,000 square meters to 68,000,000 m², while imports of these goods declined from 180,000,000 m² to 169,000,000 m². The government also helped by selling to the two firms stockpiled cotton, and it provided them with a subsidy of twenty piasters for every qantar of cotton used in their factories.[45] It encouraged them to negotiate marketing and pricing agreements.[46]

The history of the Sugar Company in the 1930s was analogous to that of the textile firms, except that the role of the state was even greater. The Sugar Company continued to enjoy a near monopoly over domestic production. Its only internal competition was provided by a few small family firms with limited output.[47] But the ad hoc arrangements that had enabled the Sugar Company to survive in the 1920s did not suffice once the depression struck. The world price of sugar declined sharply, with the result that Japanese and Cuban sugar sold at 80 and 60 percent, respectively, below the price on the Egyptian market.[48] The only recourse was tariff protection and the regulation of production and prices.[49] In February 1931, under Isma'il Sidqi's premiership, the state and the Sugar Company reached an agreement. This *régie* reserved the Egyptian market to local production by means of protective tariffs. Only if local production was insufficient would sugar imports be allowed. The wholesale price of sugar was to be determined each year in negotiations between the state and

[44] "Appel de la Filature Nationale d'Égypte aux Pouvoirs Public," *L'Économiste Égyptien*, June 8, 1930, and *L'Informateur*, June 19, 1930.

[45] *L'Informateur*, May 3, 1938.

[46] Bank Misr, *Taqrir*, 1931, p. 22.

[47] *Sahifa al-Tijara*, 1 (April 1925), 25–29.

[48] *L'Économiste Égyptien*, August 3, 1930.

[49] Ibid., February 23, 1930.

Table 4.7.

Imports of Cotton Yarn and Cloth and Consumption of Cotton,
Yearly Average by Five-Year Periods, 1910-1914 to 1946-1950

| Yearly Average during the Five-Year Period of: | Cotton Yarn and Cloth Imported | | Value of | Consumption of Cotton by Egyptian Spinning Mills (000 qantars) |
	Amount (000 tons)	Value (£E000,000)	% of Total Imports	
1910-14	31.2	3.9	15.4	26.8
1920-24	35.4	13.7	23.1	55.8
1925-29	33.1	8.0	15.0	55.8
1930-34	27.2	4.4	13.5	176.8
1935-39	21.3	3.7	10.7	513.4
1940-44	——	——	——	868.0
1946-50	4.5	5.0	3.5	1,171.0

SOURCE: National Bank of Egypt, *Economic Bulletin*, 4 (1951), 95-103.

the company. The selling price of sugar would cover the costs of cultivation, the expenses and profits of the company, and a state excise tax. After shareholders had received a statutory 5 percent profit, any remaining surplus was to be divided between the state and the company, with the state taking 70 percent of the first £E45,000 of surplus profits, and the proportion rising to 95 percent as profits increased.[50] This division of profits later became a bone of contention between the company and the state.

Meanwhile, however, the *régie* was the salvation of the Sugar Company. The company's inability to be competitive with imports was causing it to overproduce by as much as 25,000 tons per year in the 1920s. By 1929, it was losing an estimated £E1 for every ton of sugar produced.[51] Its once abundant reserves had all but disappeared, and the firm was unable to pay dividends in 1929 and 1930. In the 1930s, however, the company's output rose (table 4.8). Although the company's accounts were far from robust in the 1930s (reserves and dividend payments remained small), the company did have a guaranteed local market.

Although the foreign residential elite continued to be dominant in the Egyptian industrial sector, nonetheless some very important Egyptian industrial leaders came to the fore in the 1930s. Moreover, in the more moderate political climate of the time, native-born industrial magnates drew closer to foreign businessmen. The heart of the native-Egyptian business and industrial empire was, of course, the Misr complex. Indeed, the only manufacturing firms run mainly by Egyptian directors in 1939 were the Misr companies. In all, there was nine Misr manufacturing enterprises, with a total working capital of £E2,243,000, the great preponderance of which was in textile production. Small Misr firms were involved in cigarette-making, construction, printing, and fisheries.

[50] Ibid., February 1, 1931, and *Sahifa al-Tijara*, 7 (February 1931), 279–295.

[51] *L'Économiste Égyptien*, August 3, 1930.

Table 4.8.

Sugar Production and Cultivation, 1929-1939

	Production of the Sugar Company (metric tons)		Area Cultivated (feddans)	Sugar Produced (qantars)
	Raw Sugar	Molasses		
1929	108,952	56,922	53,953	39,915,702
1930	107,391	53,983	53,519	38,489,324
1931	121,800	58,530	65,298	47,352,682
1932	147,394	76,954	70,055	50,295,524
1933	170,284	88,176	70,799	51,248,248
1934	154,498	80,223	60,238	47,406,015
1935	136,546	68,516	60,282	46,506,382
1936	131,879	66,565	64,270	47,354,853
1937	137,908	75,538	67,783	53,035,510
1938	160,211	78,831	68,216	51,220,146
1939	162,053	77,543	72,363	54,898,565

SOURCE: Egypt, Ministry of Finance, Statistical Department, Annuaire Statistique, 1929-1930 to 1939-1940.

At its inception, the Misr empire had been stridently nationalist. But within a short time it began to shed some of its populist nationalism and its antiforeign qualities. In 1927, when the bank founded four new companies, it stipulated that only three Egyptians were required to serve on their boards.[52] Moreover, as tariff autonomy approached and the bank's directors contemplated crating large-scale textile enterprises, they recognized the need for foreign experts. In 1929, the bank established the Misr Cotton Export Company. Recognizing the intricacies of the cotton exporting business, the bank appointed a German businessman, Hugo Lindemann, as the export firm's managing director. For the first time, a foreigner had been placed at the head of a Misr company. Lindemann had vast experience in exporting cotton from Egypt. At the time he was appointed, Tal'at Harb asserted that the bank's nationalist tradition remained intact. Lindemann, he claimed, had spent most of his life in Egypt, and though a foreigner, he was described as being infused with Egyptian nationalist sentiments.[53]

In the 1930s, the bank went further and commenced to collaborate with British capital. There were accommodations on both sides. By this time, the opposition of British embassy officials to the bank had softened. They were now willing to concede that the bank and its affiliated companies were permanently established, and they concluded that no matter how inexpertly run, Misr enterprises had acquired such national stature and popular support that the government would always ensure their survival. They began to counsel British investors to treat with the bank. The bank, for its part, modified its anti-British sensitivities and expressed willingness to collaborate with British firms and advisors. The result was a series of new joint venture enterprises which mingled British and Misr capital and board members. In 1931, the newly formed Misr Air worked out

[52] *Sahifa al-Tijara*, 4 (January 1928), 21–22.
[53] Bank Misr, *Taqrir*, 1929, p. 9.

an alliance with a British aviation company (Air Work Limited); three years later, the Misr Insurance Company was founded, with 40 percent of the capital held by C. T. Bowring and Company of Lloyds.[54] In the following year, the Misr Travel Bureau joined with Cox and Kings Ltd.[55] Subsequently, in 1937, the Misr Spinning and Weaving Company negotiated a complicated agreement with Bradford Dyers for the creation of two joint-venture textile firms in Egypt.[56]

Outside the Misr complex, the number of native-born Egyptian industrialists who were influential in the 1930s was extremely small. Egyptian industrial efforts were largely controlled by the same individuals who had already appeared on the scene in the previous decade.

An exception was Sayyid Yasin, the one Egyptian businessman to catapult to prominence in the manufacturing sector in the 1930s. In many ways, Yasin was the most committed Egyptian businessman of his age, though his enterprises were never as large as those of the industrial giants. He did not spring from landed wealth, and even after he had made a fortune, he resisted the temptation to invest in the land.

Sayyid Yasin both inherited some wealth and absorbed a great deal of business acumen from his father, who had worked as an agent of European firms and a private contractor. Yasin first established himself in business as a successful bus-line owner in Cairo, but he was driven out of this enterprise by larger, more heavily capitalized businessmen, among them Ahmad 'Abbud, who represented the British transportation firm of John Thorneycroft and Company. Determined to pursue an independent business career, Yasin spurned 'Abbud's offer to join the General Omnibus Company and instead sought another field of

[54] Larkins to Department of Trade, October 24, 1933, PRO FO 371/17034.

[55] Larkins to Department of Trade, February 24, 1934, PRO FO 371/18015.

[56] See chapter 5.

activity. An interview at the Department of Commerce and Industry persuaded him to start a glassware factory, and though the technical advice provided at the department proved almost entirely wrong, he made a success of the enterprise. By the outbreak of World War II, the Yasin glassworks plant was on a sound footing. During the war, it prospered by supplying glass products to British troops and hurricane lamps to Egyptian farmers.[57]

The 1930s, also witnessed the emergence of the Yahya business empire as a rival to the Misr complex. The first company to be founded by Amin Yahya was an export firm, the Alexandria Produce and Trading Company. Yahya subsequently created the Alexandria Pressing Company, the Alexandria Insurance Company, and the Alexandria Navigation Company. He also served as president of the Egyptian Salt and Soda Company, was vice-president of the Banque Belge et Internationale en Égypte, and sat on the boards of numerous other firms.[58]

Amin Yahya's economic empire was markedly different from that of the Misr companies. Far from being suspicious of foreign economic influences, Yahya celebrated a close working relationship with foreigners. His Alexandria associations enabled him to exploit the business talents of foreigners living in Egypt; his companies relied heavily on the expert financial assistance of foreigners like Ladislas Pathy and Marcel Messiqua.[59] Symbolic of his belief in Euro-Egyptian cooperation was the Union Alexandrine, an interest-group organization he founded in the 1930s to

[57] The material on Yasin is drawn from many sources. Nearly all of the persons I talked to commented on Sayyid Yasin's life and contributions to economic development. His struggle to retain his bus line can be followed in the Foreign Office archives, especially: Turner to Department of Trade, January 21, 1932, and April 19, 1932, PRO FO 371/16123; and Jardine to the Secretary of State, April 11, 1932, USNA 883.602/10, and Jardine to the Secretary of State, April 30, 1932, USNA 883.509/9.

[58] *Majalla Ghurfa al-Qahira*, 1 (April 1936), 3–5, and *L'Informateur*, April 10, 1936.

[59] Interviews with Ladislas Pathy, August 25, 1976, and Louis van Damme, September 9, 1978.

monitor city government and to link foreign and Egyptian interests in the city.[60] At his death in 1936, he passed on his economic interests to his son, 'Ali Amin Yahya, whose American university education provided him with even wider scope for foreign associations.

Another dynamic entrepreneur who became prominent during the depression was Ahmad 'Abbud. Although he did not become a major industrialist until 1941, when he took over the management of the Sugar Company and later created the Egyptian Fertilizer Company, a brief look at his rise offers further insight into the methods of capital accumulation in Egypt.

'Abbud's origins are obscure.[61] All accounts agree, however, that he was raised in Cairo, went to local schools, and then studied engineering at Glasgow University, where he met his future wife, a Scottish woman. Upon graduation, he took up employment in the Ottoman empire but returned to Egypt around 1920, having amassed capital under rather questionable circumstances.[62] Possessing talents ideally suited to the business and political climate of interwar Egypt, he quickly became the leading Egyptian agent-entrepreneur of the era. In the 1920s and early 1930s, he was a comprador par excellence, increasing his capital by serving overseas, mainly British, trading and contracting firms in Egypt. 'Abbud presented himself to the directors of metropolitan firms as the one Egyptian agent able to secure contracts and orders from the Egyptian government. In awarding building, concessionary, and purchasing contracts, the government usually employed a tendering system. While tenders were ostensibly decided in an open and fair competition, their final determination was not free

[60] No. 142, Lloyd to Chamberlain, February 16, 1928, PRO FO 371/13145, and *L'Informateur*, June 8, 1934.

[61] Personalities File, January 1, 1931, PRO FO 371/15420; interview with Mona Abbud Husayn and Muhammad Ali Husayn, July 18, 1977.

[62] His partner in a Palestinian railway contract was convicted of fraud and sentenced to a prison term. Personalities File, January 1, 1931, PRO FO 371/15420.

of political influence and even bribery. At one time in the 1930s, the British commercial officer estimated that 'Abbud was agent for no fewer than thirty-two British firms, including such financially powerful companies as Metropolitan Wagon and Carriage Company, Dudley Docker, Thorneycroft and Company, English Electric, Humphrey Dywidog, Topham, Jones, and Railton Engineering and Contracting, and Tilbury Dredging Company.[63]

During the 1930s, 'Abbud was involved in nearly all of the government's major tendering awards. The British embassy was inclined to believe that the secret of his success was bribery pure and simple.[64] But his talents were varied and subtle. Striving to overturn the award of a massive contract to English Electric, Imperial Chemical Industries, and Lazard Frères to heighten and electrify the Aswan dam, 'Abbud charged the government with irregularities and stirred up a nationalist press campaign against the foreign firms.[65] Seeking to protect the interests of a British client, he brought a suit in the English courts against the J. W. Gibson firm in connection with the Gebel Awlia dam contract.[66] He used his influence with Sidqi and the king to drive Yasin and other Cairo bus operators out of business and to win the concession for the Egyptian General Omnibus Company. He was involved in the Alexandria harbor dredging tender, the Gebel Awlia dam construction, and the ill-fated and controversial construction of a corniche in Alexandria.[67] Between 1933 and 1935, so pervasive and in many ways corrupting was his influence over the government that British embassy officers waged a campaign against him. They endeavored to persuade British businessmen

[63] R. Campbell to Lampson, February 27, 1935, PRO FO 371/19088.

[64] Lampson to Campbell, March 16, 1935, PRO FO 371/19088.

[65] See chapter 3.

[66] Tel. No. 79, Loraine to Foreign Office, November 1, 1933, PRO FO 371/17002.

[67] Hugh-Jones to Financial Adviser, April 16, 1934; No. 836, Peterson to Simon, September 22, 1934, PRO FO 371/18014; and No. 245, Lampson to Simon, April 15, 1934, PRO FO 371/17996.

not to employ 'Abbud as their agent.[68] But the attempt was futile. 'Abbud's talents remained indispensable to British businessmen.

Despite the Great Depression, the 1930s were a decade of some progress for Egyptian import substitution industries. A number of industries were able to make a place for themselves in the Egyptian economy. Textiles and sugar, both land-related, were especially favored, but the state also assisted a developing cement industry by purchasing locally made cement for public construction projects. Moreover, the Egyptian Federation of Industries remained a successful pressure group.

In the 1930s, Egyptian industry acquired certain well-defined characteristics which were to prove long-lasting. In the modern sector, a few large firms predominated. They sought assistance from the state and received it through tariff protection, special governmental contracts, and undemanding labor legislation. Modern sector industrialists favored oligopolistic arrangements. They fixed prices and divided up the market. A tendency to develop cartels was enhanced by the small number of directors who ran the modern industrial establishments and created interlocking directorships. Already Egyptian industry displayed a certain flaccidity, a degree of inefficiency and uncompetitiveness, and a penchant for looking to the state rather than within the firm whenever business faltered. All of these traits were magnified in the industrial crises which firms faced after World War II.

THE ELEMENTS OUTSIDE THE SIDQI ALLIANCE

Like any alliance, the Sidqi coalition of landed grandees and domestic merchants and industrialists was forged at the expense of other groups. To some extent, it undermined metropolitan financial and commercial interests. But since Sidqi valued economic and even political ties between

[68] Note from Farrer to Peterson, April 23, 1935, PRO FO 371/19088.

Egypt and Europe, the reordering of Egypt's international economic posture was relatively mild.

Sidqi's tariff reform and debt consolidation entailed financial loss or sacrifice from powerful and entrenched metropolitan interests. Even more revealing of the nationalist and antimetropolitan impulse of Sidqi's policies was his handling of monetary problems that arose when Egypt followed England off the gold standard in September 1931. Almost from the very moment of Egypt's departure from gold, an outcry was raised by European investors in Egyptian joint stock companies and public debt. These groups demanded that their dividends and interest payments be made in gold or its monetary equivalent. In their defense, they cited charters of incorporation, even though most of these documents were vague and subject to differing interpretations. Agents for the bondholders of the Egyptian public debt cited article 3 of Law No. 17 of 1904, which they claimed forbade the Egyptian government from paying in paper currencies.[69] But if Egypt were to be compelled to pay in gold, its private and public debts would skyrocket. Many private business firms would lapse into bankruptcy, while a huge proportion of the state's revenues would be absorbed by debt payments. The bondholders' case was mainly argued by large European banking establishments, who were holders of substantial amounts of Egyptian public debt.[70] The Egyptian government, on the other hand, felt that Egyptian interests were being sacrificed for European concerns. It argued that if certain European powers, guarantors of the international order, had the right to depart from the gold standard and to devalue their currencies, then Egypt was within its rights in doing the same.

The Sidqi government therefore refused to make its debt payments in gold, and the joint stock companies followed the government's lead, believing the issues to be linked. Although the Mixed Tribunals in Egypt found on behalf

[69] *La Revue d'Égypte Économique et Financière*, 5 (December 5, 1931).
[70] Hoare to Foreign Office, September 28, 1931, PRO FO 371/15409.

of the public debt bondholders, Sidqi and his successors remained adamant. They finally won the support of British officials, who feared that the whole edifice of international treaties and institutions in Egypt would be jeopardized if metropolitan interests did not yield.[71]

Fortunately for the well-being of the international economic system the Mixed Court of Appeal issued a verdict in 1936 that the gold debt coupon case was not a judicial issue but a political matter. By refusing to adjudicate, the court in effect allowed the Egyptian government to pay off its public debt in paper. The Egyptian joint stock companies quickly followed suit.[72]

The main groups to suffer from Sidqi's policies were Egypt's less affluent. Although the poorer classes in general were certainly injured by the depression, Sidqi's specific policies had an additional direct and devastating impact on the urban poor. In the first place, his tariff reform raised the prices paid by urban consumers for such essentials as textiles, bread, and sugar. Secondly, because of the government's inability to control the production, distribution, and pricing of oil products sold by oil concessionaires located in the country (Anglo-Egyptian Oil in particular), the price of these commodities, indispensable for heating, cooking, and lighting, remained high during the depression.

Although prices in Cairo fluctuated a great deal during the 1930s, the prices for wheat flour and for oil, after falling more sharply than the general cost of living in the early 1930s, rebounded and then rose more rapidly than the cost of living for most of the years up to the outbreak of the war. No doubt much of this was due to Egypt's tariff policy. Sugar suffered no fall in price, and by 1939 it was 60 percent more expensive than it had been in 1929. (See table 4.9.)

[71] Tel. No. 16, Loraine to Foreign Office, January 30, 1933, and Tel. No. 21, Loraine to Foreign Office, February 3, 1933, PRO FO 371/17011.

[72] L'Informateur, February 21, 1936.

Table 4.9.

Indices of Wholesale Prices in Cairo of Commodities
of the First Necessity, 1929-1939

	Wheat	Wheat Flour	Maize Flour	Sugar	Petrol	Wholesale Prices	Cost of Living	Expenses of Families of Government Employees Living in Cairo
1929	100	100	100	100	100	100	100	100
1930	85	92	89	100	86	90	98	95
1931	85	91	87	125	69	84	91	83
1932	77	84	72	132	67	73	87	74
1933	67	75	58	132	96	62	83	70
1934	99	101	95	131	92	77	84	75
1935	99	101	88	131	96	83	86	79
1936	80	83	69	132	97	74	86	77
1937	80	81	74	134	100	77	85	77
1938	97	101	91	152	87	79	87	80
1939	93	97	88	159	91	77	87	77

SOURCE: Compiled from indices in *Annuaire Statistique*. The original base period was January 1, 1913 to July 31, 1914, but the indices have been recalculated here with 1929 = 100.

Sidqi also revealed the state's elite bias and its disinterest in the welfare of the urban poor in his approach to labor legislation. In 1927, the second short-lived Wafdist government had undertaken to draft a comprehensive code of labor laws. Egypt desperately needed such a code, for its labor legislation at the time was primitive, consisting merely of a law drafted in 1909 to protect children working in ginneries and amended in 1920 to include tobacco factories and spinning and weaving establishments.

Attaching importance to its support among the working class, the Wafd was eager to draw up an effective and advanced code. Its recommendations included proposals for imposing responsibility on employers for the housing, food, schooling, and health of workers, a nine-hour day, no work for children under twelve years of age except under certain carefully regulated circumstances, and permission for laborers to organize unions and federations of unions.[73]

Even before the draft legislation had appeared, it met strong opposition from capitalist groups. At the Egyptian Federation of Industries, I. G. Lévi claimed that European labor codes were not suitable for Egypt, which was at a more primitive stage of economic development. Lévi's view of the Egyptian laborer, shared by other business leaders, was that the worker's needs were limited and his social horizon narrow. Moreover, Lévi believed that the government should not try to pass everything at once. It should elaborate one piece of legislation at a time and should modify the legislation as it gained greater understanding of the laborers' circumstances in Egypt.[74]

Under mounting pressures, the Wafdist program was held in abeyance, and in 1930 a special Labor Bureau was established. Shortly thereafter, Sidqi selected a new and more conservative labor committee, under the chairmanship of Yunus Salih and with I. G. Lévi among its members.

[73] See "Watha'iq Ta'rikhiya 'an al-'Amal wa-l-'Ummal fi Misr," *al-Tali'a*, 1, (May 1965), 143–162.
[74] *L'Égypte Industrielle*, 1 (1928), 47–51.

In keeping with the Lévi strategy, the committee undertook
to consider first the questions of child and female labor
and workmen's compensation, eschewing the comprehensive approach adopted by the earlier committee.[75]

In order to obtain outside technical advice, the committee
invited Harold Butler of the International Labour Office
to Egypt. This invitation was full of irony. At an earlier
stage, Lévi and others had accused the ILO of trying to
foist inappropriate European labor codes on the rest of the
world. They implied that this strategy was designed to impede
industrialization by raising labor costs. Butler did not dis-
appoint the employers, however. In his recommendations,
he argued against "a rigid and comprehensive code regulating the conditions of employment on Western European
lines." Rather, he suggested that Egypt look toward Japan,
India, Palestine, and North Africa, and averred that it was
premature for Egypt to contemplate the institution of health
insurance, old-age pensions, or unemployment insurance.[76]

Labor Laws No. 48 and No. 80 of 1933 were the conservative documents that emerged from these delibera-
tions. Although the normal minimum age of work was fixed
at twelve, children as young as nine were permitted to work
in textile factories. The rationalization was that work rou-
tines in these plants were simple and not arduous. In fact,
however, working conditions were appalling.[77] The law
merely sanctioned the continuation of the widespread use
of children in textile plants. Children between the ages of
twelve and sixteen and women were not allowed to work
for more than nine hours a day.[78]

[75] Mahmud Jamal al-din Zaki, "Qanun al-'Amal," in al-Jam'iya al-Misriya lil-Iqtisad, *Buhuth al-'Id al-Khamsini,* pp. 595–618.

[76] Egypt, Ministry of the Interior, *Report on Labour Conditions in Egypt
with Suggestions for Future Social Legislation,* p. 6.

[77] On child labor, see W. A. McKnight to Henderson, March 18, 1930,
PRO FO 371/14628.

[78] R. M. Graves to First Secretary, Residency, February 20, 1933, PRO
FO 141/760, and *L'Égypte Industrielle,* 9 (1933), 7.

A workmen's compensation code was enacted in 1936; its proposals also reveal the outlook of the ruling elite. Any worker making more than £E21 per month or 70 piasters per day was not eligible for compensation, on the ground that he made a large enough income to look after his own welfare. Also ineligible were laborers whose injuries cost them only three days' loss of work. No indemnity was allowed for the loss of a toe or of a finger other than the thumb; the argument given was that laborers should not be given an inducement to mutilate themselves. In reality, the employing class was eager to ensure that labor costs were kept to a minimum, in the belief that a cheap labor force would be an inducement to investors and entrepreneurs to channel their resources into Egyptian industry.[79]

The labor legislation enacted during the 1930s was thus quite weak. It could not have been otherwise under a Sidqi administration and in the midst of the depression. Sidqi, as a close confidant of I. G. Lévi, the ideologue of Egyptian industrialization, believed that Egyptian capitalism would expand if labor remained cheap and docile. Labor itself was weak and poorly organized. Union membership was small, and control of the unions was fought over by the Wafd and 'Abbas Halim.[80] The proletariat had little influence in the political arena, and not surprisingly the rather progressive legislation offered by the Wafd was swept aside in favor of the Lévi-Butler formulas.

Egyptian reactions to the depression were tempered ones. Whereas in tropical Africa, colonies were integrated more tightly into the world economy as exporters of raw materials, and whereas in Latin America major efforts were made to create indigenous and autonomous economic institutions, Egyptian leaders sought both to maintain the high level of cotton exports and at the same time to encourage industrial growth. The pace of industrialization

[79] *L'Égypte Industrielle*, 9 (1933), 24–25.
[80] No. 385, Loraine to Henderson, April 18, 1931, PRO FO 371/15411.

was, in fact, relatively impressive despite the hard economic times. Industries which had languished in the 1920s began to expand because of the transfer of resources from the hard-hit agricultural export sector to manufacturing. An additional impetus stemmed from the enactment of tariff reform in 1930.

The Sidqi prime ministership was crucial for the interwar years. Sidqi was the first to implement many of the projects which he and others had laid out in the immediate postwar years. In seeking to achieve a linking of interests among elite groups in Egypt, he did not hesitate to challenge the metropole. But those most disadvantaged by his policies were the working poor. Sidqi's program, however, was elaborated with Egypt's majority party, the Wafd, out of office. Although the Wafd would have favored many of Sidqi's policies, their populist orientation made them sensitive to the bias against the lower classes in these programs. In 1932, a split within the Wafd had removed some of its more conservative leaders, leaving the more radical leaders (Nahhas, Ahmad Mahir, Nuqrashi, and Makram 'Ubayd) in charge of the party. When the Wafd finally returned to power in 1936, it brought a more socially conscious emphasis back into state policies.

CHAPTER 5

FISCAL AUTONOMY, THE BANK MISR CRISIS, AND THE WAFD IN POWER, 1936–1945

In 1936, the Wafd returned to power, with British encouragement and for the purpose of negotiating a treaty with the British. The treaty signed in that year did not realize the complete independence which the Wafd had set for itself. It was signed under the pressure of an impending world war and the widespread fear in Egypt that British officials would use the outbreak of war as a pretext for abridging Egypt's hard-won liberties. Although the nationalists made some damaging concessions, including authorizing the stationing of British troops on Egyptian soil, albeit in the Suez Canal zone rather than in Cairo and Alexandria, the treaty marked another advance in Egyptian autonomy.[1]

The most important consequence to flow from the treaty was a British pledge to support an Egyptian demand for the abolition of the Capitulations. At the conference of Montreux in the next year (1937), the Egyptian delegates succeeded in getting the capitulatory powers to renounce their long-standing privileges. To do so, the Egyptian government promised not to introduce any legislation discriminatory against foreigners, and as an earnest of its intention the state allowed the Mixed Tribunals to remain in existence for an additional twelve years (until 1949).

During much of the decade between 1936 and 1945, the Wafd exercised political power. The party was in office for

---

[1] The treaty may be found in No. 258, Text of Anglo-Egyptian Treaty of Alliance, August 26, 1936, PRO FO 407/220.

fifty-two months during this ten-year interval, though its longest tenure of office (from February 4, 1942 to October 7, 1944) began when British troops compelled King Faruq to appoint Mustafa al-Nahhas as prime minister and was carried out under the strained circumstances of the war. While the Wafd's assumption of power did not mark a complete break with the Sidqi period, it did herald a readjustment in political alignments. Sidqi's policies favored the domestic bourgeoisie, landed magnates, the British, the king, and to a lesser extent traditional metropolitan financial groups. The Wafdists, on the other hand, with their populist perspectives (though by then somewhat diluted) tilted their policies away from the very narrow interests of the elite groups. Party leaders demonstrated a concern for the social consequences of capitalism. Moreover, with their greater nationalist impulse, they wanted to favor native-born Egyptian businessmen and landed oligarchs over foreign capital, whether from overseas or locally resident. No doubt the Wafdist concern with social welfare was also spurred by the appearance in the 1930s of Young Egypt and the Muslim Brotherhood, political groupings openly critical of Egyptian parliamentarianism and the predominant influence of foreign capitalists in the Egyptian economy.

During this decade of power, the Wafd continued to experience fragmentation. Two splits proved to be highly significant for the political economy, since they involved major party leaders, the formation of new parties as serious competitors to the Wafd, and some loss of prestige for the Wafd itself. In 1937, following the signing of the Anglo-Egyptian treaty, several cabinet members resigned their offices, complaining about the rise of the Blue Shirts within the party and the autocratic methods of Nahhas and of Makram 'Ubayd. Those resigning cited in particular the government's intention to award a lucrative contract for the electrification of the Aswan dam to a group of powerful foreign firms. They asserted that the contract was being made without proper safeguards and without open tendering and that it would give metropolitan capital an inordinately powerful position within the local economy. Subsequently, Ahmad Mahir resigned from the Wafd, and later he and Mahmud Fahmi al-Nuqrashi formed the Sa'dist party, which—particularly after World War II, when the Sa'dists were in office for long periods—endeavored to champion the interests of local, particularly native-born, capitalists.

The second significant breakaway occurred during the war, when the party's chief orator and customary minister of finance, Makram 'Ubayd, resigned and formed his own party, the Kutla bloc. Though there was little doubt that his resignation was prompted by an apprehension of loss of power (to Madame Nahhas and others), his issuing of the famous *Black Book*, an exposé of widespread corruption and mismanagement within the Wafd, damaged the standing of the party in educated circles.

The loss of such outstanding figures—even household names—as Nuqrashi, Mahir, and 'Ubayd, was bound to shake the foundations of the Wafd. One would have expected some diminution in the populist appeal, since the three departed leaders had always had a following among workers and students. Moreover, as the party began to reform itself, a number of large landlords joined the higher party echelons. But Nahhas, as leader of the party, continued to enjoy the prestige of being Zaghlul's successor. Young, leftist intellectuals also enlisted in the ranks during and after the war, thus enabling it to maintain a rapport with students and workers.

In this era, Makram 'Ubayd emerged as the most dynamic spokesman for a more socially conscious and state interventionist approach to economic questions. 'Ubayd served as minister of finance for thirty-nine months between 1936 and 1946, first as a Wafdist and then in various Sa'dist, Kutla bloc, and Liberal coalition ministries. His economic perspective came to dominate Egyptian politics much as Sidqi's had in the previous decade and a half. The parliamentary clashes between Sidqi and 'Ubayd over economic policy proved to be classical confrontations. Although both shared a broad set of assumptions about the capitalist road to development, their emphases were far apart. Sidqi was the proponent of big business and agriculture and believed that the economic environment should be arranged to favor the entrepreneur and the landed magnate. 'Ubayd, as befitted a Wafdist, demonstrated greater concern for the social costs of capitalist growth.

'Ubayd's budget speeches were ringing affirmations of the populist orientation of the Wafd. In 1936 and 1937, his addresses turned on the terms "equilibrium" and "democracy." While affirming his desire to maintain fiscal equilibrium and a balanced budget, he also asserted the need to achieve social equilibrium. He claimed that one entire class, the peasantry, lived in "shameful misery," and stated that if a just distribution of the tax burden and an attack on problems of unemployment were not undertaken, the poor would soon be enslaved to the rich and the rich to the foreigner.[2]

In 1942 and again in 1945, 'Ubayd articulated the same themes. He described the 1942 budget as a democratic one, in contrast to previous autocratic and bureaucratic budgets, in which the interests of the people were sacrificed to those of privileged groups. With the gap growing between rich and poor, Egypt's chief enemy was internal exploitation rather than British domination.[3] In 1945, 'Ubayd returned to the theme of equilibrium and summed up his vision by decrying the "disequilibrium between agriculture, industry, and commerce, disequilibrium between capital and labor, disequilibrium between government functionaries and the

---

[2] *Annales de la Chambre des Députés*, 6th Legislature, 1st Session, July 8, 1936, pp. 43 ff., and 6th Legislature, 2nd Session, March 17 and 18, 1937, pp. 78-138. See also *La Revue d'Égypte Économique et Financière*, 10 (May 31, 1936), 5–9.

[3] *Annales de la Chambre des Députés*, 8th Legislature, 1st Session, April 27, 1942, pp. 35–37.

liberal professions, and disequilibrium between the workers and the unemployed."[4]

'Ubayd's themes disturbed some Egyptian leaders. Sidqi and 'Ubayd had a sharp exchange in the 1945 parliamentary session. Sidqi asserted that 'Ubayd's proposals for labor legislation would slow industrial growth by increasing the wage bill and would have the long run effect of injuring the very groups 'Ubayd was seeking to help. 'Ubayd countered that Sidqi's faith in the market and in ironclad laws of supply and demand was producing economic slavery among the Egyptian workers and needed to be tempered by humanitarian values.[5]

Although 'Ubayd's attacks on the rich and privileged worried the elite, the landed magnates and native-born entrepreneurs applauded his assault on foreign privilege. 'Abd al-Hamid al-Rimali, the editor in chief of the *Bulletin* of the Cairo Chamber of Commerce, featured 'Ubayd's 1936 condemnation of foreign privilege in his journal.[6]

TAX REFORM

With the abolition of the Capitulations, the Egyptian government gained a power it had long sought—the power to impose new taxes on the foreign communities without first securing the permission of their governments. Egypt had a great need for increased revenue. The Anglo-Egyptian treaty imposed heavy military and financial burdens on the state. Egypt was expected to construct a substantial military base in the Suez Canal zone for the British army and, as befitted an ostensibly independent power, it decided to increase the size and efficiency of its own army. The cost of these programs, estimated by some at £E7,000,000, put added pressure on the government to expand revenues.

[4] *Exposé de S. E. Makram Ebeid Pacha, Ministre des Finances, sur le Projet de Budget de l'Exercice, 1945–46* (Cairo, 1945), p. 3.

[5] *Annales de la Chambre des Députés*, 9th Legislature, 1st Session, February 19, 1945, pp. 7 ff.

[6] *Majalla Ghurfa al-Qahira*, 1 (July 1936), 3–7.

Although military revenues did not rise dramatically until after World War II and the creation of the state of Israel, the military budget doubled between 1937–1938 and 1938–1939 (see table A.15).

The state also intended to be more interventionist than it had been under Zaghlul and Sidqi. Concern with the consequences of the depression caused politicians to address themselves to the issues of unemployment, street violence, and the rise of new antiparliamentary organizations. Many of the leaders came to the conclusion that Egypt's social problems were deep-seated, not likely to disappear even if the world economy revived, and that the state was required to expend more on education, public health, and other projects of social welfare.

Although there was widespread agreement on the need for taxation reform, the specific nature of the reform produced disagreements. Industrialists and merchants were accustomed to exemption from taxes and justified their privileged status on the ground that it provided incentives for economic innovation. On the other hand, the landed magnates complained bitterly that most of the burden of direct taxation fell on their shoulders. The implementation of new laws was, not surprisingly, a controversial matter, exacerbating tensions between the different segments of the ruling elite.

The taxation issue was joined in 1937, when 'Ubayd put forward a budget which sought to shift tax burdens from the shoulders of Egypt's hard-pressed landed class to the owners of industrial and commercial wealth. The Wafd was ousted from power before these new taxes could be enacted, and they were passed by the Sidqi and successor regimes amidst swirling controversy and acrimonious debate.

The Egyptian government implemented its first comprehensive taxation revision in 1939. Law No. 14 of that year introduced three new taxes. The first was a tax on dividends from stocks and bonds and interest on bank deposits. The second was a tax on industrial and commercial wages and salaries, and the third an inheritance tax.[7] At the same time, the land tax was also revised. A new land evaluation was carried out (the last one having take place in the 1890s), and the land tax rate was fixed at 16 percent of rental value. The goal of the reform was to enable the state to continue to realize approximately the same total revenue from the land tax, but to allow revisions of the incidence of taxation in light of changes in the value of land. During and after World War II, the state also exempted small holders, or reduced their land tax rate as part of a campaign to make tax rates more equitable. Land valuations increased dramatically during and after the war, following steep rises in prices for Egyptian agricultural products. But the land tax was not altered; a clause in the land tax decree had stipulated that there be no change in land valuation for a period of ten years. By 1948–1949, the land tax constituted only 2.6 percent of total revenue, after having been 14 percent in 1932–1933.

Taxation proposals were hotly contested and accentuated divisions within the ruling elite. Whereas the landed notables had complained loudly in the 1930s, the industrial and commercial groups were heard from most after 1939.[8] The tax most resented by these groups was the excess profits or war profits tax of 1941. This tax was levied on surplus joint stock company profits, defined as profits which exceeded those made in one of three previous years (1937, 1938, or 1939) or which exceeded 12 percent of the real capital invested on January 1, 1940.[9] The new tax was strongly endorsed by ʿAli al-Manzalawi, a member of the Conseil Économique and a large landowner. He asserted that the tax would be used to assist the agricultural sector,

[7] *Stock Exchange Yearbook of Egypt*, 1939, p. 9.

[8] *Monthly Journal of the British Chamber of Commerce of Egypt*, 25 (July 1938). Strong opposition was registered by landed companies, which protested that they had to pay double taxation—the land tax as well as the tax on dividends. *Bulletin de l'Union des Agriculteurs*, 36 (April 1938), 180–183, and 36 (August-September 1938), 407–416.

[9] *L'Économiste Égyptien*, January 5, 1941.

especially the fellahin, who, he claimed, had borne the brunt of all taxes until then.[10] The industrialists, on the other hand, were united in their condemnation of this fiscal measure. Stalwarts of the industrial and commercial community—Isma'il Sidqi and Hafiz 'Afifi—argued that Egypt's only hope for ameliorating the standard of living of the population lay in industrial development and that this measure would impede economic growth.[11]

Tax squabbles were a harbinger of future ruling class discord. Even though landed notables had begun to diversify their economic acivities, as yet there was not a unity of interests between landowners and industrialists. The rulers had yet to determine which sector of the economy was to pay for increased military expenditure and new programs of social welfare. The calm was broken during these years.

THE RESPONSE OF THE METROPOLE

Using its increased political power, the Egyptian elite accelerated the drive to reduce the authority of metropolitan groups and to enlarge the sphere of Egyptian economic autonomy. The abolition of the Capitulations, taxation reform, and the creation of an Egyptian central bank (see chapter 6) were major steps in this direction. But metropolitan influence was not swept aside so easily, especially in the areas of banking and trading where its forces had been so powerfully established ever since the end of the nineteenth century.

Financial groups from the metropole were never monolithic. They were divided along national lines and by economic interests. Once local industrial, commercial, and even financial firms began to rise, metropolitan businesses were forced to adjust their activities.

The European powers with smaller financial interests in

[10] Ibid., March 2, 1941.
[11] *La Revue d'Égypte Économique et Financière*, 15 (February 1, 1942), 5–6, and 15 (February 8, 1941); also *L'Économiste Égyptien*, February 2, 1941.

Egypt were quicker to accommodate to Egyptian economic nationalism. In the 1920s, the Italians founded two locally based banks, and the Belgians followed in 1929, establishing the Banque Belge et Internationale en Égypte. These banks worked closely with local commercial and industrial groups; this was especially true of the Belgian bank, which exploited its close ties with Henri Naus, one of Egypt's industrial giants.

The two great metropolitan powers moved more slowly. Despite pleas from the French embassy, French metropolitan financial interests failed to create a purely Egyptian-based bank. In the opinion of French officials, the Crédit Lyonnais and Comptoir Nationale d'Escompte lost business because they remained subsidiaries of the parent firms.

Britain's substantial economic interests were affected by tariff reform and local industrialization. Although their investments in Egypt were somewhat less than those of the French (or at least they had been at the end of the nineteenth century), their trading contacts were enormous. Moreover, through the influence of their officials within the Egyptian government and the existence of the London Consulting Office of Engineers, their businessmen expected to be Egypt's main contractors for large construction projects on the Nile and the main supplier of railway equipment.

No doubt one of the reasons that British businessmen were slow to adapt to the rise of a local industrial elite was their belief that British power would be used to favor metropolitan groups. The official British establishment was skeptical of local industrial capabilities and scorned local businessmen. In particular, the British groups paid little attention to the rising Misr empire, believing that it would not last. Although there are surprisingly few references to Misr enterprises in the British archives for the 1920s, the following comment written by the British commercial attaché in 1930 typified the attitude of the British community to this undertaking:

It is an open secret that were the local bank compelled
to meet a rush or a panic it could not meet its obligations owing to the extent of its commitments due to
its industrial enterprises and rather rash cotton advances. . . . The whole object of this native bank appears to be directed toward Arab competition with European (particulary British) banking, industrial, and
transport enterprises which in ordinary circumstances
might be considered commendable were it not for the
fact that this institution endeavors to attain its end by
relying entirely upon official support and by means of
subversive xenophobic propaganda.[12]

The high point of British trade with Egypt was reached
in 1919 and 1920, and the investment peak probably occurred just before the outbreak of World War I. From then
onward, Britain's economic position in Egypt declined. By
1938, British investments in Egypt were less than one-fourth
of what they had been before 1914. British imports, which
had constituted 30 percent of the value of all Egyptian
imports in 1913 and 46 percent in 1919, had fallen to 21
percent by 1929. In 1913, Britain had supplied 60 percent
of Egypt's textile imports (and 70 percent in 1919). As
cheap Japanese, Italian, and Indian cotton piece goods
poured into the country, however, the British share of Egypt's
textile imports declined to 26 percent by 1933. (See figure
5.1 and tables A.11–A.14.)

At first, the British endeavored to use political influence
and pressure-group methods to preserve their share of the
local market. They agitated with the Egyptian government
to alter its tariffs so that British exporters would be favored
over against their leading competitors. Various Manchester
trade missions were despatched to Egypt and, though they
did persuade the Egyptian government to impose a 40 percent surtax on Japanese imports, they did not succeed in
checking the decline in British textile imports.

[12] L.S.B. Larkins, Memorandum on the Subject of the History and Activities of Bank Misr, September 6, 1930, PRO FO 141/560.

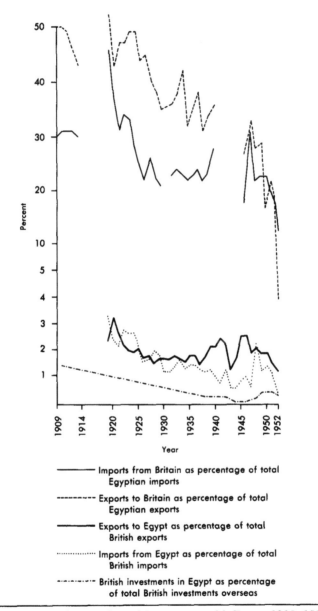

Figure 5.1 British Trade and Investment with Egypt, 1909–1952

In 1938, Lancashire used its one potentially effective economic sanction: it threatened to stop purchasing Egyptian cotton unless its manufacturers were accorded a privileged position in the Egyptian market.[13] Part of this threat was bluff. To be sure, Britain was a primary purchaser of Egyptian cotton, but the Egyptian product was essential in Lancashire manufacturing techniques. To do without certain types of Egyptian cotton would have required expensive re-equipment. Still, this ultimatum worried Egypt's powerful cotton growers, who proposed in response a quota arrangement, guaranteeing a proportion of the Egyptian textile market in exchange for assured British purchase of Egyptian cotton. This import-quota convention was on the verge of being enacted when war broke out.[14]

But British officials also realized that a changing Egyptian economy required alliances between metropolitan and local capital. Impressed by the influence of Belgian and German interests on local businessmen, United Kingdom trade mission officials promoted the formation of an Anglo-Egyptian Finance Corporation, which would link British overseas capital with local entrepreneurs. The proposal envisioned a local company with an initial capital of £100,000, provided by two or three London financial houses as well as British businessmen in Egypt and firms with large amounts of overseas British capital. The Anglo-Egyptian Finance Corporation was intended to combat the Belgian group under Naus and the German interests being coordinated by the Deutsche-Orient Bank and Siemens-Orient. This British "société d'étude" was to examine openings for investment in Egypt.[15]

The Anglo-Egyptian Finance Corporation never did become a powerful force in the Egyptian economy, but a far more significant accommodation to local capital occurred

[13] Tel. No. 252, Foreign Office to Lampson, April 15, 1938, PRO FO 371/21952.

[14] Lancashire Commercial Mission to Egypt, Shackle, Board of Trade, to Kelley, November 16, 1938, PRO FO 371/21957.

[15] Minute at Residency, May 22, 1931, and E. Cook to Turner, June 3, 1931, PRO FO 141/766.

several years later. Two large Lancashire textile firms decided to salvage their declining Egyptian market by erecting factories in Egypt itself. Although these firms—Calico Printers and Bradford Dyers—succeeded in creating factories in Egypt in the 1930s, they did not establish their own plants, as they had originally intended. Instead, they set up joint ventures with the two major Egyptian textile firms.

Calico Printers and Bradford Dyers were two of the largest British textile companies in the twentieth century. In 1905, Calico Printers was the fifth most heavily capitalized firm in the entire country, and Bradford Dyers the seventeenth.[16] Both declined after World War I, especially during the depression. According to the annual stockholders' report issued by Bradford Dyers in 1937, the yearly profits of the company, which had averaged £563,000 for the six years prior to 1929, fell to £38,000 in 1936 and £29,000 in 1937.[17]

Calico Printers was the first to enter the Egyptian industrial arena. The firm was encouraged by a British commercial attaché, who wrote that "it is . . . now time that all participation of United Kingdom capital in this rapidly developing Egyptian industry should be welcomed in official British circles"—a statement which represented a volte-face from Cromer's dismissal of Egyptian industrial efforts and reflected a changing balance of economic power in Egypt.[18] Larkins, the British commercial attaché, advised Calico Printers to align with Filature Nationale d'Égypte as a "more businesslike and commendable company" than Tal'at Harb's Misr Spinning and Weaving Company.[19] An amalgamated firm was created, called La Société Égyptienne des Indus-

[16] P. L. Payne, "The Emergence of the Large-Scale Company in Great Britain, 1870–1914," *Economic History Review*, 20 (1967), 539.

[17] This report is referred to in Bert Fish to the Secretary of State, March 28, 1938, USNA 883, 695 Dyes/1.

[18] No. 610, Lampson to Eden, enclosing memorandum by Selous, May 1936, PRO FO 371/20140.

[19] Larkins to Department of Trade, December 23, 1933, PRO FO 371/19985.

tries Textiles, with a capital of £E80,000, later increased to £E400,000, contributed equally by Calico and Filature, and with a board of directors drawn from the two parent firms. This new company, exploiting the textile expertise of Calico Printers, manufactured a higher grade of fabric than Egyptian operatives were capable of producing at that time.[20]

Bradford Dyers followed. It appeared in Egypt in 1937 in a much bolder way, engaging Alexander Keown-Boyd to head its Egyptian operations and drawing great attention to itself. Keown-Boyd was a formidable personality. For many years he had been head of the European Department of the Egyptian Ministry of the Interior, where as an intelligence gatherer for the British embassy he claimed to know more about the intricacies of Egyptian politics than any other British official. Bradford Dyers' emergence in Egypt alarmed Egyptian nationalists and financial leaders. The Egyptian press published articles holding out the specter of this powerful British company planting itself in Egypt and quickly assuming control over the country's entire textile industry.[21]

It may well have been Bradford Dyers' intention to establish an independent company in Egypt, but Keown-Boyd and Selous, another British commercial attaché, quickly persuaded company officials otherwise. Both believed that a Bradford Dyers foray into Egypt would be successful only if linked to an important Egyptian establishment. By this time, Selous was counseling alliance with the Misr Spinning and Weaving Company. Not that earlier skepticism of the Misr complex had changed; indeed, Bank Misr was only two years away from its great financial crisis, and it was widely known to have management problems. But Selous had learned that Tal'at Harb was displeased when Calico Printers chose to amalgamate with Filature rather than with Misr, and therefore he recommended an approach to Tal'at

---

[20] *La Revue d'Égypte Économique et Financière*, 8 (September 16–23, 1934), 10, and *l'Informateur*, January 3, 1936.

[21] See *Majalla Ghurfa al-Iskandariya*, 1 (July 1937), 10.

Harb "whose influence in all Egyptian circles . . . [is] immense."[22]

An agreement was struck, similar in many respects to the Calico-Filature arrangement but on a grander scale. Two new joint venture companies were established, one in which Bradford Dyers had a majority of the capital (£E200,000) and Bank Misr a minority (£E50,000), and a second firm with Bank Misr in the majority and Bradford Dyers in the minority. What eventuated was a substantial textile complex, located at Kafr al-Dawar, just outside of Alexandria. The leading firm was called La Société Misr de Filature et de Tissage Fin en Coton Égyptien (Usines Kafr al-Dawar), and it specialized in fine thread and high-quality material not previously produced in Egypt. As part of the complex, the Bradford Dyers firm ran a dyeing plant at Kafr al-Dawar.[23]

Although some Egyptian economic nationalists were displeased that this powerful British textile firm had established itself in Egypt, most were relieved that Bradford Dyers did not enter Egypt as an independent entity and that its considerable textile expertise benefited the Misr textile enterprise. This was the message promulgated by Tal'at Harb himself, who congratulated the Misr complex for having rebuffed this threat to the development of an autonomous Egyptian capitalism.[24]

This fascination story is revealing of the interwar Egyptian economy. It demonstrates how much diminished was the influence of British officials and private interests in Egypt. At a time when British textile manufacturers were desperately trying to maintain overseas markets, they were not able to reverse their declining position in a country where British political power was still great. Morcover, the foray into Egyptian manufacturing by two once-powerful

[22] Selous to Department of Trade, May 14, 1937, PRO FO 371/20897, and Selous to Department of Trade, February 1, 1934, PRO FO 371/19985.

[23] Bank Misr, *al-Yubil*, p. 195.

[24] Bank Misr, *Taqrir*, 1937, p. 10.

British textile firms enhanced the expansion and the productive capabilities of Egypt's two most important textile firms. Clearly British capitalism lost this battle to Egyptian capitalism.

THE BANK MISR CRISIS

In September 1939, a crisis at Bank Misr resulted in the abrupt resignation of Tal'at Harb and the appointment, under government pressure, of a new board. Egyptian nationalists saw in these happenings the malevolent hand of British imperialists, anxious to throttle this expression of Egyptian economic autonomy. They contended that British business and political leaders in Egypt, in league with Egyptian collaborators, turned a small run on the bank into a major crisis, precisely in order to oust Harb and replace him with two persons—Hafiz 'Afifi and 'Abd al-Maqsud Ahmad—more amenable to metropolitan British economic interests.[25]

The truth in this matter was far more complex, however. To be sure, at its inception Bank Misr was not warmly received by the British or by foreign economic groups. Its charter, prohibiting foreigners from holding stock in the bank or sitting on its board, manifested a suspicion of foreign economic aspirations. Foreign business groups in Egypt, supported by the British embassy, were suspicious of the Misr plans. They believed the bank's ideology to be tinged with nationalist xenophobia and the bank's programs beyond it capabilities.

However, as the bank shed its populist, nationalist, and antiforeign characteristics during the 1930s, it won acceptance from influential foreigners. The one potentially explosive area of discord between the British and Bank Misr involved the bank's aviation company, Misr Air. For military reasons, British officialdom wished to control avia-

[25] See especially Bank Misr, *al-Yubil,* pp. 74 ff., and Muhammad Rushdi, *al-Tatawwur al-Iqtisadi fi Misr* (Cairo, 1972), vol. 1, pp. 45–57.

tion development in Egypt, and Misr Air founded in 1931 threatened that objective. Nevertheless, by forcing Misr Air into an alliance with a British aviation company (Air Work Limited), the British were able to supervise Misr Air's activities and preclude an alignment with a non-British firm.

The details of the banking crisis are simple and easily recounted. In August and September of 1939, with a European war in the offing, there was a run on the bank. In the midst of the crisis, the Egyptian government withdrew £E1,000,000 of post-office savings deposited with the bank. When Tal'at Harb turned to the National Bank of Egypt for assistance, he was rebuffed.[26] He looked next to the Egyptian government, where Prime Minister 'Ali Mahir and Finance Minister Husayn Sirri said that the price of government support must be his resignation from the bank. He was given three days to accept the ultimatum.[27] In September 1939, Harb did resign from the board, citing poor health. He was replaced by Hafiz 'Afifi and 'Abd al-Maqsud Ahmad.

That this revered pioneer of Egyptian business was so hastily and unceremoniously replaced by two persons well known for their British sympathies and their commitment to close collaboration between foreign and Egyptian capital led many to suspect a plot. Moreover, the governor of the National Bank who refused to provide the desperately needed assistance was Edward Cook, well connected with the British official community in Egypt and with overseas British financial groups. These suspicions and rumors grew in magnitude when 'Afifi, as the new head of the Misr empire, began to extol the contributions of foreigners to Egyptian economic development in numerous speeches and articles. Under his leadership, the bank became much less active in establishing new companies. These facts persuaded Egyptian nationalists that the bank's crisis could

[26] Rushdi, *al-Tatawwur al-Iqtisadi fi Misr*, vol. 1, pp. 45–57.

[27] Muhammad Husayn Haykal, *Mudhakkirat fi-l-Siyasa al-Misriya*, vol. 2, pp. 166–168.

have been averted by timely financial assistance from the National Bank. That Bank Misr's accounts were again healthy by 1942 seemed to offer additional evidence of collusion.

In reality, the bank's financial situation was much more serious than these interpretations suggest. No annual shareholders' reports were issued in 1939 and 1940; the 1941 meeting was postponed until the end of March.[28] The bank was able to function during these difficult times only by contracting loans totaling £E2,000,000 from the Egyptian government in 1940 and by virtue of a promise made by the Council of Ministers and approved by parliament guaranteeing the present and future deposits of the bank and assuring the necessary steps to consolidate and continue the bank's prosperity.[29] This calming statement was issued in March 1940, at a time when the bank's failure to issue a shareholders' report threatened to set another run in motion.

The bank's crisis had been caused by a multitude of factors, well known to members of the board of directors and other financial experts in Egypt long before the crash.[30] According to a report issued by Hewitt, Bridson, and Newby, an independent firm of British auditors, by 1939 the bank's losses totaled over £E3,000,000. These had wiped out the entire £E1,000,000 operating capital of the bank, its £E800,000 reserve, and between £E1,000,000 and £E2,000,000 of the £E17,000,000 of depositors' money. One Foreign Office official commenting on the report noted that "the auditors are of the opinion that the former directors are criminally responsible for this state of affairs."

[28] L'Économiste Égyptien, April 7, 1940.

[29] Majlis al-Shuyukh, Majmu'a Madabit, al-Jalsat al-Sirriya (Secret), March 28, 1940, pp. 3–8, and June 12, 1940; Annales de la Chambre des Députés, 7th Legislature, 4th Session, July 22, 1941; and l'Économiste Égyptien, March 31, 1940.

[30] See, for example, Cook to Hornsby, April 20, 1939, Hornsby Papers, where Cook reported that Bank Misr was "now beginning to feel the pinch" and warned that the situation at the bank might create a problem which the government would have to face in six months.

Another British official cynically observed that "it is the kind of Bank in which I would prefer to be a director rather than a depositor," to which a wag added, "best of all would be the happy role of a director's friend."[31]

The basic problem of the bank was liquidity, brought about because of the bank's aspiration to be an aggressive instrument of local capital accumulation. In the 1930s, the bank was not as dependent as it had been in the previous decade on the landed magnates for financial support. It was able to draw capital from local merchants and industrialists and even from metropolitan groups. But its ambition to accelerate the process of industrial and commercial growth caused it to continue to pursue the same risky financial policies it had followed in the 1920s. To be specific, it neglected to build up large and relatively liquid reserve funds. Its deposits grew steadily throughout the 1930s and were allowed to become 90 percent of the Bank's total liabilities. Since many of its depositors were small investors, rather than government agencies or large firms, the bank ran clear risks from financial panics (table 5.1).

In the 1930s, the bank played an even more energetic role in starting up its Misr companies. It was especially preoccupied with the success of the Misr Spinning and Weaving Company, which, with the bank's backing, increased its working capital from £E300,000 in 1927 to £E2,000,000 by 1938. In 1938, with war clouds gathering, the bank created five new companies with a total capitalization of almost £E400,000 (table 5.2). In the same year, it held in its own portfolio of assets no less than 25 percent of the shares of all Misr companies. Moreover, in 1938 and 1939 it made advances of over £E4,000,000 to its Misr companies—loans that constituted about one-third of all of the advances made by the bank in those two years.[32]

Thus, a great deal of the liquidity crisis arose from Harb's

---

[31] The report is summarized in No. 384, Lampson to Halifax, April 16, 1940, PRO FO 371/24603. The remarks of the Foreign Office officials quoted in the text are notations to this report.

[32] Bank Misr, al-Yubil, passim.

Table 5.1.

Uses of Assets and Liabilities of Bank Misr, 1931-1938

	Advances as % of Total Assets	Reserves as % of Total Liabilities	Deposits as % of Total Liabilities	Misr Co. Securities Held by Bank as % of Total Securities in Bank's Portfolio
1931	74	4.0	72	24
1932	73	3.9	75	13
1933	71	3.9	83	15
1934	71	4.0	87	16
1935	71	3.6	85	14
1936	62	3.4	87	14
1937	60	3.3	88	14
1938	67	3.9	88	5

SOURCE: Bank Misr, *al-Yubil*, pp. 172-173.

Table 5.2.

Misr Companies Founded in 1938
and Their Capitalization

	Total Capitalization (£E)
Misr Company for Fine Spinning and Weaving	250,000
Misr Dyeing Company (Beida)	50,000[a]
Misr Clothing Company	30,000
Misr Cement Company	6,000
Misr Mining Company	40,000
Total	376,000

SOURCE: Bank Misr, *al-Yubil*, p. 191.

[a]Misr contribution only.

eagerness to found a Misr textile complex and his need to draw upon the financial resources of the bank to do so. Textile industrialization required more capital than Harb envisioned when he founded the Misr Spinning and Weaving Company. Much of the additional capital, including a loan of nearly £E3,000,000, was provided by the bank itself because of the enormous difficulties of raising private risk capital in Egypt. In addition, Harb was able to keep Beida Dyers from founding an independent textile complex in Egypt only by establishing the two joint venture firms with Bradford Dyers, and this required a Bank Misr shareholding participation of over £E100,000 and a loan in 1939 of over £E150,000.

A complicated set of governmental arrangements was required to put the bank on its feet. These generated further controversy. The government renounced interest and principal on agricultural and industrial loans which it had made to firms and individuals through the bank (£E1,000,000). It also turned over to the bank £E1,150,000 worth of Egyptian government debt bonds. Still, £E500,000 worth of debts remained outstanding, and the government's first proposal was that the capital of the bank should be reduced from £E1,000,000 to £E500,000 to cover these losses. Arguing that the stockholders must assume responsibility for such catastrophic losses and mismanagement, the minister of finance, ʿAbd al-Hamid Badawi, became the proponent of this view in parliament.[33] His position was accepted in the Chamber of Deputies but resisted with great vigor in the Senate. There, Wahib Duss and Yusuf Ahmad al-Jindi contended that this reduction in capital would penalize the bank's many small shareholders, who were not responsible for the mismanagement, and would severely weaken Egypt's one and only powerful economic institution.[34]

The government relented. In Law No. 40 of 1941, the additional £E500,000 was realized by taking £E350,000 from the profits of affiliated Misr companies and by the government's contributing an additional £E150,000 to the bank from the unified and privileged debt.[35] The government's contribution may have seemed substantial, but it was really not so. The state stood to lose a great deal more if the bank failed, since its own loans and deposits at the bank were substantial. Moreover, its depositing of government debt certificates with the bank was largely a paper transaction. The state debt was overvalued and difficult to dispose of on the open market. In return for its assistance, the government received 1,000 founders' shares and a portion of future profits, as well as representation on the board of the bank. The bank was required to introduce a system of independent auditing and to establish separate administrations for its affiliated companies.

Bank Misr advocates blamed the National Bank of Egypt

[33] *Annales de la Chambre des Députés* 7th Legislature, 4th Session, July 22, 1941, pp. 551-555.

[34] Majlis al-Shuyukh, *Majmuʿa Madabit*, al-Jalsat al-Sirriya (Secret), May 28, June 2, June 3, June 4, and June 9, 1941.

[35] The law is printed in Bank Misr, *al-Yubil*, pp. 158 ff.

for failing to come to its rescue. But the National Bank had not yet turned itself into a central bank, even though Cook, its governor, wanted it to occupy a central position within the Egyptian economy. It addition to being a commercial and private bank, responsible to its shareholders, it was also experiencing considerable pressure in 1939. Its assets had contracted by 20 percent between 1937 and 1939. At the very moment the Bank Misr crisis was occurring, the National Bank's financial situation was causing great worry. Its advances to cultivators and merchants were double what they had been in 1937, and its investments were half and its holdings of government deposits only one-quarter of their 1937 value (table 5.3).

In his annual report for 1939, Cook summed up the financial problem at that time: "Our liquid resources were thus very fully employed to provide cash both for the administration to be carried on and for the cotton crop to be purchased."[36] Cook was not trying to destroy the Misr empire when he spurned Tal'at Harb's request for a loan. He had, in fact, granted Bank Misr a large advance in the previous year. He was merely acting as a prudent banker.

The Bank Misr crisis was a severe one, not the stage-

Table 5.3.

Financial Position of National Bank of Egypt, 1937-1939
(£E)

	1937	1938	1939
Total assets	36,577,930	30,768,231	29,988,934
Investments	22,483,156	14,478,297	10,034,388
Advances	6,428,085	8,258,833	12,017,148
Total liabilities	36,577,930	30,768,231	29,988,934
Government Deposits	8,953,512	4,835,932	2,633,049
Other Deposits	18,522,003	17,204,810	16,961,768

SOURCE: National Bank of Egypt, *Annual Report*, 1939.

[36] National Bank of Egypt, *Annual Report*, 1939, p. 5.

managed production depicted by Egyptian nationalists. The bank's finances were in a chaotic condition. Without the government's show of support and the special arrangements hammered out in Law No. 40 of 1941, the bank might have collapsed. Finally, the British intervention must not be exaggerated. The outbreak of the war brought at least a temporary resolution to the dispute between the British embassy and the bank over Misr Air. The declaration of war gave the British the necessary justification to prohibit foreign airlines from obtaining aviation privileges in Egypt.

Nor is it even correct that, as many have contended, the crisis was a major turning point in the economic history of modern Egypt—an end to the effort to industrialize and to build a more autocentric capitalism in Egypt. To be sure, the crisis bought to an end Tal'at Harb's distinguished public career, but the bank and its economic empire were not radically transformed after his resignation nor did the bank repudiate Harb's vision. The new bank directors followed more prudent fiscal practices. While the main liabilities of the bank were tied up in deposits, as they had been previously, the bank's management drastically curtailed its advances to cultivators and other firms, kept a larger proportion of its assets in securities and banknotes, and increased its reserves. (See table 5.4.)

Although the parliament had mandated separate administrations for the Misr companies, they continued to be run by a small group of administrators, notably Hafiz 'Afifi and 'Abd al-Maqsud Ahmad. The bank did not create any new companies during World War II, but it could not have been expected to, since plant equipment was not available. At the conclusion of the war, however, the bank, in league with an American industrialist, Henry von Kohorn, started up a huge rayon factory (capitalization, £E2,000,000) and also created other commercial and manufacturing firms.

Although the crisis was not contrived, the politicians were quick to exploit it. The Misr economic empire was a rich prize, and Harb's resignation was foreordained. The ap-

Table 5.4.

Uses of Assets and Liabilities of Bank Misr,
1941-1952

	Advances as % of Total Assets	Reserves as % of Total Liabilities	Deposits as % of Total Liabilities
1941	47	0.8	90
1942	40	0.8	88
1943	32	2	88
1944	32	3	89
1945	23	4	90
1946	20	5	89
1947	26	5	87
1948	41	5	88
1949	53	6	86
1950	50	7	85
1951	51	6	86
1952	56	7	87

SOURCE: Bank Misr, *al-Yubil*, pp. 174-176.

pointments of ʿAfifi and Ahmad were certainly welcomed by the British. No doubt the British forcefully presented their views to ʿAli Mahir and Husayn Sirri, who chose Harb's successors.

Harb's resignation was a crushing disappointment to a person whose career to that point had been crowned only with success. Many countries have produced propagandists campaigning for national banks, shipping companies, airlines, and textile factories as manifestations of national pride, wealth, and power. But few individuals have realized so much of their vision as Talʿat Harb did. Yet his final resignation, amidst reports of gross mismanagement and corruption, raises many questioins. How does one evaluate Harb's contribution to Egyptian economic development? What were his strengths and weaknesses?

An Egyptian patriot and devout Muslim, Tal'at Harb realized that genuine independence could be achieved only by wedding the vitality and optimism of nationalism with the political might generated by economic development. Even before World War I, when he was laboring for the Umma party and writing for and supporting its newspaper, *al-Jarida*, he championed the bonding of economic development with political nationalism. His forte was as a publicist, at first through his books and articles and later much more effectively through his speeches and writings at Bank Misr. The bank's annual report was much less a statistical account of its yearly activities than a presentation of Harb's economic philosophy. There he affirmed his belief that Egypt would not be restored to its exalted place in the world without gaining control over its own economic resources or without industrializing. To this end, once the government had rejected his idea of establishing an industrial bank, he used the resources of Bank Misr to found industrial and commercial firms. He incurred the risk of a run on the bank, which finally could not be averted in 1939. But as many observers commented, he was ahead of his time as a banker. In an age accustomed to commercial banking, he was already a development banker.

His skills as publicist and visionary were never so much in evidence as when he fashioned the Misr business empire. He coaxed support and money out of the landed classes by appealing first to their self-interest and engaging the bank heavily in the purchase and export of cotton. But Harb also played upon Egyptian national vanity and visions of grandeur. His Misr Air, Misr Cinema, and Misr Shipping Company were intended to project Egyptian prowess throughout the Middle East and even beyond. Harb was a pan-Arab and a pan-Muslim. Misr Air was designed to link the capitals of the Arab world, and the Misr Shipping Company wrested from the Egyptian government a concession for transporting Muslim pilgrims from Egypt to the Arabian peninsula. In the 1920s, he opened Misr branch banks in Syria and Lebanon and prophesied Arab economic unity.

In all of these areas, Harb was a master. But as a banker and administrator, he was lacking. A graduate of the Egyptian Law School, he was not trained in finance. Perhaps some of the difficulties that occurred in the late 1930s were not entirely his fault. By that time, he was ill and unable to devote long hours to his work, as he had done previously. But he did not compensate adequately for his technical deficiencies. His understandable suspicion of foreigners and his fear that foreigners would try to take over his enterprise made him reluctant to seek outside assistance. A major aim in founding Bank Misr was to show that Egyptians had financial skills and to provide employment opportunities for Egyptians. Thus, Harb was ideologically committed to delegating responsibility to Egyptians whose qualifications were often not the equal of foreigners.

The major new economic development after 1936 (the date of the Anglo-Egyptian Treaty and the return of the Wafd to power) was the abolition of the Capitulations. The opportunity to revise the tax system and to use this powerful instrument to facilitate industrial development and economic diversification was not immediately realized, however, because of ministerial turnovers and the outbreak of World War II in 1939.

The late 1930s also saw concerted efforts by metropolitan capital, led by British textile operatives, to recoup some of its trade losses by creating joint venture industries in Egypt. The Bank Misr crisis of 1939 was not, however, part of a metropolitan campaign to challenge local capitalist initiatives. Perhaps Bank Misr's difficulties were foreordained. In order to break into the banking sector and to lead an industrializing thrust, the bank's directors had to adopt bold, even risky, financial policies—certainly not those that were traditional in the conservative commercial banking environment of interwar Egypt. But the bank also had management problems, and the depression created unanticipated additional pressures. Although Tal'at Harb was ousted and the bank subsequently proved more sympathetic to metropolitan financial concerns, the bank's directors continued to pursue the same industrial and cartelization policies that had marked the Tal'at Harb years.

CHAPTER 6

EGYPTIANIZATION AND INDUSTRIALIZATION, 1945–1952

The period preceding the seizure of power by Gamal Abdel Nasser in 1952 was an era of intense political and economic nationalism. Egyptian politicians tried to wrest full-fledged independence from the British, and the country fought a war with the newly founded state of Israel. Nationalism also manifested itself in the economic arena, where the state resumed in a particularly strident fashion its efforts to liberate the economy from metropolitan finance. Under populist pressures, the government enacted a series of corporate laws designed to regulate business firms and to increase the proportions of Egyptian capital, employees, and directors in these companies. The Egyptian currency was separated from sterling. The National Bank was transformed into a central bank and given powers to regulate the other commercial banks in Egypt, which had always been the cornerstone of metropolitan financial influence. Not surprisingly, given the decidedly nationalist thrust of these efforts, a great deal of local industrial growth occurred in this period.

Until the Wafdists returned to power in 1950, the Sa'dist party was the predominant parliamentary force in postwar Egypt. Ahmad Mahir and Mahmud Fahmi al-Nuqrashi were the prime ministers from the end of 1944 until the middle of 1948, except for a ten-month hiatus when Isma'il Sidqi held the office. The Sa'dists never enjoyed a clear parliamentary majority, and hence they had to form coalition governments. At first they aligned with Makram 'Ubayd's Kutla bloc and the Liberal Constitutionalists, and then, after quarreling with 'Ubayd, with the Liberal Constitutionalists alone.

The Sa'dists revived the Sidqi alliance of the 1930s, largely neglected under Wafdist rule. Their policies favored local industrialists and merchants as well as large landlords. But under the nationalist pressure of the period, their legislation had a much more powerful Egyptian thrust to it. The coalition governments challenged metropolitan and even domestic but non-Egyptian capital much more aggressively than any previous regime had. For instance, the laws requiring an increase in Egyptian capital, directors, and employees in joint stock companies were intended to benefit Egyptian nationals and made no allowances even for those nonnationals who had been living in Egypt and who looked upon Egypt as their homeland. Not surprisingly, then, foreign residential business leaders opposed much of this legislation and found themselves in an unexpected alliance with metropolitan groups. (See figure 6.1.)

The ties between the two wings of Egypt's bourgeoisie had always been tenuous: witness, for example, the suspicion that foreign residentials originally manifested toward Bank Misr and its nationalist orientation. But some of this hostility had been overcome in the 1930s, when the native-born bourgeoisie, led by Bank Misr itself, had begun to work more closely with foreign capital, even in some cases with metropolitan capital. In the intense populist nationalism of the postwar years, however, the latent antagonisms resurfaced.

EFFECTS OF THE WAR

World War II proved to be an even more powerful stimulant to the domestic bourgeoisie and the development of local economic initiatives than World War I had been. Egypt was once again cut off from its traditional European trading and investment partners and was thrown back on its own resources. On this occasion, however, it had a more substantial industrial base and thus was better able to take

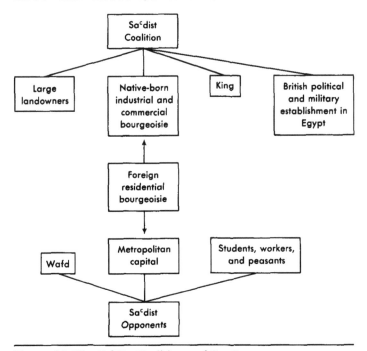

Figure 6.1 The Saʿdist Coalition and Its Opponents

advantage of this opportunity. In addition, the presence of large numbers of allied troops stationed in Egypt increased the demand for Egyptian manufactures. The output of most of the leading industries, including cotton piece goods, yarn, seed oil, petroleum, and alcohol rose sharply during the war (table 6.1).

The wartime demand for local industrial products was so intense that many plants were forced to work on twenty-four-hour shifts. The companies themselves made large profits and accumulated large reserves. In 1939–1940, the textile industries consumed 650,000 qantars of cotton to produce 38,000 tons of textiles. By war's end, these factories were using 1,067,000 qantars of cotton annually and manufacturing 45,000 tons of textiles. The net profits of the Misr Spinning and Weaving Company rose from

Table 6.1.

Industrial Production in Egypt, 1939-1945

	Cotton Yarn[a]	Cotton Woven Fabrics[a]	Cottonseed Oil	Crude Oil	Mazout	Benzine	Cement	Refined Sugar	Alcohol
1939[b]	24.0	100.8	49.2	749	282	104	368.3	233	4.6
Indices:									
1939	100	100	100	100	100	100	100	100	100
1940	96	89	121	124	140	130	99	101	109
1941	109	97	169	158	260	151	114	83	117
1942	120	109	160	150	205	158	103	70	133
1943	125	113	132	167	232	163	88	68	172
1944	126	117	123	180	239	170	115	67	187
1945	134	127	161	175	233	169	117	64	196

SOURCE: National Bank of Egypt, *Economic Bulletin*, 1951, p. 242.

[a]Production of large factories only.

[b]Output in thousand tons, except cotton woven fabrics in thousand square meters and alcohol in thousand liters.

£E200,000 in 1941–1942 to £E393,486 in 1944–1945; at that point they constituted 39 percent of nominal capital. The Filature Nationale and the new Misr textile firm at Kafr al-Dawar also realized profits ranging from 20 to 40 percent of nominal capital.[1] In addition, the industrial work force grew from 288,260 in 1942 to 361,936 in 1946, and this figure must be increased by more than 200,000 persons who were employed in the latter stages of the war by the British and also the American forces stationed in Egypt.[2] As a consequence, the proportion of Egyptians living in cities rose from 28 percent of the total population in 1937 to 33 percent in 1947, when the next census was taken.[3]

Corporate Legislation

In 1947 and 1948, with Mahmud Fahmi al-Nuqrashi and a Sa'dist coalition government in power, the state passed a series of decrees designed to bring Egypt's joint stock companies under greater state control and to enlarge the influence of Egyptian nationals in the management of these firms. Egypt's corporate legislation had hitherto been very limited. To be sure, the state had laws—and fairly stringent ones—for the incorporation of joint stock companies. Egyptian law required a khedivial act of incorporation, fixed the smallest share at £E4, and obligated each shareholder to have paid at least 25 percent of the nominal value of his shares at the outset.[4] But the only major corporate law existing in 1947 was a mild decree dealing with joint stock companies, first enacted in 1923 and revised in 1927. This legislation required that at least two directors of every com-

[1] *L'Économiste Égyptien*, December 15, 1940, December 7, 1941, and December 26, 1948; and Misr Spinning and Weaving Company, *Taqrir*, 1941, p. 10, and *Taqrir*, 1944, p. 8.

[2] Mahmoud Amin Anis, *A Study of the National Income of Egypt*, pp. 773–775.

[3] See Egypt, Ministry of Finance, Statistical and Census Department, *Population Census of Egypt*, 1937, 1947.

[4] Issa, *Capitalisme et Sociétés Anonymes en Égypte*, p. 75.

pany be Egyptians, that one-quarter of the shares of new companies be offered for purchase in Egypt, that annual stockholders' reports be published in a French and an Arabic newspaper prior to the stockholders' meeting, and that 25 percent of the white-collar employees be Egyptian.[5]

The 1947 law was more far-reaching and controversial. It had a long gestation period. First introduced into the Egyptian parliament in 1941, its proposed provisions produced cries of outrage among the foreign community at that time.[6] As it was refined, it became more radical. In its final stages, it came under the influence of 'Ata 'Afifi, one of Egypt's most outspoken critics of foreign predominance.[7] When finally passed, the law proved to be a powerful instrument of the native-born Egyptian bourgeoisie. Many foreign businessmen believed that it would ultimately result in the exclusion of all foreign investment from the country.

The new legislation had many purposes. First, it sought to Egyptianize. It requried that at least 40 percent of the board members of companies be Egyptian, 51 percent of the stock of new companies be held by nationals, 75 percent of the white-collar employees be Egyptian and receive 65 percent of the salaries, and 90 percent of the workers be Egyptian and receive 80 percent of the wages. It also sought to separate the public and private sectors by barring government officials or recent government officials from sitting on the boards of joint stock companies. Finally, the law sought to dissolve interlocking directorships in order to ensure that companies received the time and energy from their board members that they deserved. It stipulated that no person could serve on the boards of more than ten companies or be managing director of more than three.[8]

[5] *Bulletin Commercial*, September 2, 1923, and *L'Économiste Égyptien*, December 4, 1927.

[6] For the British protest, see No. 289, Lampson to Foreign Office, April 1, 1941, PRO FO 371/27470 f. 696.

[7] *Majalla Ghurfa al-Iskandariya*, 5 (April 1941), 4–5.

[8] *L'Économiste Égyptien*, June 29, 1947.

Foreign business executives residing in Egypt led the opposition to the 1947 law. They were especially critical of those clauses which increased the number of Egyptian directors and the proportion of capital to be held in Egypt. They feared that Egyptian ownership of 51 percent of the capital would result in the ousting of foreign directors. Foreign business leaders claimed that they could not implement such far-reaching changes in three years, as required. Most firms, however, did respond quickly to the law by hiring Egyptian directors, employees, and workers between 1947 and 1952. What impact the requirement on indigenizing capital would have had on Egypt's attractiveness as an area of foreign investment is difficult to tell. In 1952, the military came to power and amended the law, requiring only 49 percent Egyptian capital rather than 51 percent. But then it Egyptianized most foreign holdings following the Suez Canal invasion of 1956.

The joint stock company in general was not Egypt's only concern. Particular nationalist attention was focused on one type of joint stock company: the foreign concessionaire. Concessionaires differed from other joint stock companies in that the state conferred economic privileges on them in their acts of incorporation. Some were given access to special markets; others received territorial grants. But the most important privilege extended was a promise of absence of competition. Although some of these firms had come under the control of the domestic bourgeoisie, the majority—including the largest and most visible economically—were still run by metropolitan capital in the 1940s. Hence, they were a natural object of nationalist concern.

Most Egyptian concessionaires had come into being in the second half of the nineteenth century, when Egyptian rulers (and later their British advisors) were trying to attract European capital and business firms into the country. During that era, concessionary companies were a popular device employed, for example, by Belgian King Léopold in the Congo and by the French in Equatorial Africa to lure European capitalists into Africa. In Egypt, the stakes were somewhat different, although the largest of the Egyptian concessionaires, the Suez Canal Company, enjoyed the same massive economic and even political power which some of the African concessionaires possessed. Otherwise in Egypt, concessionary companies were brought in to run power companies (e.g., Lebon and Company for gas and electricity in Cairo and Alexandria), build railways (Delta Light Railways) and tramways (Alexandria and Ramleh Railway Company), supply cities with potable water (Alexandria Water Company and Cairo Water Company), develop agricultural lands (Behera Land Company), and build urban housing estates (Cairo Electric Railway and Heliopolis Oasis Company).

Many of these firms were given extremely generous terms. The liberality of the concessions appalled latter-day Egyptian nationalists and was a constant source of friction between them and the business interests. The best known of the concessions, that granted to the Suez Canal Company in 1854 and 1856, accorded the company a ninety-nine-year lease and did not obligate it to appoint Egyptians to the board. Nor was the company compelled to employ a proportion of Egyptians, share profits with the Egyptian government, or pay Egyptian taxes. After Khedive Isma'il sold Egypt's shares in the company and also bartered away his founders' shares, for many years Egypt's only remaining financial return on this extraordinarily lucrative venture was a small annual payment from the canal company.[9]

There were other examples of one-sided concessions. The Alexandria Water Company, established in 1879, had a perpetual concession which provided that all the profits up to 10 percent of the capital would go to shareholders; only then would any surplus be divided between shareholders and the municipality. The charter of the Tramways of Cairo, granted in 1894, made no provision for payments

[9] D. A. Farnie, *East and West of Suez*, and Bent Hansen and Khairy Tourk, "The Profitability of the Suez Canal as a Private Enterprise, 1859–1956," *Working Papers in Economics*, Institute of International Studies, University of California at Berkeley, October 1976.

to the state and imposed no obligation to turn over equipment to the state at the end of the concession. The Cairo Electric Light and Power Supply Company (1906) was awarded a sixty-year concession and had no obligation to make payments to the state. The Cairo Electric Railway and Heliopolis Oasis Company (1906) won a concession to construct an electric tram line linking Cairo with urban quarters rising on the outskirts of the city; for installing the tram line, the company was granted 2,500 hectares at Heliopolis, where it was permitted to develop and manage a housing estate. Each of these companies derived its financing from Europe and was managed by Europeans. In every case, the firms were granted economic privileges, ususally of a monopolistic nature, for which the Egyptian government and people often received no return other than the provision of the services.[10]

The Egyptian rulers of the twentieth century attempted to rectify the inequities in the concessionaire system. When occasions arose for renegotiating charters, the government sought to increase Egyptian control. It demanded the appointment of Egyptians to the board of directors, a fairer division of profits, and more consultation about rates and the quality of service.[11] A good example was the 1936 agreement between the Suez Canal Company and the Egyptian government. This agreement guaranteed two places on the board to Egyptians and required the company to make an annual payment of £200,000 to the government.[12] Other European-run concessionary companies, subject to the same pressures, were forced to make similar changes in their charters.

[10] This information comes from various Egyptian financial handbooks, especially those edited by Papasian. On the Cairo Tramway concession, consult Note au Conseil des Ministres, June 25, 1908, from Ahmad Mazloum, Minister of Finance, Egyptian Archives, Council of Ministers, Box 2-A.

[11] See Makram 'Ubayd's speech in the parliament: *Annales de la Chambre des Députés*, 6th Legislature, 2nd Session, March 17, 1937, pp. 113–116.

[12] *La Revue d'Égypte Économique et Financière*, 10 (April 29, 1936).

In the late 1940s, the state attempted to go further. Despite intense opposition from metropolitan financial groups, Egyptian nationalists introduced into the parliament a concessions bill, which became law in 1947. The main provisions of the law were that new concessions could be granted for no longer than thirty years and that profits payable to shareholders were not to exceed 10 percent of capital. Surpluses beyond that figure could be used to create a reserve fund, provided the reserve did not exceed 10 percent of capital, either. Any additional surpluses were to be employed to improve services or lower rates.[13]

The bills on concessionaires and other joint stock companies were accompanied by another piece of legislation regulating business activity. A mining ordinance approved by the parliament in 1948 tightened the requirements for prospecting and developing oil wells in Egypt. Its most important provision stipulated that new prospecting licenses would be granted only to Egyptian companies. Since the 1947 joint stock company law required Egyptian companies to offer 51 percent of their stock to Egyptians and to place Egyptian nationals on 40 percent of the board seats, the oil companies were threatened with a greater degree of Egyptian control than they had ever experienced.[14]

Although various oil firms were involved in Egypt, three large multinationals predominated: Shell Oil, whose affiliate in Egypt was Anglo-Egyptian Oilfields; Socony-Vacuum (later Mobil); and Standard Oil of New Jersey. These were in fact the only multinationals that played an important role in Egypt's interwar economy.[15] Others, like Im-

[13] Ibid., 13 (January 28, 1939); *L'Économiste Égyptien*, January 29, 1939; and No. 878, Campbell to Bevin, October 22, 1947, PRO FO 371/63097.

[14] *L'Économiste Égyptien*, March 21, 1948, and Tuck to the Secretary of State, March 26, 1948, USNA 883.6363/3-1848; Tuck to the Secretary of State, March 26, 1948, USNA 883.6363/3-2648; and Tuck to the Secretary of State, August 11, 1948, USNA 883.6363/8-748.

[15] In thinking about multinationals, I have consulted: Robert Gilpin, *U. S. Power and the Multinational Corporation: The Political Economy of Direct Foreign Investment* (New York, 1975); Raymond Vernon, *Storm over the Multinationals: The Real Issues* (Cambridge, Mass., 1977); W. J. Reader,

perial Chemical Industries, American Cyanamid, Dunlop Tyres, and Firestone, became influential in Egypt only at the end of World War II.

Egypt's experience with the oil multinationals had not been a happy one. It would not be fair to generalize from the actions of three firms, but many of the charges that critics have leveled at multinationals in the third world apply to these oil companies. Their size and vast economic and political resources made it difficult for the Egyptian government to control them. They were not above employing sharp practices to swell their revenues, and their profits in the 1920s and 1930s were unconscionably high, at least in the opinion of officials at the British and Amercian embassies.[16] For a long time, Anglo-Egyptian Oilfields refused to permit Egyptian inspection of its refinery, on the grounds that its secret production processes would be revealed. In fact, its intention was to keep the Egyptian government from obtaining information on the costs of production and regulating the sale of oil products in the local market. When the Egyptian representatives were finally allowed admittance to the plant, they of course discovered that the production techniques in operation there

---

Imperial Chemical Industries: A History, 2 vols. (London, 1970); Anthony Sampson, *The Seven Sisters: The Great Oil Companies and the World They Shaped* (New York, 1975); Richard Sklar, *Corporate Power in an African State: The Political Impact of Multinational Mining Companies in Zambia* (Los Angeles, 1975); Grant L. Reuben, *Private Foreign Investment in Development* (Oxford, 1973); Lawrence G. Franko, *The European Multinationals: A Renewed Challenge to American and British Big Business* (Stamford, Conn., 1976); Frederick Pedler, *The Lion and the Unicorn in Africa: A History of the Origins of the United Africa Company, 1787–1931* (London, 1974); D. K. Fieldhouse, *Unilever Overseas: The Anatomy of a Multinational, 1895–1965* (Stanford, Cal., 1978); Christopher Tugendhat, *The Multinationals* (London, 1971); Norman Girvan, *Corporate Imperialism: Conflict and Expropriation* (White Plains, N.Y., 1976); Stephen Hymer, "The Multinational Corporation and the Law of Uneven Development," in *Economics and World Order from the 1970s to the 1990s*, ed. Jagdish N. Bhagwati (London, 1972), pp. 113–140.

[16] W. M. Jardine to the Secretary of State, January 30, 1933, USNA 883.6363/39, and No. 139, Yencken to Peterson, June 24. 1933, PRO FO 371/17025.

were not different from those in use everywhere else in the world.

The major oil firm in Egypt was Anglo-Egyptian Oilfields. It owed its primacy to Lord Kitchener, who, as British consul-general, had persuaded the Egyptian government to grant an extremely generous concession to the firm. Anxious to secure British predominance in Egyptian oil exploration, Kitchener in 1913 made concessions to Shell Oil, including royalty and other arrangements, which were more liberal than those prevailing in standard oil treaties of the period. The royalty payable to the Egyptian government was fixed at a paltry 1.5 percent and was only gradually increased to 5 percent, well below the oil royalties being paid at the time.[17] By obtaining a minority of the stock of the newly created Shell affiliate for the Egyptian government, Kitchener secured a position on the board for a government representative. But for a while this concession proved hollow, since the main Egyptian officials were British. For many years, the advisor to the Egyptian government on oil matters was a British official and the Egyptian government delegate on the board of Anglo-Egyptian Oil was Henry McMahon, a former British high commissioner in Egypt.[18]

Anglo-Egyptian Oil began prospecting in the Red Sea area. Its first strike was at Gamsa in 1910, but its most important well proved to be Hurghada, which began to yield oil in 1914.[19] The subsequent history of Egyptian oil development revolved around Egyptian efforts to reacquire the control which Kitchener had given away. According to the 1913 treaty, Anglo-Egyptian Oil was obligated to supply Egypt with its oil needs at or below world market prices. But in the 1920s and 1930s, Anglo-Egyptian

[17] No. 970, High Commissioner to Foreign Office, September 12, 1919, PRO FO 141/426.

[18] As an example of British influence over oil matters, see E. M. Dowson, Financial Adviser, to Henry McMahon, July 11, 1921, PRO FO 141/426.

[19] Egypt, Ministry of Finance, Mines and Quarries Department, *Report on the Mineral Industry of Egypt*, 1922, p. 1.

Oil was able, through devious practices, to evade this requirement, compelling Egyptian consumers to pay high prices.[20] Since the Egyptian populace used kerosene for fuel, lighting, and cooking, these marketing practices affected large numbers and had an impact on standards of living.

At the time the mining ordinance was passed, in 1948, the oil companies were already greatly distressed about their financial situation in Egypt. The government had introduced oil price controls during World War II and retained them after the war. The primary object was to make cheap kerosene available to Egyptian consumers. To do so, the government compelled the oil companies to sell kerosene at a loss, but it permitted them to market their other oil products at higher prices. A price stabilization fund was created, designed to secure reasonable profits to the oil companies by ensuring that losses on certain products were offset by gains on others. The companies were greatly troubled, however, by the fact that this fund was running a deficit of £E1,000,000 in 1949.[21]

Given these unsettled conditions, the companies embarked upon no further exploration work. Never having enjoyed financial success in Egypt, Standard Oil of New Jersey closed down its entire Egyptian operation.[22] Although the other firms enjoyed a reprieve when the military came to power in 1952, it lasted only four years for Anglo-Egyptian Oilfields, which was sequestered following the Anglo-French invasion of the Suez Canal zone in 1956.

At the time of the sequestration, Anglo-Egyptian Oil was the largest British firm in Egypt. Its refinery and five oilfields were worth an estimated £20,000,000. Unlike many joint stock companies based in Egypt, the majority of the

[20] E. M. Dowson to Henry McMahon, July 11, 1921, PRO FO 141/426.

[21] Petroleum in Egypt: A Report Prepared for the Ambassador, November 29, 1949, USNA 883.6363/11-2949.

[22] "Memorandum of Conversation by Mr. Richard Fundhouser of the Office of African and Near Eastern Affairs," January 25, 1950, United States Department of State, *Foreign Relations*, 1950, pp. 15–18.

stock of the firm continued to be held overseas. Sixty percent of the shares were divided equally between Shell and
British Petroleum, 22 percent were in the hands of Egyptian shareholders, 10 percent belonged to the Egyptian
government, and 6 percent were held by private British
shareholders.[23]

Indigenization of Boards and Shareholding

The campaign against foreign firms which culminated
in these legislative enactments was intended to increase the
local direction of companies, stimulate Egyptian investment, and provide greater job opportunities for Egyptians.
Actually, a considerable amount of Egyptian capital was
already invested in local companies and the control of many
firms had already passed into the hands of the domestic
bourgeoisie, albeit its foreign residential wing.

A steady Egyptianization of capital had been occurring
ever since 1914, which may be considered the high-water
mark of metropolitan financial dominance of Egypt. The
years between 1914 and 1933 saw the formation of 153
companies. In 51 of them, the majority of capital came
from overseas, but 102 were subscribed locally. The proportion of shares held in Egypt rose from £E28,899,000
out of £E100,152,000 in 1914 to £E49,723,333 out of
£E99,371,000 in 1933, though a great deal of this Egyptianization was the holding by Egyptian companies of their
own stock.[24] This trend was maintained between 1933 and
1948, during which period the proportion of local capital
in new joint stock companies increased to 79 percent.[25] (See
table 6.2.) Indeed, according to one estimate the
£E357,000,000 of foreign capital—both metropolitan and
locally based—in Egypt in 1948 constituted only 15.5 per-

---

[23] *Times* (London), November 30, 1956.

[24] Crouchley, *Investment of Foreign Capital*, p. 39–43.

[25] *Majalla Ghurfa al-Qahira*, 16 (July and August 1951), 642–648.

Table 6.2.

Egyptian and Foreign Capital in Joint Stock Companies, 1948

| | Value of Capital, 1948 (£E) | | | Percentage |
	Egyptian-Held	Foreign-Held	Total	Egyptian-Held
Companies founded before 1933	6,006,635	60,733,751	66,740,386	9
Companies founded 1933-1948	21,041,566	5,677,048	26,718,614	79
Increase in capital, 1933-1948	19,260,632	5,213,378	24,474,010	79
Total	46,308,833	71,624,177	117,933,010	39

SOURCE: Articles by ᶜAbd Allah Fikri Abaza, in *Majalla Ghurfa al-Qahira*, 16 (July and August 1951).

cent of Egypt's national wealth, and even that figure is almost certainly too high.[26]

Another prominent aspect of Egyptianization or at least indigenization was the increasingly important role played by Egyptians and foreigners resident in Egypt in the direction of joint stock companies. By the end of World War II, the number of Egyptians serving on boards had increased dramatically. Nor were they serving merely for political purposes or to appease nationalist sensitivities or even to satisfy the 1927 joint stock company law requiring two Egyptians on every board. Many were appointed because of their financial acumen, though their numbers were so limited that the same small group served on numerous boards. An even more noticeable trend was the increased number of persons of foreign nationality but permanently resident in Egypt serving on these boards. This group also represented an important indigenization tendency.

Any effort to assess the Egyptianization and indigenization of joint stock companies through membership on boards of directors is fraught with difficulty. Minutes of the meetings have not been preserved. It is impossible to know the influence individual members exercised. On the basis of a general understanding of Egyptian business history, however, one can identify persons, Egyptian and foreign, who were influential, experienced businessmen and whose opinions as board members on company matters

[26] 'Abd Allah Fikri Abaza, in *Majalla Ghurfa al-Qahira*, 16 (September 1951), 761–771, cited data showing that 13.7 percent of all capital in Egypt in 1948 was foreign capital. However, he pointed out that his calculations did not include branches of foreign companies operating in Egypt, of which there were 242 in that year. He estimated that their worth was £E45,000,000 and that the proportion of foreign capital was therefore actually about 15.5 percent. On the other hand, his figures included only the nominal capital of the joint stock companies; his estimate of £E300 per feddan for the worth of agricultural land must be considered too low; and his estimate of capital in the informal sector, based on the building tax, also surely yielded a figure far below the true value of that amorphous but important sector. It seems clear, then, that foreign capital was less than 15 percent of the total.

were presumably taken seriously. The boards themselves set the broad and general policies of the firms, for most Egyptian firms were not so large or so complex that board members were not able to understand the operations of the firm and determine its general policy. Moreover, in most Egyptian companies the top one or two management figures sat on the boards. The separation of ownership from management and the rise to power of a managerial elite, so characteristic of nineteenth-century American businesses, had not yet emerged in most twentieth-century Egyptian business concerns.

Nonetheless, in analyzing the direction of companies one cannot focus attention on the boards to the exclusion of shareholders and the actual shareholding situation. If the majority of the shares of a company were held overseas, the board of such a company, no matter how indigenous it might be, could not neglect this reality. Still, there were wide variations in the influence that shareholders had over boards. French capital, for example, was dispersed, and French companies in Egypt were easily threatened by local management takeovers. Even so powerful a French firm as the Crédit Foncier Égyptien had to be responsive to its Egyptian board members, particularly during the 1930s when Tal'at Harb was buying up all the available shares of the firm in hopes of being able to hold a majority of the voting shares at stockholders' meetings.[27] At the opposite

[27] In 1934, for example, the Crédit Foncier Égyptien had 500,000 shares; of the 201,123 of these that were reported at the annual stockholders' meeting that year, 104,274 were in Egyptian hands, 82,259 belonged to French citizens, and 14,590 to nationals of other countries. Thus, it was not unrealistic for Tal'at Harb to hope for an Egyptian management takeover. In 1934, he was estimated to be holding 30,000 shares on behalf of the Egyptian government. (No. 20, French Ambassador to Ministry of Foreign Affairs, January 24, 1934, FEA, Box 225.) The total French holdings were estimated at between 225,000 and 250,000, but as can be seen, the ordinary shareholder took little interest in the affairs of the management. (Vincenot to French Minister, Cairo, January 30, 1935, FEA, Box 225.) These shareholder figures appear not to have altered much from that point onward. When the Crédit was nationalized in 1956,

extreme was the Banque Belge et Internationale en Égypte, which appointed a large number of impressive Egyptians to its board. Its policies, however, were always determined by its managing director, an appointee of the Société Générale de Belgique which was in turn the majority shareholder of the bank.[28]

These qualifications notwithstanding, an examination of the *Egyptian Stock Exchange Yearbook* for 1946 reveals a dramatic rise in the indigenous direction of joint stock companies. Of 342 joint stock companies described in the yearbook, only 43 were dominated by overseas foreigners, though it must be conceded that many of these companies were the most heavily capitalized. The remaining 299 companies had significant indigenous participation, in all cases far beyond the two Egyptian board members required by the 1927 law. Many important Egyptian businessmen served, but the most powerful group was the foreign community of Egypt. These men were permanently domiciled in Egypt; they intended to live out their lives there and to have their children succeed to their properties and fortunes. There were 18 firms in which the board was predominantly constituted of Syrians, 22 Greek companies, and 38 Jewish firms; these firms were almost exclusively in the hands of foreign persons resident in Egypt. Another 60 firms were run by Egyptians. Of the remaining companies, the largest number were directed by mixed boards of Egyptians and foreigners resident in Egypt. (See table 6.3.)

The transformation that had taken place between 1920 and 1950 was striking. In 1920, business firms were organized on national lines. Firms depended on large European branch banks and were managed by board mem-

the French shareholders estimated that French nationals still possessed over 200,000 of the shares. The Egyptian holdings were approximately what they had been in 1934. (Représentation des Actions du Crédit Foncier Égyptien at stockholders' meetings of January 18, 1955, and January 18, 1956, FEA, Box 225.)

[28] Interview with Louis van Damme, managing director of Banque Belge et Internationale en Égypte, September 8, 1978, and *Ruz al-Yusuf*, December 15, 1961, pp. 26–28.

Table 6.3.

Number and Capitalization of Joint Stock Companies
Operating in Egypt, 1946, by Nationality of
Board of Directors

Nationality of Board of Directors[a]	Number of Companies	Total Nominal Capitalization (£E)
Armenian	1	100,000
Italian	1	25,000
French (not including Suez Canal Company)	3	10,046,898
Belgian	18	6,921,821
British	18	6,759,777
Syrian	18	3,091,759
Greek	22	3,861,887
Jewish	38	7,020,048
Egyptian	60	25,094,185
Mixed	163	38,173,263

SOURCE: Names of board members and capitalization of companies from *Egyptian Stock Exchange Yearbook*, 1946. Affiliated and branch companies of metropolitan firms were not included in this yearbook.

[a]A board is designated here as being of a given nationality if a large number, though not necessarily all, of its members were of that nationality. The names of the individual members were the basis for determining nationality. The Jews were, of course, drawn from many different national groups.

bers based overseas. By 1950, such firms were no longer so prominent; those that existed were much more "Egyptian." They were now directed by foreigners resident in Egypt. Even more prevalent were companies run by a mixed board of Egyptians and foreigners resident in Egypt.

The elite in Egypt endeavored to assert control over for-

eign capital through legislation and the purchase of stock
of foreign companies on the bourse. By 1952, this effort
had certainly not liberated the country from overseas economic dominance (and consequently a spate of Egyptianization decrees was carried out in the 1950s), but considering the fact that Egyptians eschewed radical approaches
to the problem in favor of gradual, negotiated arrangements, they had accomplished more than most observers
would have thought possible in 1920.

Of the two methods for asserting control, legislation proved
less effective than stock and bond purchase. The Egyptian
political elite seemed unable to strike a happy balance in
its corporate legislation between regulation and encouragement of foreign investors. The laws passed in the 1920s
and 1930s imposed only minimal Egyptianization requirements on local firms. Those passed after World War II,
framed under strong nationalist pressures, aroused the resentment of the foreign resident business groups as well as
of metropolitan financiers. The joint stock company law of
1947 and the mining law of 1948 threatened all foreign
enterprises because of their insistence on Egyptians holding a majority of the shares.

Although a proposal to nationalize foreign capital through
local purchase may on the face of things seem naively optimistic, in fact Egyptians accomplished a great deal. By
1948, Egyptian nationals held 39 percent of the total capital
invested in joint stock companies of the country. Moreover,
most of these companies were run by persons residing in
Egypt. Many of the directors in the 1940s were native-born
Egyptians, though an even larger number were foreigners
who were permanently domiciled in the country. But the
two wings of the domestic bourgeoisie had hardly forged
a solid alliance. The nationalist effervescense of the late
1940s, coupled with the nationalist business legislation, had
heightened suspicion. Moreover, the foreign business leaders, by separating themselves from the main stream of
Egyptian life and embracing European ways, aroused deep-
seated resentment against themselves from all segments of

Egyptian society and even from within the lower strata of their own communities.

CREATION OF A CENTRAL BANK

Egyptian economic nationalists had been anxious for a long time to create a central bank and to use its powers to gain control over the money and banking system, thereby reducing the influence of foreign banks over the local economy. Foreign banks were of course the centerpieces of metropolitan business empires in Egypt. Under nationalist pressures, many had turned themselves into "Egyptian" joint stock companies, but they were still controlled by overseas business interests and were more responsive to the needs of the metropole than to those of Egypt. While they gave Egypt access to the enormous financial resources of the metropole, they took their cue from overseas. Because of their overseas backing, it was virtually impossible for the Egyptians to regulate them and to ensure that their policies operated in the interests of the Egyptian economy.

Beginning in the 1930s, under the impact of the depression, demands were made to create a central bank. The nationalists envisioned an institution that would have control over the finances of the country, that would be a bank of issue and a banker's bank, holding government funds and the deposits of other banks in Egypt, and that would regulate the money supply by rediscounting bills from other banks and by purchasing currencies on the open market.

The nature of the Egyptian economy, however, made it difficult to create a genuine central bank. The link between the British and Egyptian currencies established during World War I gave foreign banks operating in Egypt easy access to the London money market. They could convert funds into Egyptian currency at par at any time. Thus, no rediscount market could develop. As long as currency and exchange controls were lacking, foreign firms had no obligation or incentive to deposit funds in an Egyptian bank, and thus no single bank in Egypt was in a position to ex-

ercise control over the expansion or contraction of credit
or the money supply. Since most of the banks in Egypt
were foreign affiliates, they tended to expand or withhold
credit on the basis of overseas financial concerns.

The Egyptian financial institution which bore the closest
resemblance to a central bank was the National Bank of
Egypt, created in 1898. It was a bank of issue and held
many of the government's deposits. But it was not a banker's bank, since other banks in Egypt deposited funds with
parent metropolitan firms. In 1938, the National Bank held
only £E600,000 of the deposits of other Egyptian banks.
Nor did it rediscount bills or enter into the money market
to expand or contract the supply of money.

In fact, the National Bank was, as many Egyptians pointed
out, neither national nor central. Founded by foreign investors, it had a foreign board of directors and even a formal
London Consulting Committee. Nor was the National Bank
a banker's bank, as central financial institutions are meant
to be. It was primarily a commercial bank like most of the
other banking institutions in Egypt, obligated to protect the
interests of its depositors.

A first effort to turn the National Bank into a central
bank occurred just before the outbreak of World War II.
It was led by Ahmad 'Abd al-Wahhab, other economic
nationalists, and the nationalist press, and it was opposed
by many of the metropolitan groups with financial interests
in the National Bank.[29] The support of Edward Cook, the
powerful governor of the National Bank from 1931 to 1940,
proved decisive, however, in achieving change. The
reforms enacted in 1939–1940 produced a considerable
Egyptianization of the bank and some increase in its "central" position within the local economy.

Cook met the challenge of the call for a central bank in
a pragmatic and conciliatory fashion. He conceded the va-
lidity of the Egyptianization demands and tried to strengthen
the central position of the bank. In 1939, the bank's charter

[29] *L'Informateur*, April 3, 1936.

was revised: Egyptians were to become a majority of the board by 1945, the number of Egyptian personnel employed by the bank was to be increased, an Egyptian president was to be named when Cook left the post, and the overseas committee of the bank was abolished, although overseas experts would continue to counsel the board.[30] Cook also talked about the bank's becoming more responsible for currency matters by maintaining the exchange value of the Egyptian pound and conducting the banking business of the state.

The next steps toward creating a central bank occurred during and just after the war. Upon the outbreak of war in 1939, Egypt imposed exchange and currency controls. By an informal understanding, the commercial banks operating in Egypt agreed to keep a certain proportion of their assets with the National Bank. But the National Bank's status as a quasi-central bank was still based solely on these tacit understandings, and the state was anxious to formalize these arrangements and establish its control over monetary policy. In 1947, Egypt decided to leave the sterling zone and to create an independent currency backed by gold and foreign securities. The linking of British and Egyptian currencies had served the Egyptian economy well up until 1939. It facilitated trade with Europe and inspired investor confidence in Egypt. The postwar decision to depart from the sterling zone was less an assertion of economic nationalism (though this was certainly a factor) than a realistic assessment that the war had exhausted the British economy and that sterling was no longer the powerful and stable international currency it had once been. Indeed, when Egypt withdrew from the sterling zone, huge sterling balances were owed to it.

All of these changes were important for the central banking law which was enacted in 1951. They separated Egypt

[30] No. 222, Lampson to Halifax, February 28, 1939, PRO FO 371/23314; No. 335, Lampson to Halifax, March 28, 1939, PRO FO 371/23315; and Ahmad Mahir, minister of finance, to governor of the National Bank, March 7, 1939, Hornsby Papers.

from the European economies and established a framework of control around the commercial banks. By 1951, Egypt had its own monetary system. Its notes were still issued by the National Bank, but their backing was now determined by Egyptian officials rather than British. The government also regulated the flow of funds in and out of the country.

The 1951 law made it mandatory for commercial banks in Egypt to maintain a proportion of their reserves with the National Bank. In order to legitimize the state's role in determining monetary policies, the law also established a Supreme Monetary Council within the National Bank. It consisted of three representatives of the government and three representatives of the National Bank, presided over by the Egyptian minister of finance. Although the National Bank remained a private bank for its ordinary commercial transactions, all matters relating to monetary, credit, and exchange policy were decided by the Supreme Monetary Council.[31]

This law marked the culmination of the long-drawn-out process of asserting control over Egyptian finance. It gave the Egyptian government regulatory powers over foreign commercial banks which had operated with a free hand for nearly a century. Still, the government was not satisfied with the amount of control it exercised, and, following the British, French, and Israeli invasion of the country in 1956, it further tightened state control of banks.

INDUSTRIALIZATION

Industrial expansion, so impressive during the war, continued apace after the war and slowed only in the early 1950s, when Egypt's traditional trading partners were once again able to compete in world markets. Most of the expansion was carried out in those manufacturing branches which had been established before 1939. The textile industry led the way, enjoying a remarkable burst of activity

[31] National Bank of Egypt, *Economic Bulletin*, 3 (1950), 80–85.

immediately following the war. Fifteen new textile firms were set up at this time, with a total capitalization of £E3,750,000, while sixteen already established firms increased their capital by just under £E2,000,000. In 1946 alone, Egypt imported textile machinery worth more than £E4,000,000, and it continued to make heavy investments in machines in the succeeding three years.[32]

Although the first few postwar years witnessed an especially rapid expansion of textile production, the industry continued to increase its output in most of the years leading up to 1952. Moreover, Egyptian manufacturers began to develop new product lines. The joint venture agreements negotiated by Filature Nationale d'Égypte and the Misr Spinning and Weaving Company with major Lancashire firms in the 1930s had resulted in the production of a better quality, more finely woven, and more expertly dyed cloth. This diversification was resumed after the war, particularly as a result of the creation of a large rayon factory, which had the capacity in 1948 to produce five tons of thread and one ton of cellophane per day.[33] As local textile production increased, the value of Egyptian textile imports continued to decline as a proportion of the total (table 6.4).

The other main import-substitution industries also expanded. Even before the outbreak of the war, Egyptian

Table 6.4.

Value of Textile Imports as a Percentage of Total
Egyptian Imports, 1946-1952

1946	1947	1948	1949	1950	1951	1952
17.5	19.6	16.7	13.6	12.9	9.4	8.3

SOURCE: Egypt, Ministry of Finance, Statistical Department, *Annuaire Statistique*.

[32] Great Britain, Board of Trade, Overseas Economic Surveys, *Egypt: Economic and Commercial Conditions in Egypt, 1947*, p. 37.

[33] No. 17, Killearn to Foreign Office, January 14, 1946, PRO FO 371/53362, and *L'Économiste Égyptien*, February 17, 1946, and January 18, 1948.

industrialization had rendered the country self-sufficient, or nearly so, in sugar, alcohol, cigarettes, common salt, cereal milling, lamp glass, boots and shoes, soap, cement, tarbooshes, and furniture.[34] In the five years after the war, the output of refined sugar from the Sugar Company, for instance, rose by about 10 percent per year, and cement production increased 2.5 times during the same period. (See table 6.5.) However, Egyptian manufacturing continued to be concentrated in nondurable consumer branches, mainly textiles and food processing. Five main manufacturing groups (food processing, beverages, tobacco, cotton ginning and textiles, and clothing and footwear) accounted for around two-thirds of the capital invested in manufacturing companies, of value added in manufacturing, and of industrial employment (table 6.6).

The difficulties Egyptian industrialists had previously experienced in raising capital were greatly alleviated after the war. During the years from 1945 to 1952, savings averaged approximately 8.5 percent of gross national product, and investment, 9.5 percent. (See table 6.7.) Most of the savings and investment were channeled toward industrial enterprises for the first time. Of the £E72,366,000 of new capital invested in joint stock companies between 1946 and 1954, nearly two-thirds went to industrial firms (table 6.8). The two largest industrial enterprises of the era, the Misr Rayon Company (original capitalization, £E2,000,000) and the Egyptian Fertilizer Company (£E4,000,000), were subscribed as soon as their stock was offered to the public. Indeed, the public pledged more than £E17,000,000 for the £E750,000 of stock which the Misr Rayon Company originally made available.

Continuing Limitations

Yet many of the same problems which had plagued Egypt's industrial growth in the interwar period persisted after

---

[34] Anis, *National Income of Egypt*, p. 778.

Table 6.5.

Industrial Production in Egypt, 1945-1952

	Cotton Yarn[a]	Cotton Woven Fabrics[a]	Cottonseed Oil	Crude Oil	Mazout	Benzine	Cement	Refined Sugar	Alcohol
1945[b]	32.1	128.5	79.4	1,314	657	176	432.1	149	9.0
Indices:									
1945	100	100	100	100	100	100	100	100	100
1946	102	106	105	97	93	107	136	112	102
1947	101	111	102	101	106	113	150	124	109
1948	103	121	112	143	193	113	178	134	104
1949	105	118	117	172	233	122	206	145	104
1950	99	123	128	197	248	110	237	155	162
1951	97	135	112	177	227	109	261	146	118
1952	100	131	116	181	244	100	219	141	160

SOURCE: National Bank of Egypt, *Economic Bulletins.*

[a]Production of large factories only.

[b]Output in thousand tons, except cotton woven fabrics in thousand square meters and alcohol in thousand liters.

Table 6.6.

Importance of Consumer Nondurables in Egyptian Manufacturing,
1950 and 1952

| | Percentage of Total of: | | |
	Paid-up Capital[a]	Value Added[b]	Employment[b]
Food processing	15.2	15.4	19.0
Beverages	6.1	2.1	1.5
Tobacco	6.2	6.5	3.4
Cotton ginning and textiles	28.8	43.0	43.0
Clothing and footwear	2.8	1.3	2.3
Total	59.1	68.3	69.2

SOURCE: United Nations, *Development of Manufacturing in Egypt, Israel, and Turkey*, passim.

[a]1950, all establishments.

[b]1952, establishments with ten or more employees.

Table 6.7.

Gross National Product, Industrial Growth, Savings, and Investment, 1945-1952

	GNP (£E000,000, constant 1954 prices)	% Increase in GNP	% Increase in Industrial Production	% Increase in Textile Production	Savings as % of GNP	Investment as % of GNP
1945	711	—	—	—	12.9	4.5
1946	744	5	1	4	4.9	7.3
1947	776	4	9	10	5.4	9.0
1948	877	13	12	15	10.4	11.6
1949	927	6	12	17	10.1	10.6
1950	945	2	5	0	8.5	9.7
1951	971	3	-1	6	8.0	11.5
1952	992	2	3	8	7.4	10.8

SOURCE: Bent Hansen and Girgis A. Marzouk, *Development and Economic Policy in the UAR (Egypt)* (Amsterdam, 1965), pp. 318-325.

Table 6.8.

Capital Issues of Joint Stock Companies, 1946-1954

	1946-50		1951-54		1946-54	
	Value (£E000)	Percentage	Value (£E000)	Percentage	Value (£E000)	Percentage
Industry	28,251	59	17,773	73.2	46,024	64
Commerce	9,119	19	3,930	16.2	13,049	18
Banking and insurance			800	3.3		
Building and land	10,725 }	22 }	1,190	4.9	13,293 }	18 }
Transport			578	2.4		
Total	48,095	100	24,271	100.0	72,366	100.0

SOURCE: National Bank of Egypt, *Economic Bulletins.*

1945. Manufacturing was still confined to a few branches, entrepreneurship was limited, institutions for mobilizing savings for industrial development had not been established, and industrial expansion did not offer employment for nearly as many persons as its advocates hoped that it would.

Entrepreneurs in Egypt had founded few consumer durable factories and even fewer firms concerned with the production of intermediate goods and capital goods. Illustrative of the timidity of private enterprise was the foundation of the Egyptian Iron and Steel Company in 1953. Although businessmen and politicians like Sidqi had been calling for such an industry since the 1920s, this firm was established only when the state itself put up virtually all the capital and invited a German steel manufacturer to lend managerial expertise.[35]

Although industrial firms had begun to win a larger share of the investors' savings, the country had not developed reliable markets and institutions for raising risk capital for new undertakings. There were no financial houses for distributing stocks and bonds to the interested investing public. The great public interest in the Misr Rayon Company and the Egyptian Fertilizer Company notwithstanding, most new firms began as they had in the 1920s and 1930s, with large contributions from a small group of backers. Subscriptions were usually drawn from a few wealthy Egyptian and foreign families, well known for their backing of industrial endeavors. Once under way, companies had only two methods for increasing their capital: self-financing and the contracting of loans. A bond market hardly existed at all. Even as late as 1952, debentures constituted only 2 percent of the liabilities of 103 of the main Egyptian joint stock companies (table 6.9). As a consequence, firms endeavored to create large profit margins in order to be able to lay aside funds for future expansion.

The entrepreneurial elite also remained a small one. The

[35] National Bank of Egypt, *Economic Bulletin*, 7 (1954), 110–111.

Table 6.9.

Form of Liabilities of 103 Joint Stock Companies, 1952

Type of Companies	Total Liabilities (£E 000)	Percentage in the Form of:				
		Paid-Up Capital	Debentures	Reserves	Creditors	Profits
Industrial	62,468	46	3	13	32	6
Building	15,627	42	—	13	43	2
Land	10,571	50	—	20	25	5
Utilities	7,428	37	3	14	40	6
Hotel	2,010	47	1	26	24	2
Commercial and other	18,260	35	—	19	40	6
Total	116,364	43	2	15	35	5

SOURCE: National Bank of Egypt, *Economic Bulletin*, 1955, Vol. 8, No. 2, p. 102.

same men served on the boards of numerous firms. No doubt this practice was encouraged to secure tight managerial control, but it also reflected the dearth of managerial and entrepreneurial talent. And most of the directors of joint stock companies continued to be foreigners resident in Egypt, though aside from the increased Syrian contingent, the number of new entrepreneurs in the foreign-resident group was small. Native-born Egyptians remained in a distinct minority; their contribution to Egypt's entrepreneurial cadre was disappointing.

Of the 351 joint stock companies with a capitalization of £E10,000 or more listed in the *Stock Exchange Yearbook* for 1946, sixty were run predominantly by native-born Egyptian businessmen. Their total capitalization was £E25,094,185. But twenty-seven of these companies, representing nearly two-thirds of the total capitalization, were the creation of Egypt's four great economic entrepreneurs. No fewer than twenty-two were part of the Misr conglomerate. Three large-scale companies were under the direction of Tal'at Harb's aggressive competitor, Ahmad 'Abbud. They were the Egyptian Sugar Company, the Egyptian Fertilizer Company, and the Khedivial Mail Line. The other two leading wealthy Egyptian businessmen were well known for their cooperation with foreign businessmen, but they each directed one purely Egyptian firm. Muhammad Farghali was serving on the boards of twenty-nine firms in 1946, including the National Bank and various Misr companies. His own company was the Farghali Cotton and Investment Company. 'Ali Amin Yahya, son of Amin Yahya, served on the boards of Bank Misr, the Filature Nationale d'Égypte, and the Egyptian Salt and Soda Company. His predominantly Egyptian company was the Alexandria Navigation Company, which his father had founded in 1930. It had a capitalization of £E400,000.

There were three main areas from which Egyptian entrepreneurs might have been expected to emerge in large numbers: large-scale firms, small workshops, and the land. None of them performed this function. Although the Misr firms inculcated entrepreneurial values among Egyptians, they did so almost in complete isolation. Elsewhere, even in companies run by other Egyptians or by foreigners resident in Egypt, there was a profound prejudice against employing Egyptians or promoting them into responsible high-level positions. The usual practice in filling these openings was to look for a qualified foreigner in Egypt, and if the appropriate person could not be found there, to advertise overseas.

Substantiation of this point comes from examining the careers pursued by graduates of the Egyptian Higher School of Commerce between 1914 and 1936. Of the 724 graduates for whom career information could be found in 1937, 478 entered that traditional preserve of Egyptian career aspirations—government service. Private business attracted only 179, the professions 54, and 4 went into other careers. Of the 179 who entered the private sector, no fewer than 100 worked for Misr companies. Only 25 were employed by large foreign firms, 16 of these by the National Bank, which came under heavy pressure to Egyptianize in the 1930s. No other predominantly foreign-run and foreign-financed firm had engaged more than a single Egyptian graduate of the Higher School before 1936. Indeed, only the Anglo-Egyptian Bank (later taken over by Barclays Bank, Dominion, Commonwealth, and Overseas) and the Sugar Company hired a graduate before 1933, when the government of Isma'il Sidqi launched a campaign to persuade business firms to employ Egyptians.[36]

This imbalance in staffing had not altered much by the late 1940s. At the time of the enactment of the joint stock company law of 1947, the French embassy observed in a report that French companies had a long way to go before they would be in compliance with the requirement for employing a minimum percentage of Egyptians. At the Alexandria branch of the Crédit Lyonnais, only 45 percent of the employees were Egyptians, and they were earning

---

[36] Kulliya al-Tijara, *al-Yubil al-Fiddi*, pp. 181–221.

only 31 percent of the salaries. Moreover, embassy officials believed that the French bank counted as Egyptian many Syrians, Lebanese, and Greeks, as well as many Jews who still had not acquired Egyptian nationality. The same situation existed at the Crédit Foncier Égyptien, where 50 percent of the employees and 72 percent of the workers were Egyptians. At Air Liquid, a branch of a French company, only 33 percent of the employees and 83 percent of the workers were Egyptians. The French firms thought to have a high proportion of Egyptian workers and employees were the insurance companies, Air France, Messageries Maritime, Savon, Orosdi-Back, Hannault, Chalons, the Egyptian Sugar Company, and the Egyptian Water Company. The embassy report concluded that banks and concessionary companies required the most radical adjustment, while the newer companies, especially many of the French industrial firms, had taken greater heed of Egyptian nationalist sentiments.[37]

Not all the blame belongs to the foreign firms. Egyptian aspirations were biased against business careers. ʿAbd Allah Fikri Abaza, a graduate of the Higher School of Commerce, admitted that young Egyptians preferred the Schools of Law and Medicine and that the School of Commerce attracted less qualified candidates.[38] Despite the fact that the School of Commerce boasted some truly exceptional teachers, including for a short time Ahmad Mahir and Ahmad ʿAbd al-Wahhab, the quality of education left something to be desired. In the early years, before the school was absorbed into Cairo University, its curriculum was at a rudimentary level. It was generally conceded that the foreign-language training, so essential for successful business careers in interwar Egypt, was not of a high standard.[39]

Furthermore, graduates of the school faced enormous

[37] No. 1150, Arvengas to Ministry of Foreign Affairs, August 25, 1947, FEA, Box 229.

[38] Kulliya al-Tijara, *al-Yubil al-Fiddi*, pp. 167–169. This was also the view of Talʿat Harb: ibid., pp. 21–23.

[39] Ibid., pp. 174–175.

prejudice from foreign businessmen. ʿAbd Allah Fikri Abaza, who graduated in the first class (1914), recounted the hostility he encountered from foreign engineers while employed with the Suez Canal Company.[40] The situation had not changed greatly three decades later, when H. M. al-Zeini, an engineering graduate of Cairo University, was offered employment, along with seven other graduates, by the Egyptian Sugar Company. All eight were shunned by the company's entirely foreign managerial staff. Dr. al-Zeini was told to stay in the laboratory and for a time was forbidden to enter the refinery.[41] The foreign businessman's arrogance and insensitivity is well summed up in the reply given by Baron Edouard Empain to a request that he employ more Egyptians: "Why? Who would compel me? I control the affairs, and I am not interested in your national considerations."[42]

Despite some change in its activities, the small-scale manufacturing sector continued to be important in production and employment. Although smaller establishments lost some of their prominence in food production, they remained largely responsible for the local production of wearing apparel and wood and metal products. (See table 6.10.) Yet, with some notable exceptions (Sayyid Yasin, Ahmad al-Lawzi, and a few wearing-apparel industrialists), hardly any of the small operatives were able to break into the world of big business. The small businessmen in Egypt lacked capital and vision. They knew how to manage a small workshop, but could not contemplate administering a large factory. More importantly, they lacked the business and political contacts so essential for success in pre-Nasser Egypt. In most cases, they had only a smattering of formal education, and if they lacked fluency in English and French they would have great difficulty entering the modern economic sector.

[40] Ibid., pp. 55–61.
[41] Interview with H. M. el-Zeini, May 31 and June 4, 1979.
[42] E. I. Politi, *L'Égypte de 1914 à Suez*, p. 99.

Table 6.10.

Proportion of Employment in Small-Scale Industrial Establishments, 1947

Industrial Sector	Percentage of Employees in Industrial Sector Indicated Employed in Small-Scale Establishments	Percentage of Employees in Small-Scale Establishments Employed in Industrial Sector Indicated
Food products	34	11
Beverages	19	} 1
Tobacco	3	
Textiles	45	17
Apparel	95	30
Wood products	90	16
Metal products	71	19
Total	55	94

SOURCE: See Table 6.7. Small-scale manufacturing establishments are those with fewer than ten employees.

The final group from which much was expected was the landed grandees. Not only were they encouraged to invest in the new industrial and commercial joint stock companies, but it was hoped that they would transfer their administrative and business talents to this arena. In fact, this transfer never occurred, at least not in large numbers. There were a few important landed magnates-industrialists. One example was Muhammad Khalil, a large estate owner who was even better known for his interest in industry and commerce. But most large landowners, if they invested in companies at all, were like the Badrawi-'Ashur family, which held stock in Egyptian firms, partly out of patriotic reasons, but took no active part in the management of the firms even when chosen as members of the board of directors. In 1946, of the 227 Egyptians on the boards of joint stock companies, 46, or approximately 20 percent, were individuals who were to become subject to the land reform law in 1952. This is a relatively small proportion in light of the facts that land was the major source of wealth in Egypt and that industrial and commercial joint stock companies were eager to attract the financial backing of landlords.

By 1951–1952, the number of Egyptians serving on the boards of joint stock companies had risen to 501, a consequence of the 1947 law requiring 40 percent of the directors to be Egyptian. Seventy-one of them were individuals who were to lose land as a consequence of the land reform law. This was 14 percent of the number of Egyptian board members—a decline from the proportion of five years earlier. While it is true that certain large landowning families were represented on the boards by members who were not large landowners themselves, it is also the case that some of the 71 individuals like Ahmad 'Abbud, 'Ali Amin Yahya, 'Abd al-Rahman Hamada, and Hafiz 'Afifi, who, though they owned large estates, must be considered first and foremost industrialists who had diversified their holdings by investing in the land.

The leading spokesman of Egyptian industrialization, especially those worried about social turmoil in the country, looked to industrial expansion to offer jobs to Egypt's expanding urban population. Unfortunately, although industries in Egypt provided employment for about twice as many people in 1947 as they had in 1907 (553,000, compared with 281,000), the proportion of the total work force employed in manufacturing rose from 6.0 percent only to 8.4 percent. Agricultural employment declined from 69.5 percent in 1937 to 61.7 percent in 1947, but it was the tertiary sectors of commerce and transportation that absorbed the largest numbers (table 6.11).

Finally, although real industrial wages rose impressively in the postwar years, after a sharp decline during the war, labor's share of value added declined precipitously over the same years. In large part, the reasons for the declining labor share were management's policy of paying high dividends to its shareholders (10 percent of nominal capital in 1951) and a desire to increase reserves as a means of self-financing. Thus, despite impressive industrial growth rates in postwar Egypt, industrialization did not solve the country's pressing social problems.

In many ways, the postwar years leading up to the Nasser *coup d'état* realized some of the economic aspirations so forcefully articulated by economic nationalists after World War I. The Egyptianization of joint stock companies was accelerated by legislation, by purchase of stock, and by appointment of Egyptians and foreign residents to directorships. Firms themselves came under a greater degree of regulation than they had experienced in the laissez-faire era of the 1920s and 1930s. A central bank was established, and Egypt extricated itself from the sterling monetary bloc, though suffering considerable financial loss in doing so. Industrial growth was impressive.

But, as the next chapter will show, the changes came at a late date; they were insufficient for Egypt's burgeoning and no longer quiescent population. Industrial growth was limited to standard branches and failed to generate substantial new employment opportunities. Wealth was maldistributed; very little trickled down to the lower orders.

Table 6.11.

Distribution of Employment among Economic Sectors, 1937 and 1947

Economic Sector	1937		1947	
	Number Employed (000s)	Percentage	Number Employed (000s)	Percentage
Agriculture	4,020	69.5	4,075	61.7
Mining	11	0.2	13	0.2
Manufacturing	345	6.0	553	8.4
Electricity, gas, and water	21	0.4	23	0.3
Construction	117	2.0	112	1.7
Trade and finance	436	7.5	588	8.9
Transport and communication	137	2.4	202	3.0
Services	696	12.0	1,046	15.8
Total	5,783	100.0	6,612	100.0

SOURCE: Samir Radwan, *Capital Formation in Egyptian Industry and Agriculture, 1882-1967* (London, 1974), p. 283.

CHAPTER 7

DENOUEMENT

Postwar Egypt was marked by violence, although not so intense as the violence which had followed World War I. The primary issue of these years was full, unqualified independence.[1] However, while most of the assassinations, strikes and other confrontations occurred over the issue of independence, socioeconomic dislocations underlay the violence. Capitalism had proved to be neither the social panacea nor the protection against political revolutions which its advocates expected. The most militant political actors in Egypt tended to be those with deep-seated socioeconomic grievances; they fulminated against capitalism as well as against imperialism.

THE ECONOMIC SITUATION AT WAR'S END

The social problems of the postwar years were very grave ones. The war itself had imposed a heavy burden on Egyptian society, especially on the lower classes, which were hurt by the sharp inflation. Although the state and the British Middle East Supply Center endeavored to regulate the economy so as to insure a minimum basic standard of living to all, British officials were forced to admit that Egypt's resources were not substantial enough. In particular, the Middle East Supply Center was concerned about its inability to distribute more than seven meters of "popular cloth" to persons among the common people. It concluded that "many

[1] See especially Aide Memoire of Egyptian Delegation in Reply to Memorandum of the British Delegation, April 29, 1946, May 8, 1946, PRO FO 371/53295; No. 920, Campbell to Foreign Office, May 22, 1946, PRO FO 371/53297; and Cabinet Paper entitled "Revision of Anglo-Egyptian Treaty," Memorandum by Secretary of State for Foreign Affairs, June 1946, PRO FO 371/54301.

amongst the poorer classes will remain partially naked—a situation which has already manifested itself in several regions in the provinces and in the poorer quarters of the metropole."[2] Moreover, whenever the rural or urban dweller had to enter the black market, because of the unavailability of necessities on the controlled market (and this happened often), he was compelled to pay exorbitant prices.[3]

The per capita national income probably declined somewhat between 1913 and 1939, perhaps by about 10 percent overall. The war years witnessed another 10 percent reduction. Thus, Egypt emerged from the war in an even more precarious economic situation than it had entered it in.[4]

For a half decade after the conclusion of the war, the country enjoyed a high economic growth rate of 7 percent per year. (See table 7.1.) But there seems little question that the distribution of this wealth was highly skewed. Notwithstanding the government's efforts to control prices and to fight increases in the cost of living, the enormous incidence of poverty persisted and may even have worsened.

In the absence of formal income-distribution figures for this period, one must rely on literary sources for intimations of poverty and income maldistribution. A picture of inequality emerges very clearly. Whether the spokesmen were left-wing novelists like Nagib Mahfuz or parliamentary officials speaking in the Chamber of Deputies, they left no doubt that the poor in Egypt eked out a meager existence, if they were fortunate enough to avert death itself. They lived in primitive homes, spent 60 to 70 percent of their income on foodstuffs (which did not afford them an adequate diet), and lacked access to essential health and educational services. An economic officer attached to the British embassy estimated in 1946 that 93 percent of the rural

[2] Memorandum from the Commercial Counsellor to Headquarters, RAF, ME, January 9, 1945, PRO FO 371/45937.

[3] Anis, *National Income of Egypt*, p. 756.

[4] Hansen and Marzouk, *Development and Economic Policy in the UAR*, p. 5.

Table 7.1.

Gross National Product, 1945-1954

	Gross National Product [a]	Index (1939 = 100)
1939	711	100
1940	707	99
1941	687	97
1942	707	99
1943	664	93
1944	699	98
1945	711	100
1946	744	105
1947	776	109
1948	877	123
1949	927	130
1950	945	133
1951	971	137
1952	992	140
1953	981	138
1954	1010	142

SOURCE: Hansen and Marzouk, *Development and Economic Policy in the UAR*, pp. 318-319.

[a] £E million at constant 1954 prices.

population in Egypt were living "below the line of health and decency."[5]

By the late 1940s, Egypt had reached a crisis point in the provision of necessities, especially foodstuffs. From the on-

[5] Speaight to Scrivener, May 23, 1946, containing a note by the Financial Counsellor, W. J. Johnson, May 17, 1946, PRO FO 371/53246.

set of the depression, the amount of grain available in Egypt, grown locally or imported, declined, and this in spite of the fact that during and after the war the Egyptian government required local cultivators to plant a certain proportion of their lands in wheat and also spent massively on the importation and distribution of wheat and maize. (See table 7.2.) By 1952, nearly one-quarter of Egypt's import bill represented the cost of foodstuffs (table 7.3). The consumption of tobacco also fell, and, though the consumption of textiles remained on an even keel, the annual average of approximately 2.5 kilograms per person meant that each person in Egypt could purchase only seventeen meters of cloth each year—an average that was far below that of the United States and Western Europe.[6]

At the other end of the spectrum, a very few lived in splendor. The maldistribution of land is well known. In 1952, approximately 12,000 families owned 35 percent of the land, while 2.5 million families holding estates of five feddans or less also owned another 35 percent of the land.[7] Egypt's landless population had risen to 1,600,000 families and constituted sixty percent of the total rural population.

Table 7.2.

Net Supply of Grains Per Capita,
1935-1939 to 1950-1954 (kg/year)

	Wheat	Maize	Millet	Rice	Barley	Total
1935-39	70.3	96.8	28.6	20.0	13.0	228.7
1940-44	61.4	81.3	38.7	22.4	13.2	217.0
1945-49	65.6	79.1	30.5	24.6	8.0	207.8
1950-54	82.5	70.7	24.0	20.0	4.9	202.1

SOURCE: National Bank of Egypt, *Economic Bulletin*, 11 (1958), 228 ff.

[6] National Bank of Egypt, *Economic Bulletin*, 4 (1951), 100.
[7] Samir Radwan, "The Impact of Agrarian Reform on Rural Egypt, 1952–75," p. 6.

Table 7.3.

Proportional Value of Major Imports, 1946-1952

	Percentage of Total Value (£E) of Imports Represented by Each Category in:						
	1946	1947	1948	1949	1950	1951	1952
Foodstuffs	10.2	8.3	20.2	16.5	16.2	19.9	24.8
Processed foods	11.0	7.4	4.9	5.4	7.8	3.5	6.5
Mineral products	11.0	9.0	6.3	6.9	5.0	5.7	8.1
Chemical products	10.8	10.8	9.8	11.0	10.7	9.6	11.4
Textiles	17.5	19.6	16.7	13.6	12.9	9.4	8.3
Machines	8.1	10.1	9.8	11.7	9.5	8.0	11.0

SOURCE: Egypt, Ministry of Finance, Statistical Department, *Annuaire Statistique.*

The land reform of 1952 was applied to 1,758 landholders, who thereby lost 656,640 feddans or approximately one-tenth of Egypt's arable surface.[8] Of these, 1,758 landowners, 425 were members of the royal family, whose land-holdings totalled 179,157 feddans.[9] The largest landowner was King Faruq himself, with estates comprising 28,109 feddans.[10] Three other families had estates larger than 10,000 feddans: Badrawi-'Ashur, Siraj al-Din Shahin, and 'Amr.[11]

Although landownership was highly concentrated throughout Egypt, it was particularly pronounced in a few provinces. More than half of Behera province was in the hands of large owners, while Gharbiya was the location of the family estates of the Badrawi-'Ashur (18,000 feddans) and Siraj al-Din (3,300 feddans).[12] In Upper Egypt, land in Minya, Qena, and Aswan provinces was heavily concentrated. Seventy Qena families owned a total of 44,325 feddans, and in Aswan thirteen owned 74,350.[13] In the area around Nag Hammadi, a rich sugar-cultivating region, a great deal of the land belonged to Ahmad 'Abbud (over 5,000 feddans), Prince Yusuf Kamal (over 16,000 feddans), and King Faruq (over 6,500 feddans).[14]

The same concentration of wealth existed in the industrial and commercial sectors. A few individuals sat on the boards of numerous joint stock companies and formed interlocking directorates. Sixteen superwealthy personages served on the boards of twelve or more companies in 1946: Hafiz 'Afifi (33); Husayn Sirri (30); Muhammad Ahmad Farghali (29); 'Ali Amin Yahya (23); 'Abd al-Maqsud Ahmad (22); Muhammad Mahmud Khalil (20); Hasan Mazlum (17); Maurice Mosseri (15); Ahmad Saddiq (15); Michel

[8] *al-Ahram*, August 4, 1954.

[9] *al-Ahram*, May 28, 1954.

[10] *al-Ahram*, May 28, 1954.

[11] 'Asim al-Disuqi, *Kibar Mullak al-Aradi al-Zira'iya*, p. 31.

[12] *al-Ahram*, September 10, 1954.

[13] Gabriel Baer, *A History of Landownership in Modern Egypt, 1800–1950*, p. 137.

[14] *al-Ahram*, April 3, 1955.

Salvago (14); Aslan Qattawi (14); Muhammad Shukri (14); Tawfiq Duss (13); Silvio Pinto (13); 'Abd al-Rahman Hammada (13); and Henry A. Barker (12).[15]

Rarely is one afforded an intimate view of the assets of members of the upper bourgeoisie. The estate of Ralph Green, however, which became a subject of legal proceedings in 1966, gives some idea of the diverse holdings of these families. A member of an industrialist family, Green in 1966 had accounts in the Banque d'Alexandrie, the Banque de Port Said, the Banque du Caire, the National Bank, Bank Misr, and Banque al-Gumhuriya. He had property holdings all over Egypt and owned stock in forty-five Egyptian joint stock companies. His total estate, no doubt undervalued for legal purposes, was estimated in excess of £E3,500,000.[16]

DISCONTENTED GROUPS

Soon after the end of the war, private enterprise capitalism came under heavy and mounting criticism for the first time. Workers, students, and peasants did not succeed in seizing power, but they challenged the parliamentary order and undermined the legitimacy of private enterprise. They created new and powerful anti-establishment political organs, which spread left- and right-wing anti-capitalist ideas among the population.

Turning first to labor, it would appear that the industrial labor force in 1950 was slightly over one-half million and was concentrated in Cairo, Alexandria, and a few delta cities like al-Mahalla al-Kubra. It was capable of making its political influence felt.

Labor's grievances were legion. They comprised a lack of protective legislation, low wages, harsh and unhealthy working conditions, and repeated violations of the admit-

[15] *Stock Exchange Yearbook of Egypt*, 1946.
[16] Typescript translation of the Tribunal of First Instance of Cairo, July 13, 1966, kindly lent by Solomon Green.

tedly weak labor laws. The war years had been particularly
hard on industrial laborers, whose real wages plummeted
steeply in the early years of the war and did not return to
their 1937 level until 1947.[17] A number of firms, particularly cigarette manufacturers, were frequently found in vi-
olation of the child labor laws. The Matossian firm was
reported to employ 5,000 workers of whom 2,000 were
children under the age of 13.[18] Working conditions in the
sugar processing plants of Upper Egypt were notoriously
unhealthy. These factories did not have proper ventilation
and were veritable ovens during the summer months. Their
antiquated and improperly guarded machinery was responsible for numerous injuries.[19] Many Egyptian factories,
notably the textile plants run by the Misr Spinning and
Weaving Company, were biased against hiring educated or
urban persons, fearing labor agitation. According to the
leftist paper *al-Fajr al-Jadid*, anyone applying for a job in
the al-Mahalla al-Kubra plant needed to be dressed like a
fellah and appear hungry and poor.[20]

The Misr plant at Mahalla illustrates labor's plight. One
of the reasons for locating the Misr plant at al-Mahalla al-
Kubra was accessibility to cheap peasant labor. The plant
suffered from the typical problems of high labor turnover
and absenteeism associated with the transition from a peasantry to a proletariat. The firm's managers used harsh and
autocratic techniques, including fines, demotions, and
transfers, to hold and motivate the workers. These labor
arrangements were still in effect at the end of the war and
were a cause of tense labor-management relations.[21] An
additional irritant was the enormous disparity in income
and living styles separating labor and management. From

[17] Robert Mabro, "Industrial Growth, Agricultural Under-Employment,
and the Lewis Model: The Egyptian Case, 1937–1965," *Journal of Development Studies*, 3 (1967), 335.

[18] *al-Jamahir*, August 11, 1947.

[19] *al-Jamahir*, February 22, 1948.

[20] *al-Fajr al-Jadid*, 1 (May 1, 1946).

[21] William Norris Carson, *The Mehalla Report*, p. 1.

the massive profits made during the war, the Mahalla company constructed thirteen spacious homes for its general manager and division foremen. The homes of the division foremen cost £E16,000 each and, according to the Amercian ambassador, "would be very fine residences anywhere in the world."[22]

The Mahalla factory cultivated a reputation for enlightened labor practices. It boasted of its housing estate and its various social and recreational facilities. Important political figures came to Mahalla to praise the firm. The reality was quite different, however. Though originally constructed for workers, the housing quarters were taken over by the state during the war. The American ambassador concluded after a guided tour that the living conditions of the work force were "deplorable. . . . Frequently as many as 4 or 5 families live in one mud house in shifts of three— in other words approximately 15 families to a house."[23] Hafiz ʿAfifi, head of the Misr complex, later admitted that inadequate housing was a major cause of labor unhappiness.[24]

A prolonged and sporadically violent strike at the plant in 1947 forced the firm to improve working and living conditions. Still, the recreational areas and other social facilities were not much used by the employees, who felt that these conveniences were intended for management and who wanted the firm to expend the funds on wage increases instead.[25]

During its tenure of power in the early 1940s, the Wafd passed legislation legalizing labor unions. Though there had been unions before that time, their unrecognized status made their existence precarious. The Wafd itself controlled unions with 47,000 members, half the total union membership. Another 47,000 workers belonged to independent

[22] Report by Lyon visit to Misr Textile Mill, June 22, 1945, USNA 883.655/7-945.

[23] Ibid.

[24] al-Muqtataf, 114 (1949), 292–303.

[25] Carson, Mehalla Report, p. 10.

unions, while 3,500 more were led by the former *nabil* (prince) 'Abbas Halim. Although Halim's following was small, his unions were influential. They included the well-organized and often radical transport unions (Cairo Tramways and Egyptian General Omnibus) as well as public utilities unions.[26] Although the number of union members was growing—according to one estimate, it had reached 140,000 in the 1940s—the membership was fragmented into small groupings and lacked effective coordination and leadership.[27] Many unions were run by company managers. The largest members of unionized workers were in textiles (37,470), road transport (11,913), railway transport (4,854), and sugar (4,606).[28]

Though divided, labor nevertheless organized some paralyzing strikes and sit-ins. During the postwar years, the city of Shubra al-Khayma became a center for labor agitation; in 1946, a series of strikes and worker confrontations with the police turned it into a veritable armed camp.[29] Located on the outskirts of Cairo, Shubra al-Khayma had become a heavily industrialized region in the 1930s. By 1946, its work force numbered between 10,000 and 16,000. Its largest single industry was textile manufacturing. Labor organizers concentrated on Shubra al-Khayma, and a strong sense of labor consciousness was instilled among the work force.[30] Strike activity was initiated in 1946 when a textile firm, the Nile Weaving Company, decided to move its plant from Shubra al-Khayma to Alexandria. The workers sus-

[26] Report by M.T.E. Evans on Condition of Labor and Trade Unions in Egypt, July 28, 1944, PRO FO 371/41380.

[27] See *L'Egypte Industrielle*, 25 (May 1949), 43–45, and No. 1684, Carol B. Lyons to Secretary of State, July 8, 1946, USNA 883.504/7-846.

[28] Killearn to Eden, June 30, 1944, PRO FO 371/41380.

[29] S. P. Tuck to Secretary of State, April 12, 1946, USNA 883.5045/4-246, and No. 83, Killearn to Bevin, January 16, 1946, PRO FO 371/53327.

[30] Ahmad Sadiq Sa'd, *Safahat min al-Yasar al-Misri fi A'qab al-Harb al-'Alamiya al-Thaniya, 1945–1946*, and Taha Sa'd 'Uthman, "Mudhakkirat wa Watha'iq min Ta'rikh al-Tabaqa al-'Amma," *al-Katib*, 11 (July 1971), 170–188; (August 1971), 176–191; (September 1971), 172–190; and (November 1971), 111–126.

pected that the motive for the move was to relocate in an area less troubled by labor disputes. Their suspicions were confirmed when the company agreed to move all of its work force to Alexandria with the exception of thirty-two persons who were the leading labor organizers. The company decision provoked opposition, which spread to other firms and led to encounters with the police and a wave of arrests.

Other firms also experienced strikes during this period. The Filature Nationale d'Égypte had serious labor disputes, and the 1947 strike at the Misr plant in Mahalla brought operations to a halt for a month and a half.[31] Workers struck the Hawamdiya Sugar Refinery in 1950, much to the embarrassment of the Wafdist regime, which enjoyed financial backing from Ahmad 'Abbud, chairman of the board of the Sugar Company.

Students remained a volatile political force and were involved in political turbulence. Although the government bureaucracy began to expand following the retrenchment of the 1930s, and although businesses made a more concerted effort to hire educated Egyptians, Egyptian university and secondary-school graduates still faced employment problems and the prospect of low salaries. The government bureaucracy grew from 219,872 in 1939 to 258,707 in 1949. But the educational system also expanded. The proportion of those with some form of education rose from 15 percent of the total population in 1937 to 25 percent in 1947.[32] By 1952, Egypt's three modern universities (Cairo, Alexandria, and 'Ain Shams) were instructing over 19,000 students.[33] The student population was barraged by opinion on the left and the right, and students soon comprised an

[31] No. 1179, Robert du Bardier to Bidault, September 6, 1947, FEA, Box 45; S. P. Tuck to Secretary of State, September 9, 1947, USNA 883.5045/9-947; and *La Revue d'Égypte Économique et Financière*, 21 (October 18, 1947), 3.

[32] Egypt, Central Agency for Public Mobilization and Statistics, *Population and Development*, p. 15.

[33] Egypt, Ministry of Finance, Statistical Department, *Annuaire Statistique*, 1951–52, 1952–53, and 1953–54 (one volume), pp. 98–99.

important constituency in the Muslim Brotherhood, Young Egypt, and communist and socialist organizations.

The lot of the peasantry appears not to have improved and may even have worsened between 1920 and 1945. Beginning in the 1930s, it came to be widely recognized that the deplorable condition of the peasantry required remedy. But peasant discontent itself did not go beyond jacqueries, which, however, were becoming more prevalent in the postwar years. Between 1945 and 1952, peasants were beginning to challenge the status quo. In one locale, they encroached on crown land; elsewhere, they engaged in thefts and banditry, struck against the picking of cotton, sent a deputation to the parliament to petition for the reduction of land rents, and rose against the autocratic control of Egypt's largest nonroyal landowning family, the Badrawi-'Ashurs.[34]

Despite the atrocious condition of the peasantry, the countryside did not pose a serious threat to Egypt's political order in this period. A few political parties had been organized to represent peasant interests. *Hizb al-Islah* and *Hizb al-Fallah*, established in the 1930s, purported to deal with peasant affairs, but these parties were urban-based and were led by urban educated elites. Their efforts to go among the peasantry to win support did not succeed.[35] The peasants were poor and beholden to the large and medium landowners. Their existence depended desperately on securing wage employment or rental agreements with large estate owners. Some small holders—owners of one or two feddans—had to find off-farm employment in order to supplement their income. A population pressing so heavily

[34] On rural violence see Tareq al-Bishry, "Aperçu Politique et Social"; pp. 11–71; Ibrahim 'Amir, *al-Ard wa-l-Fallah*, p. 143; No. 45, Filliol to Arvengas, February 10, 1948, FEA, Box 45; No. 508, Killearn to Eden, April 5, 1945, enclosing memorandum by W. Smart, March 30, 1945, PRO FO 371/45920; *al-Ahram*, March 11, 1950; *al-Ahram*, June 24, 1951; and *al-Ishtirakiya*, August 25, 1950, and September 23, 1951.

[35] *Shubra*, October 13, 1938, and "Watha'iq Baramaj Ahzab al-'Ummal wa-l-Fallahin fi-l-Thalathinat," *al-Tali'a*, 6 (October 1970), 154–159.

on the land would think only about staying alive, not about revolution.

POLITICAL ORGANIZATIONS

These groups spawned ideas and organizations critical of parliamentary governance and capitalism. Although the Egyptian communist movement never enlisted a large following (probably not more than 3,000 members in 1952), its ideological influences were widespread.[36] Communism was barely kept alive in the 1920s and 1930s by a handful of students and intellectuals.[37] World War II, however, witnessed a proliferation of communist organizations. A new society called *Jam' al-Buhuth* came into being, and at the end of the war communist and socialist groups began to issue pamphlets and newspapers and to promote their ideas among the industrial proletariat.[38] The most influential of numerous leftist publications were the weekly newspapers *al-Fajr al-Jadid* and *al-Damir*. Leftist labor organizers had some success organizing the textile workers at Shubra al-Khayma, al-Mahalla al-Kubra, and Alexandria, although the strikes in those three plants cannot be attributed entirely to their influence.

At various moments in postwar Egypt, the fragmented socialist and communist organizations attempted to federate. In 1946, two of the leading groups, *Lajna al-'Ummal l-il Tahrir al-Qawmi* and *Iskra*, merged to create a students' and workers' committee, which then called for a general strike.[39] But unity was not achieved. In July 1946, the Sidqi government launched an attack on leftist elements, arrest-

[36] Walter Laqueur, *Communism and Nationalism in the Middle East*, pp. 42 ff.

[37] Sa'd, *Safahat*, p. 44.

[38] See Rif'at al-Sa'id, *Ta'rikh al-Munazzamat al-Yasariya al-Misriya* and *al-Sihafa al-Yasariya fi Misr 1925–1948*.

[39] In addition to the references in note 38, see also G. J. Jenkins, Defense Security Office, General Headquarters, Middle East Forces, to W. Smart, March 12, 1946, PRO FO 371/53327.

ing numerous leaders and banning publications. Over 100
persons were arrested, including Muhammad Mandur, editor of the left Wafdist paper, *al-Wafd al-Misri*; Salama Musa,
an Egyptian socialist; and Henri Curiel, a leading Egyptian
communist. Eleven organizations and clubs were closed and
eight journals were suppressed, including *al-Wafd al-Misri*,
al-Damir, *al-Tal'ia*, *Umdurman*, and *al-Fajr al-Jadid*. Although Sidqi's actions may have been intended to ham-
string the Wafd, as his critics contended, they also destroyed the leftist unity campaign.[40]

Even if the socialist and communist political groups did
not achieve marked political success, their ideas permeated
Egyptian society and challenged the political parties. Their
critiques condemned the status quo, the paralysis of the
political order, and the exploitation and oppression of capitalism, and extolled income redistribution, the nationalization of property, and friendship with the Soviet Union.

Nearly all political parties felt the sting of this attack, but
none more so than the Wafd, which aspired to be the champion of the people. The left wing of the Wafd answered
back. Muhammad Mandur associated the Wafd with many
of the socialist and communist ideas in vogue at that time.[41]
A graduate of the Sorbonne in the 1930s and a professor
of Arabic literature at Alexandria University during World
War II, Mandur transformed the newspaper *al-Wafd al-
Misri* into a vehicle of socialist criticism.[42] Affirming that
the essence of the Wafd was populism, social justice, and
income redistribution, Mandur launched a series of articles
in 1946 directed against the "Capitalist Pashas." Com-
mencing with a listing of Isma'il Sidqi's numerous company
directorships, Mandur laid bare the interconnections between Egypt's political rulers and its major business firms.
Other articles on capitalist-politicians dealt with Ahmad

[40] Tel., Lyon to Secretary of State, July 12, 1946, USNA 883.00/7-1246;
No. 1231, Campbell to Foreign Office, July 13, 1946, PRO FO 371/53327;
and *al-Ahram*, July 12 and July 14, 1946.

[41] Sa'd, *Safahat*, pp. 134–137.

[42] "Mandur fi Turathna al-Qawmi," *al-Tali'a*, 2 (May 1966), 130–152.

'Abbud, Ahmad Farghali, Husayn Sirri, and 'Ali Amin Yahya.[43] It was these articles and Mandur's assertion that the Wafd was a socialist party, that persuaded Sidqi to suppress *al-Wafd al-Misri* and to arrest Mandur.

Two other organizations challenged private enterprise and Egypt's brand of parliamentary democracy and represented disaffected social groups: the Muslim Brotherhood and Young Egypt. At the apex of its power at the conclusion of World War II, the Muslim Brotherhood had great appeal for students, unemployed and underemployed university and secondary-school graduates, and industrial workers. Hasan al-Banna's criticism of parliamentary corruption and assertion of the fullness and sufficiency of Islam seemed to offer answers to the poverty and unhappiness that beset many people.

Although much of its social and political thought was naively framed, the brotherhood had a sophisticated political left wing which brought the exploitation and inequity of Egyptian capitalism under the spotlight of Islamic principles. Its leading members, Sayyid Qutb, Muhammad Khalil Muhammad, and Muhammad al-Ghazzali, emphasized the suffering that Egyptian capitalism had produced among the masses and claimed that Islam, properly understood, was strongly committed to social justice. Asserting that Islam stood for equity and brotherhood and that early Islamic leaders detested poverty, these Muslim intellectuals argued for an end to rampant laissez-faire capitalism and demanded that the government ensure minimum standards of living. To them, the obligation that symbolized Islam's affirmation of social justice was the *zakat*, the duty to give alms.[44]

Although Young Egypt was a much less popular group

---

[43] *al-Wafd al-Misri*, May and June 1946.

[44] See the articles by Sayyid Qutb in *al-Ahram*, September 20, 1946, and by Muhammad Khalid Muhammad in *al-Jamahir*, August 11, 1947. Also Sayyid Qutb, *Ma'araka al-Islam wa-l-Ra'smaliya*; and Muhammad al-Ghazzali, *al-Islam al-Muftara 'alayh bayn al-Shuyu'iyin wa-l-Ra'smaliyin* and *al-Islam wa-l-Manahij al-Ishtirakiya*.

than the Muslim Brotherhood, its swing to socialist ideas in the late 1940s and early 1950s was another indication of private enterprise's growing disfavor. In the 1930s, Young Egypt had espoused a mixture of nationalist, Islamic, and fascist ideals. By the next decade, it had blended Islamic nationalist appeals with powerful socialist themes. Ahmad Husayn attacked Egyptian capitalism, both its foreign and local components. Renaming the party's weekly newspaper *al-Ishtirakiya* (Socialism), he championed a fifty-feddan limitation on land holdings and called for the nationalization of major business firms operating in Egypt, including the Suez Canal Company.[45] His Socialist party succeeded in having one of its members elected to parliament in 1950, and though *al-Ishtirakiya* had a limited circulation, it was responsible for inciting the Cairo populace against the foreign presence before and during the riots of January 1952.[46]

HALF-MEASURES OF REFORM

The mounting discontent and increasingly vehement attacks on Egyptian capitalism were a cause of concern to the political elite. While Egypt's postwar ministries did not hesitate to resort to the heavy hand of coercion, there was a consensus that social reforms were needed. Most of the parties elaborated programs calling for the distribution of state lands to small peasants, the provision of potable water to the countryside, the expansion of educational facilities, restrictions on the activities of joint stock companies, price controls on essential consumer goods, and so on. Party leaders delighted in calling their parties socialist, though they carefully differentiated socialism from communism. They claimed that socialism meant a concern for equity and social justice.[47]

[45] *al-Ishtirakiya*, 1950–1952; and Ahmad Husayn, *Kayfa 'Araftu 'Abd al-Nasir wa 'Ishtu Ayyam Hukmih* and *al-Ishtirakiya Allati Nad'u Illayha*.

[46] Muhammad Anis, *Hariq al-Qahira*, pp. 52 ff.

[47] *al-Ahram*, February 20, 1950. In this interview, 'Abd al-'Aziz al-Sufani, secretary of the Watani party, argued that his party was socialist since it was concerned with the welfare of the people.

The British and American embassies in Egypt lent their support to reform. Fearing revolution, these officials exhorted Egyptian leaders to foster timely changes. Killearn, the British ambassador, lectured Egyptian politicians about the "fat Pashas" and the "extremes of wealth and poverty" and warned that the sands of time were "running out."[48] The British appointed a labor attaché at their embassy to assist the Egyptian government in formulating and implementing reforms.[49] Although the American officials were not so closely involved with Egyptian cabinets, they championed a program of land redistribution. The specter of a communist uprising was constantly in their minds.[50]

Although there was widespread agreement on the need for reform, the parliamentary leaders were much more successful in treating the symptoms of the problem, such as inflation, than its root causes. The national legislature spent lavishly—and often unwisely—on food subsidies and wage and salary adjustments while failing to carry out meaningful land reform. It did not overhaul the decrepit system of taxation, and it did not execute its five-year program of social and economic change vigorously. A basic reason for this inaction in crucial areas was the unwillingness of the different segments of the ruling elite—landed magnates and domestic bourgeoisie—to sacrifice any of their privileges. The parlimentary system was paralyzed, and the country tumbled toward social revolution.

In the postwar years, Egypt was once again plagued by ministerial instability. Between 1945 and July 22, 1952, ten ministries held power. All of them engaged in fruitless and debilitating negotiations with the British, and all were intimidated by campaigns of assassination, carried out by extremist groups. Their political orientations ranged from the strongly procapitalist stance of the Sa'dists to the populism of Makram 'Ubayd's Kutla bloc and the Wafd.

[48] No. 145, Killearn to Foreign Office, May 19, 1945, PRO FO 371/45921; also No. 362, Killearn to Foreign Office, November 17, 1945, PRO FO 371/45927.

[49] No. 640, Foreign Office to Cairo, April 9, 1946, PRO FO 371/53327.

[50] Holmes to Secretary of State, January 7, 1949, USNA 883.00/1-749.

Although these parties held different positions, they agreed that the state needed to be more interventionist and to use its powers to solve social problems. State intervention had taken place on a large scale during World War II, and many of these programs were maintained after the war. In 1942, the state passed legislation raising the wages of state employees and persons employed in large-scale industry and commerce. In subsequent years, further increases in these payments were enacted. The state also regulated the prices of sugar, kerosene, cheap textiles, bread, salt, and cement, causing in the process endless disputes with the Sugar Company, textile manufacturers, and the oil companies. All complained that the state's pricing policies produced heavy financial losses. The efforts to combat inflation and to secure a just price for necessities consumed one-quarter of all state expenditures between 1945 and 1952 (see table 7.4).

In contrast, the state was dilatory in executing its five-year plan (1946–1951) designed to promote the social and economic development of the country. The plan laid out a series of schemes for hydraulic reforms, land reclamation and distribution, the establishment of rural social centers, and the spread of education. These programs were expected to cost £E35,600,000. But between 1946 and 1951, the government underspent £E71,700,000 on all of its new works, much of which was for the five-year development program. In the first three years of the plan, the state expended only one-third of the total funds set aside to implement the projects. Many of the schemes still remained uncompleted in 1952.[51]

Similarly, the regime failed to carry out any meaningful land reform. In the postwar years, numerous voices were heard calling for land redistribution. A program of land redistribution was not simply a socialist demand; it was enbraced by a number of conservative Egyptian politicians.

[51] National Bank of Egypt, *Economic Bulletin*, 5 (1952), 53, and 2 (1949), 81–83.

Table 7.4.

Proportions of Government Expenditures to Combat Inflation
and Promote Economic Development and Social Welfare,
1945-1946 to 1951-1952

	Percentage of State Budget to Combat Inflation[a]	Percentage of State Budget to Promote Economic Development and Social Welfare[b]
1945-46	32	0
1946-47	33	4
1947-48	18	8
1948-49	19	4
1949-50	13	4
1950-51	23	4
1951-52	23	0

SOURCE: Egypt, Ministry of Finance, Statistical Department, *Annuaire Statistique.*

[a]These expenditures included income adjustments for civil servants and industrial employees and price subsidies on essential consumer commodities such as sugar, kerosene, bread, textiles, and salt.

[b]These are the expenditures for hydraulics, public health, education, and rural modernization in the five-year plan and in the campaign against poverty, sickness, and ignorance.

In 1944, Muhammad Khattab, a Sa'dist, submitted a private member's bill in the Senate limiting the size of landholdings to 100 feddans.[52] Subsequently, Marit Ghali, a large landowner himself and a member of a wealthy Coptic family, published a pamphlet in favor of land limitation and the redistribution of surplus land to small holders and the landless. Ghali's pamphlet consciously sought industrialist support. It argued that a limitation on the size of estates would redirect resources from agriculture to industry and commerce. It would reduce high land rents and lower the prices of agricultural commodities, industrial raw materials, and consumer goods.[53]

The various land reform schemes were embraced by some industrialists. 'Abd al-Rahman al-Rimali, editor in chief of the influential journal of the Cairo Chamber of Commerce, hoped that a combination of land redistribution and progressive taxation on large estates would result in greater industrial investment.[54] However, although a few enlightened landlords favored land limitation, most echoed the view of 'Ali 'Allubah that the surplus land made available for redistribution to poorer peasants would not make a significant difference in the standard of living of most.[55] Recognizing the resentment felt against large landowners, some politically experienced landed magnates pressed the government to distribute crown lands to poorer peasants.[56]

Despite the attention focused on land, little was accomplished before the military came to power. The state sold land in 1946 and 1947 in Gharbiya, Behera, and Sharqiya provinces, but most of it was purchased by large landown-

[52] Majlis al-Shuyukh, *Majmu'a*, 19th Session, 15th Sitting, p. 330.

[53] Marit Ghali, *al-Islah al-Zira'i* (1948), pp. 57–70.

[54] *Majalla Ghurfa al-Qahira*, 10 (May 1945), 407–409, and Sa'd, *Safahat*, pp. 113 ff. and 160–173.

[55] 'Ali 'Allubah, *Mabadi fi-l-Siyasa al-Misriya*.

[56] This cause was taken up by 'Abd al-Rahman al-Bayli and Sayyid Badrawi-'Ashur. See *al-Ahram*, March 21, 1946, April 2, 1946, and April 16, 1950.

ers.[57] Between 1945 and 1950, only 20,000 feddans of state land were sold to small peasants.[58] The position of the large landowners was too solidly entrenched in the parliament, the higher echelons of the established political parties, and the ministries. Nor were the industrialists energetic supporters of land redistribution. Some, like Ahmad 'Abbud, had large estates themselves. All of them feared the precedent of a land limitation law. The industrialists believed in unfettered private enterprise and were suspicious of programs calling for the redistribution of wealth. Some favored a progressive tax on large estates, but even in this area the views of industrialists were ambiguous, since they were also worried about the impact of progressive taxes on their own wealth.

Nor did the elite carry out a major overhaul of the taxation system. It failed to increase the proportion of revenue raised by means of direct taxes on land, income, and surplus profits. The state continued to rely on indirect taxes, mainly customs, for the bulk of its revenues.

Although Egypt acquired fiscal autonomy in 1937, the war had delayed a complete revision of the taxation system. By the end of the war, tax reform was desperately needed, because the state had to collect more revenue to meet new expenditure obligations. Not only was Egypt expanding its military forces in the face of an impending Palestinian war, but all of its politicians admitted that more funds were needed for welfare and redistribution programs. But where was the increased revenue to come from? Which economic sectors could afford to pay more? The industrialists asserted that agriculture was inadequately taxed, while the landed magnates countered by arguing that Egyptian industry could pay more.

Egyptian taxation rates were moderate, to say the least. Commercial and industrial profits were taxed at 14 percent. The income tax was progressive; incomes of less than £E1,000

[57] Baer, *Landownership*, p. 99.
[58] Ibid., pp. 86–87.

were exempted, the base rate of £E1,000 was only 5 percent, and the rate rose to 50 percent, but only on incomes in excess of £E100,000.[59]

By the late 1940s, industrialists and merchants believed that agriculture was too lightly taxed and that the industrial and commercial sectors bore a disproportionate share of the tax burdens. Their complaints had merit. The land tax had been revised in 1939, the first such revision since the 1890s, but the 1939 tax did not anticipate the extraordinary rise in world prices for agricultural commodities which took place during and after World War II. Nor surprisingly, as the government searched for additional sources of revenue, industrial and commercial leaders demanded that agriculture contribute more. They pointed out that most landowners were not paying even as much as 8 percent of the true rental value of their land.[60]

Industrialist opposition to agricultural privilege was vociferous and widespread. Gone were the days when, as fledgling participants in Egypt's political economy, the industrial wing quietly sought to curry the favor of the landed magnates and ignored areas of potential conflict. The main journals of industrial and commercial opinion now directed editorial comment against the privileges enjoyed by the landed. Charles Arcache, editor in chief of the *La Revue d'Égypt Économique et Financière*, wrote: "The consumer pays the indirect taxes; the merchant and industrialist pay taxes on normal and surplus profits; and employees pay taxes on their earnings. All of these are activities in the service of an agriculture which enjoys exaggerated profits without paying the least tax."[61]

Finally, in 1949, the land tax was again revised, and land

[59] *L'Égypte Industrielle*, 25 (December 1949), 57–60, and *L'Économiste Égyptien*, May 16, 1948.

[60] al-Mu'atamar al-Iqtisadi al-Awwal, *Majmu'a*, p. 149.

[61] *La Revue d'Égypte Économique et Financière*, 21 (February 19, 1949), p. 3. See also *L'Économiste Égyptien*, February 22, 1948; *Majalla Ghurfa al-Qahira*, 15 (April 1950), 379–384; and *L'Égypte Industrielle*, 26 (December 1950), 25–26.

values were reassessed. The tax minimum of £E1.64 per feddan was abolished, but the tax rate was lowered from 16 to 14 percent. Nonetheless, the revenues generated from the land tax rose substantially, from £E5,149,931 in 1948 to £E17,892,700 by 1951.[62]

The various postwar Egyptian ministries succeeded not only in raising more taxation revenues but also in redistributing tax burdens. Increasing numbers of small holders were exempted from having to pay tax, and the larger owners were finally compelled to pay a larger share. Other forms of income and wealth yielded more revenue. The tax on movable wealth produced £E15,650,000 in 1951, as compared with £E11,337,560 in 1948. In 1951, an income tax finally materialized (producing revenue of £E6,000,000 in that year), but nearly half of the state's revenue still derived from customs duties.[63] (See table 7.5.)

Increased revenue enabled the government to alter its spending priorities. Ministries allocated more for education; expenditures for education attained a peak of 12.6 percent of total expenditure in fiscal year 1947–1948. Public health spending also rose to a high point of 6.1 percent of total expenditure in the same fiscal year, while expenditures on public works, mainly hydraulics, declined. This spending pattern marked a sharp reversal from pre–World War I priorities, when a British-dominated Egyptian government spent four times as much on public works as on education and public health combined. (See figure 7.1 and table A. 15.)

Nevertheless, social concern came to the Egyptian government too late and not forcefully enough. By the end of World War II, military expenditures were outstripping other calls on Egyptian resources, and they were destined to increase. The vested interest groups had fought a vigorous rear-guard action to protect their wealth and had delayed

---

[62] *La Revue d'Égypte Économique et Financière*, 21 (April 30, 1949), and Misr, Wizara al-Maliya, *Mizaniya*, 1951–52.

[63] Misr, Wizara al-Maliya, *Mizaniya*, 1951–52.

Table 7.5.

Main Sources of Government Revenue,
1945-1946 to 1951-1952

Source of Revenue	Percentage of Government Revenue Obtained from Each Source in:		
	1945-46	1946-47	1947-48
Land tax	4.4	3.8	3.8
House tax	1.1	1.0	1.2
Income tax	8.7	7.0	8.7
Surplus profits tax	5.0	4.7	2.8
Stamp tax	1.7	1.6	1.6
Inheritance tax	0.3	0.4	0.3
Tax on sale of property	1.5	1.1	1.2
Customs duties and excises	35.0	43.0	46.6
Total revenue collected (£E)	103,498,761	112,793,778	101,495,312

SOURCE: Egypt, Ministry of Finance, Statistical Department, *Annuaire Statistique.*

the implementation of new taxation schedules and social legislation. The bickering over fiscal policy revealed disunity among the rulers of Egypt. It also showed that, even when faced with a clear and well-defined crisis, the elite was not able to elaborate an effective program of action.

Egypt's one last opportunity to avert social revolution and preserve civilian government occurred when the Wafd swept to power in January 1950. In a relatively free election, the voters reaffirmed their support of the Wafd by returning 226 of its members to parliament. No other party

1948-49	1949-50	1950-51	1951-52
2.2	3.4	3.0	6.2
0.8	0.9	1.3	0.4
6.7	6.7	6.3	7.1
3.1	2.3	1.6	0.4
1.3	1.4	0.7	2.4
0.5	0.4	0.3	0.3
1.1	1.1	1.1	1.2
35.3	42.7	48.4	40.1
120,476,297	173,592,682	191,806,055	232,850,531

boasted as many as thirty seats.[64] Once installed in office, the party showed its awareness of the serious tasks before it. Taha Husayn was appointed minister of education and quickly enacted a law making secondary education free and compulsory. The budget of the Ministry of Education was increased. A new Ministry of National Economy was established and charged with the duty of eradicating poverty.[65] The potentially powerful Ministry of Social Affairs was en-

[64] *al-Ahram*, January 6, 1950.
[65] *al-Ahram*, January 14, 1950.

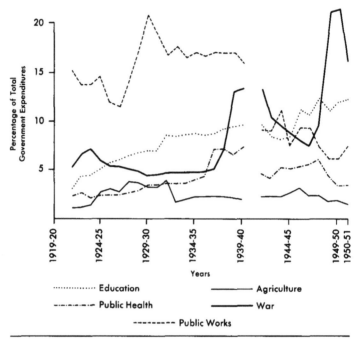

Figure 7.1 Allocation of Projected Government Expenditures, 1919–1920 to 1950–1951

trusted to Dr. Ahmad Husayn (not to be mistaken for Ahmad Husayn, the leader of the Young Egypt Party). Well known for his reformist tendencies, he had been cultivated by American officials in Egypt anxious to see the Egyptian government make a serious attack on social problems. Shortly after assuming office, he announced a £E1,000,000 program of social insurance designed to provide grants of assistance to the needy.[66] Another of the first acts of the government was a law elevating substantially the land tax to be paid by large owners and raising the income tax rate at the highest levels to 70 percent from its previous maximum of 50 percent.[67]

[66] *al-Misri*, January 18, 1950.
[67] *al-Misri*, January 22, 1950.

Yet in spite of these long overdue programs, by the end
of 1951 the Wafdist administration was in disarray, attacked from all sides and unable to maintain political stability. In the area of social reform, the party was hamstrung
by its own conservative wing. The Wafdist ministry was
dominated by large landowners. Its most energetic new
leader was Fu'ad Siraj al-Din, secretary general of the party
and the cabinet's minister of finance and the interior. Although a labor and student organizer when the Wafd had
been out of power, Siraj al-Din was one of the largest landowners in Egypt and a close associate of Egyptian industrialists.[68] His ties with Ahmad 'Abbud were the cause of
numerous press comments.[69] The cabinet included at least
two other large landowners: 'Uthman Muharram and Muhammad Muhammad al-Wakil. Moreover, the steering
committee of the Wafdist party was controlled by representatives of big business and the landed elite. Nor was the
Wafdist cabinet different from its parliamentary membership, where the wealthy were also disproportionately represented. Among the Wafdist members of the Chamber of
Deputies, 32 percent were large landowners, 27 percent
were professionals, 26 percent were medium landowners,
and 11 percent were industrialists.[70] Although the professional stratum may have been sympathetic to leftist and
reformist ideas, its influence was blocked at every turn by
landowners and industrialists.

Unable to implement major social and economic changes,
the Wafd was faced with mounting popular criticisms. Reports of special financial deals between the government and
Ahmad Farghali's Cotton Export Company cost the party
credibility.[71] The resignation of Dr. Ahmad Husayn from
the Ministry of Social Affairs seemed to symbolize the end

[68] On Fu'ad Siraj al-Din, see Jefferson Patterson to Secretary of State,
June 28, 1948, USNA 883.00/6-2848.

[69] E.g., al-Misri, January 1, 1950.

[70] 'Azzah Wahbi, "Tajarib al-Dimuqratiya al-Libraliya fi Misr," p. 176.

[71] al-Ishtirakiya, January 19, 1951 and Ya'qub Bibawi, Haya 'Isami, pp.
60 ff.

of the Wafd's effort at social transformation. Increasingly, the government resorted to coercive rule, seeking to suppress critical newspapers like *al-Ishtirakiya* and to intimidate its political opponents by putting the most outspoken on trial, as it did with Ahmad Husayn.[72] As a last desperate effort to restore its sagging popularity, the Wafd, on October 8, 1951, denounced the Anglo-Egyptian treaty of 1936. Far from calming the political climate, this bold move only inflamed the populace and led the country into chaos.

Of course, the *coup d'etat* that followed soon after cannot be attributed exclusively or perhaps even mainly to failings in Egypt's economic system. The military takeover had its own internal dynamics, and many of the most acute moments of political tension arose because of blocked nationalist ambitions. But undergirding the discontent of those years was a host of economic and social grievances—unemployment, underemployment, poverty, and maldistribution of income—which the capitalist leaders had feared from the first days. The shock troops of discontent, whether they were the assassination squads of the late 1940s or the rioters of 1952, were drawn from among the deprived. They tended to rail against the British as colonial masters, agianst established Egyptian politicians as collaborators, and against capitalists as exploiters.

[72] *al-Ahram*, July 10, 1951, and March 18, 1950.

CONCLUSION:
DEVELOPMENT WITHOUT
GROWTH

In the 1950s and early 1960s, the military government turned against the upper bourgeoisie. Besides nationalizing the main industries and commercial establishments, the state sequestrated the wealth of important businessmen. Many of the leading foreign families, and even some wealthy Egyptians, were compelled to leave the country. The passports of some foreigners bore the words "never to return to Egypt." The message was clear. Egypt's new rulers blamed the old elite for failing to modernize; they also held this group accountable for the poor showing of the Egyptian army in 1948 and for the accumulation of social and economic problems that beset Egypt in the 1950s.

The reality of these years is again more complex than this self-serving picture disseminated by the military. To be sure, the bourgeoisie fell short of many of its goals. But, as has so often been the case in Egypt's quest for modernity, its effort was a determined one. In this case, its heroes are much less well known than other Egyptian modernizers. Most of the individuals who played decisive roles in developing the Egyptian economy came from the private sector, though a few government officials warrant recognition for the clarity of their vision about economic matters (Isma'il Sidqi and Makram 'Ubayd, to mention the most prominent). Although many of the native-born Egyptian businessmen have been recognized and some of them even lionized (notably Tal'at Harb), many foreigners resident in Egypt also played important roles, which, though very meaningful to the whole process, have generally been ignored by later commentators. The names of Henri Naus, Michel Salvago, Yusuf Cicurel, and Yusuf Aslan Qattawi rarely appear in studies of modern Egypt, although their influence on events was enormous.

The outline of the economic history of these years can be quickly summarized. Beginning in 1920 with some clear advantages (a relatively high standard of living, a lucrative export crop, and substantial foreign assistance) as well as some real deficiencies (educational, entrepreneurial, and governmental), the Egyptian ruling elite accomplished much over the next three decades. Economically minded leaders had three overarching aims. They wanted to diversify the economy, rendering it less dependent on the export of cotton. They sought to make it more autonomous, enhancing the Egyptian component in it and strengthening Egyptian control over it. Finally, they believed that this bundle of changes not only would produce structural economic changes but also would lead to economic growth which would translate into material benefits for all inhabitants of the country—a goal always in the foreground. Egyptian leaders were haunted by a specter of social revolution (glimpsed clearly in the 1919 revolt and in the urbanization and general population statistics) and believed that far-reaching, transformative economic change was the only way to avert social catastrophe.

The achievement of economic growth and an increase in economic control are perhaps the supreme ambitions in the contemporary third world. The effective strategies for overcoming economic backwardness and closing the poverty gap separating third-world societies from Europe and North America are the substance of numerous cabinet meetings in Lagos, New Delhi, and Caracas. Interwar Egypt's avowedly capitalist approach and its welcoming of foreign contributions to economic growth can add to this discussion, for its programs were similar to those being promoted today in parts of Asia, Africa, and Latin America.

Two opposed perspectives compete for attention in seeking to explain and achieve economic development in the third world. One, the mainstream liberal model, assumes that the drive to innovate arises most strongly within the private sector and is responsive to profit motives and the dictates of a free market economy. While the state can aid in effecting major structural changes by increasing the savings and investment rates, transferring resources from agriculture to industry, and closing the economy through tariff and monetary controls, the decisive economic push must come from individual entrepreneurs. Although mainstreamers believe in the virtue of sheltering a local economy from the international economic environment, they also regard foreign capital and foreign technical assistance as useful substitutes for local deficiencies. In this vein, they regard the colonial period as having contributed to growth through infrastructural and agricultural improvements.

In contrast, the dependency perspective, which originated in Latin American studies but was carried over to other third world societies, stresses the international and class obstacles to change. Dependency theorists contend that only by effecting a radical break in the bonds of subordination to the developed world can real growth and economic autonomy be realized. Far from contributing to long-term economic gain, colonialism, in this view, tied Asia, Africa, and Latin America to Western Europe and North America in ways that prevented necessary structural economic change. Political independence has meant little more than the substitution of neocolonial sway for formal colonial authority.

The Egyptian interwar experience offers pertinent and suggestive insights into these perspectives. Certainly Egypt was one of the countries bound tightly to the international economy. International arrangements—formal and informal—were powerful deterrents to change. International treaties propped open the Egyptian economy for cotton exporting and the importation of manufactures. The European powers defended their privileged arrangements (in the form of tariff restrictions and the Capitulations) until finally forced to yield. European capital, specializing in commerce, agriculture, and finance, was solidly entrenched and slow to change. The prevailing attitude among the Egyptian and foreign elites—exceedingly hard to eradicate, no matter how diligently innovators tried—was that Egypt was an agricultural country with few natural industrial advantages.

The first two decades of Bank Misr's existence provide many examples of domestic and international resistance to structural changes. The bank at the outset was able to compete against its numerous and solidly entrenched European competitors only by extolling its patriotic qualities and by entering the cotton marketing arena aggressively. After its program for creating a state-supported industrial bank had been rejected, it was compelled to be the primary arm of the native-born industrial bourgeoisie. Its efforts to promote Egyptian industrial and commercial development with the use of its own deposits stretched its resources thin and jeopardized its solvency.

Yet the obstacles to change were not so unyielding as to stymie the determined efforts of local economic leaders. Egypt did acquire tariff and fiscal autonomy. The government abolished the Capitulations and challenged the predominant position of entrenched foreign financial groups. The local elite itself—foreign but residential and Egyptian—proved to be far from monolithic. Industrial and financial entrepreneurs came forward, spurred by profit motives and sometimes by patriotic visions, and undercut metropolitan finance.

The local bourgeoisie, though weak as suggested in the dependency literature, was not committed to maintaining the status quo (another dependency contention). Compradors (Egyptian and foreign) pioneered new industries; often agents of foreign trading and financial firms used their wealth and business experience to found new companies.

But the Egyptian industrial bourgeoisie never gained an upper hand in the Egyptian political economy. Landed magnates retained great power; most refused to take an interest in new economic ventures. Social, economic, and cultural divisions kept the native-born and foreign residential wings of the industrial bourgeoisie apart. The more successful the foreign residents became, the more they drew themselves away from Egyptian ways and toward a European style of existence. Even Jews, Greeks, and Syrians, despite long-standing attachments in the Arab East, behaved in this fashion. On the other hand, although the Egyptian industrial and financial bourgeoisie, as represented by the Misr group or ʿAbbud, embraced European cultural practices, they remained responsive to their Arab Muslim heritage. Their Egyptian consciousness increased as the period wore on and nationalist and anti-European sentiments intensified.

These divisions were manifested clearly in the political arena, where the bourgeoisie often failed to create conditions conducive to economic diversification. Expected to support development by means of taxation reform, large-scale development projects, and the creation of an industrial development bank, the state was slow to realize programs recommended by the bourgeoisie. Failures often stemmed from the populist and antiforeign nature of Egyptian nationalism, which rendered difficult a strategy based on using foreign assistance to overcome domestic lacks in capital and skills.

The Egyptian economic experience over this thirty-five-year period was a curiously mixed one. Perhaps it can best be described by revising the standard dependency critique of "growth without development." Egypt achieved development without attaining real growth. Use of the analytical categories suggested by Chenery and Syrquin points toward such a statement. On the basis of an examination of socioeconomic data from 101 countries during two decades following World War II, Chenery and Syrquin conclude that the development process entails transformations in four large and analytically distinct areas: accumulation, where investment, government revenue, and expenditure on education increase as a proportion of GNP; resource allocation, where demand, production, and foreign trade shift out of primary products into manufactured goods and into services; demography, where the proportion of labor in industry and services rises and urbanization increases; and finally, income distribution, where industrialization and urbanization often lead initially to a widening of income gaps.[1]

Application of these categories to Egypt shows that the country experienced change—in some ways, rather startling structural transformations—in many social and economic areas. Yet the country did not show improvement in the general standard of living. Income per capita as a nationwide figure (i.e., making no allowance for distribution) was no better in 1952 than it had been in 1914. One can only assume that an already badly skewed distribution of income (as reflected in landholding statistics) may even have worsened in the period leading up to 1952. Governmental efforts to alleviate poverty and provide avenues of social mobility were hardly impressive. The growth of the population increased the numbers of the rural landless and swelled the population of underemployed and unemployed city dwellers.

Many other characteristics of economics transformation did show significant change, however. Conventional yardsticks of measurement would indicate that the efforts of the local bourgeoisie and the state were not without effect (table C.1). Local investment and savings rates, which had been minuscule before 1914, reached the not unhealthy level of 8 to 10 percent of Gross National Product (GNP) in the postwar years—far from what was needed to produce accelerated development, but an achievement nonetheless. Moreover, savings and investment resources were being channeled into the industrial sector.

While government was not as purposeful as it might have been, government expenditures as a proportion of GNP rose between 1913 and 1952, from 15 percent to 20 percent of GNP. However, a large proportion of government re-

[1] Hollis Chenery and Moises Syrquin, *Patterns of Development 1950–1970*, pp. 23–63.

Table C.1.

Development without Growth, 1913-1952

	1907 or 1913	1947 or 1952
Gross national product (GNP) per capita	£E10	£E10
Savings as percentage of GNP	a	8.5
Investment as percentage of GNP	a	9.5
Government revenue as percentage of GNP	14.7	20
Exports as percentage of GNP	26.4	13.5
Imports as percentage of GNP	21.4	15.9
Government expenditure on education as percentage of GNP	.5	2.2
Percentage of children age 5-19 in school[b]	7	25
Percentage of labor force in primary sector[b]	68.3	61.7
Percentage of labor force in industrial sector[b]	13.0	10.6
Percentage of labor force in service occupations[b]	15.9	27.7
Percentage urban of total population[b]	19	33

SOURCES: Data on GNP from Hansen, "National Product and Income for Egypt," p. 29, and Bent Hansen and Girgis a. Marzouk, *Development and Economic Policy in the UAR (Egypt)*, pp. 318-319. All other data from Egypt, Ministry of Finance, Department of Statistics, *Population Census of Egypt*, 1907 and 1947, and Egypt, Ministry of Finance, Statistical Department, *Annuaire Statistique*, 1913 and 1952-1953.

[a]Not available.

[b]Census years of 1907 and 1947 are used for these figures.

sources had to be earmarked for the alleviation of poverty (no doubt laudatory as well as politically and socially necessary); thus, they could not be set aside for the purpose of promoting growth.

Education was one of Egypt's great deficiencies in the pre–World War I period, caused in large part by British stinginess. Though the educational effort of the interwar years would be dwarfed by the Nasser push of the 1950s and 1960s, the expenditure on education and the educational achievements of this era were far from insignificant. By 1952, the proportion of total government expenditure on education had increased nearly fivefold; Egyptian society was offering some form of education (though its quality varied immensely) to about one-quarter of eligible children, whereas less than 10 percent had had access to schooling before 1914.

Thus, these processes, which Chenery and Syrquin refer to as "accumulation processes" (investment, government revenue, and education) were far more substantial than later critics conceded.

Less striking were the resource allocation transformations (structure of demand, structure of trade, and structure of production). Although Egypt ceased to be an almost exclusively agricultural country, industry gained much less than did the service sector of the economy. Exports as a percentage of GNP declined substantially between 1913 and 1952, largely because Egypt developed no major export items other than cotton. As for imports, there was a substantial decline in consumer nondurables, like textiles, but an alarming and economically retrogressive rise in foodstuffs. No longer able to feed its burgeoning population with its own production, Egypt expended valuable foreign exchange on grains. Nor had an export-oriented industrial sector been established.

Major demographical changes did not signify economic growth; rather, they stemmed from economic problems. Agricultural employment declined as a proportion of the total labor force, but the labor force moved not into industry but into services and into a growing informal sector. An urbanization spurt accompanied labor transfers, with the proportion of the urban population rising from 19 percent in 1907 to 33 percent in 1947.

In many respects, then, Egypt witnessed some marked structural changes: a move to the cities, a growth of industries, an expansion of the services sector, an increase in government control over GNP, and educational expansion. But the standard of living did not improve. Indeed, despite the fact that nearly all of the advocates of economic change had regarded this goal as primary, the life of the rank and file was probably harsher in 1952 than it had been before World War I.

Of course, Egypt's prospects for economic success during those years could hardly have been judged favorable. The population was already large (over 12,000,000 in 1917) and was growing at a rapid rate. Even at the outset of the period, the population pressed heavily on the land, and since agriculture had expanded dramatically in the previous century, it could no longer generate high growth rates. The proportion of the young in the total population was high and illiteracy was widespread, a consequence of a continuous neglect of educational needs.

The real moving force for structural economic change during this era was a small group of wealthy foreign businessmen who resided in Egypt. One could hardly have picked a less likely group to lead the struggle for economic transformation. As non-Egyptians, they lacked formal political power; they had to influence the political process from behind the scenes. Their success had come through contact with Europeans and their knowledge of European languages and ways. They gloried in their devotion to European culture. A great paradox marked their actions and attitudes. Eager to diversify and industrialize the economy and to establish local control over financial institutions, they nonetheless lacked a sympathy for the Arabic and Muslim heritage of the country. In the face of rising Egyptian nationalism, their commitment to European values doomed them to being cast out of the country. Yet their contributions to Egypt's economic change were impressive. As a social group, they were an alien enclave; as an economic force, they were dynamic and farsighted.

APPENDIX

Table A.1

Characteristics of the Greek Population of Egypt,
1897-1947

	Total Population	Percent Living in Cairo	Percent Living in Alexandria	Literacy Rate[a]
1897	38,208	b	b	b
1907	62,973	30.8	39.1	b
1917	56,731	26.9	44.8	596
1927	76,264	26.4	48.7	863
1937	68,559	24.7	53.7	795
1947	57,427	27.3	53.6	866

SOURCE: Egypt, Ministry of Finance, Statistical Department, *Population Census of Egypt*, 1897, 1907, 1917, 1927, 1937, and 1947.

[a]Number of literate persons per 1,000 persons over five years old.

[b]Not available.

Table A.2.

Characteristics of the Italian Population of Egypt,
1907-1947

	Total Population	Percent Living in Cairo	Percent Living in Alexandria	Literacy Rate[a]
1907	34,926	38.1	45.6	b
1917	40,198	38.9	44.4	674
1927	52,462	35.4	46.3	825
1937	47,706	34.5	48.0	831
1947	27,958	44.2	44.2	886

SOURCE: Egypt, Ministry of Finance, Statistical Department, *Population Census of Egypt*, 1907, 1917, 1927, 1937, and 1947.

[a]Number of literate persons per 1,000 persons over five years old.

[b]Not available.

Table A.3.

Characteristics of the British Population of Egypt, 1907-1947

	Total Population	Percent Living in Cairo	Percent Living in Alexandria	Literacy Rate[a]
1907	20,653	41.5	39.7	b
1917	24,354	30.9	43.8	675
1927	34,169	32.8	42.1	851
1937	31,523	37.0	44.5	829
1947	28,246	40.7	34.2	881

SOURCE: Egypt, Ministry of Finance, Statistical Department, *Population Census of Egypt*, 1907, 1917, 1927, 1937, and 1947.

[a]Number of literate persons per 1,000 persons over five years old.

[b]Not available.

Table A.4.

Characteristics of the French Population of Egypt, 1907-1947

	Total Population	Percent Living in Cairo	Percent Living in Alexandria	Literacy Rate[a]
1907	14,591	44.4	29.5	b
1917	21,270	38.8	40.2	627
1927	24,332	39.2	38.8	751
1937	18,821	39.9	38.9	763
1947	9,717	46.5	33.5	889

SOURCE: Egypt, Ministry of Finance, Statistical Department, *Population Census of Egypt*, 1907, 1917, 1927, 1937, and 1947.

[a]Number of literate persons per 1,000 persons over five years old.

[b]Not available.

Table A.5.

Characteristics of the Jewish Population of Egypt, 1907-1947

1	2 Total Population	3 Percent Living in Cairo	4 Percent Living in Alexandria	5 Literacy Rate[a]	6 Number of Egyptian Citizens[a]	7 Number of British, French, and Italian Citizens[a]	8 Percent (7 ÷ [6+7])
1907	38,635	52.5	37.5	438	b	b	——
1917	59,581	49.0	41.7	438	24,980	17,056	40.6
1927	63,953	53.3	38.8	726	32,320	18,922	36.9
1937	62,953	55.6	39.2	754	40,300	15,343	27.6
1947	65,639	63.8	32.2	823	50,831	8,820	14.8

SOURCE: Egypt, Ministry of Finance, Statistical Department, *Population Census of Egypt*, 1907, 1917, 1927, 1937, and 1947.

[a]These figures must contain many errors, since in 1956 most Egyptian Jews found themselves without Egyptian nationality and had to be treated as stateless persons. The censuses apparently merely indicated what the individuals themselves reported as their nationality. It would also appear that in some households children were counted and in others they were not. The totals do not add up to the total Jewish population living in Egypt.

[b]Not available.

Table A.6.

Egypt's Foreign Trade by Country, 1885-1913

Exporting Country	1885-89	1890-94	1895-99	1900-04	1905-09	1910	1911	1912	1913
	Percentage of Value of Imports								
Great Britain	37.5	34.7	33.8	36.0	32.1	31.0	31.4	30.8	30.5
France	10.6	9.7	10.8	9.2	11.7	11.3	10.2	9.3	9.0
Turkey	18.7	20.2	17.7	14.4	12.6	12.3	10.3	10.6	9.8
Importing Country									
	Percentage of Value of Exports								
Great Britain	62.8	59.6	51.4	52.1	52.6	49.6	48.8	46.3	43.1
Germany	.1	1.9	4.0	7.2	8.6	10.7	10.9	11.2	12.8
United States	.2	1.5	6.9	5.4	6.5	6.6	7.3	12.0	7.9
France	8.2	7.6	8.9	8.1	8.2	8.5	8.1	7.8	8.8
Russia	9.2	12.4	11.6	7.8	5.7	5.7	6.3	6.0	7.1

SOURCE: Egypt, Ministry of Finance, Statistical Department, *Annuaire Statistique*, 1914, p. 294.

Table A.7.

Main Items in Egyptian Imports, 1912 and 1913

	1912		1913	
	Value (£E)	Percentage of Total	Value (£E)	Percentage of Total
Animal and animal food products	1,105,000	4.3	1,051,000	3.8
Hides, skins, and leather goods	389,000	1.5	385,000	1.4
Shoes	178,000	0.7	179,000	0.6
Other animal products	73,000	0.3	71,000	0.3
Cereals, flour, and agricultural produce	3,066,000	11.8	4,242,000	15.2
Wheat flour and maize flour	1,535,000	5.9	2,196,000	7.9
Colonial produce and general grocery	1,231,000	4.8	1,066,000	3.8
Sugar, raw and refined	424,000	1.6	380,000	1.4
Spirits, beverages, and oils	1,272,000	4.9	1,412,000	5.1
Wines, beer, and liquors	363,000	1.4	361,000	1.3
Petroleum	340,000	1.3	572,000	2.1
Vegetable oils	376,000	1.5	282,000	1.0
Paper and printed matter	434,000	1.7	437,000	1.6

Wood and coal	3,062,000	11.8	3,839,000	13.8
Stone, earthenware, and glassware	640,000	2.6	583,000	2.1
Cement	168,210	0.6	107,869	0.4
Dyestuffs, tanstuffs, and colors	281,000	1.1	252,000	0.9
Chemical and medicinal products and perfumery	1,372,000	5.3	1,343,000	4.8
Chemical fertilizer	668,000	2.6	658,000	2.4
Soap	273,169	1.1	231,894	0.8
Medicinal preparations and pharmaceuticals	113,786	0.4	120,488	0.4
Yarns and textiles	6,908,000	26.7	6,969,000	25.0
Cotton fabrics and yarns	3,948,000	15.2	4,066,000	14.6
Woolen fabrics and yarns	599,000	2.3	518,000	1.8
Silken fabrics and yarns	374,000	1.4	342,000	1.2
Metals and metalware	2,922,000	11.3	3,145,000	11.3
Iron and steel pieces	580,000	2.2	718,000	2.6
Agricultural machines	184,000	0.7	266,000	1.0
Locomotives, wagons, and automobiles	214,000	0.8	176,000	0.6
Other machines and parts of machines	569,000	2.2	646,000	2.3
Tobacco, tombac, and cigars	1,215,000	4.7	1,082,000	3.9
Miscellaneous	1,938,000	7.5	1,988,000	7.1
Total	25,908,000	100.3	27,865,000	100.1

SOURCE: Egypt, Ministry of Finance, Statistical Department, *Annuaire Statistique*, 1914, pp. 300 ff.

Table A.8.

Reserves and Profits of Eleven Large Industrial Companies in Egypt after World War I

	Associated Cotton Ginners of Egypt (£E263,250)		Kafr el-Zayat Cotton Company (E312,000)		Société Générale de Pressage et de Depôts (E445,045)	
	Reserves (£E)	Profits (%)	Reserves (£E)	Profits (%)	Reserves (£E)	Profits (%)
1919-20	a	13	a	40	a	20
1920-21	a	8	a	15	a	35
1921-22	a	12	a	15	a	175
1922-23	56,027	12	177,866	7.6	92,036	94
1923-24	58,379	7	137,765	5	107,416	81
1924-25	63,238	10	144,198	5	204,328	50

Société Générale des Sucreries et de la Raffinerie d'Égypte (£E2,798,419)		Compagnie Frigorifique d'Égypte (£E232,360)		Egyptian Salt and Soda Company (E528,539)		S.A. des Bieres Bomonti et Pyramides (£E154,300)	
Reserves (£E)	Profits (%)	Reserves (£E)	Profits (%)	Reserves (£E)	Profits (%)	Reserves (£E)	Profits (%)
a	44	a	6	a	30	a	a
a	20	a	7.5	a	22.5	a	a
a	20	a	7.5	a	17.5	a	a
341,704	28	56,226	7.5	160,731	7.5	23,652	4
372,520	29	57,295	9	155,825	0	24,177	6
274,786	6	58,759	9.5	141,781	5	24,615	5

Table A.8 (Continued)

Reserves and Profits of Eleven Large Industrial
Companies in Egypt after World War I

	United Egyptian Salt Company (£E292,500)		Clothing and Equipment Company of Egypt (£E150,000)		Filature Nationale d'Égypte (£E146,250)	
	Reserves (£E)	Profits (%)	Reserves (£E)	Profits (%)	Reserves (£E)	Profits (%)
1919-20	a	3	0	0	a	63
1920-21	a	6	0	0	a	37
1921-22	a	4	0	0	a	25
1922-23	63,814	3	0	0	84,154	4.8
1923-24	67,956	4	0	0	67,226	0
1924-25	72,729	5	0	0	78,949	4.8

Société des Huiles d'Égypte "Egolin" (£E267,883)	
Reserves (£E)	Profits (%)
a	a
a	a
0	0
0	0
0	0
0	0

SOURCE: Egypt, Ministry of Finance, Department of Statistics, *Statistique des Sociétés Anonymes par Actions*, 1925.

NOTES: Only companies with capitalization in excess of £E145,000 are included in this table; capitalization of each company is shown in parentheses beneath its name. Tobacco companies are not included because they did not report dividends.

Profits are calculated on the basis of the nominal value of ordinary shares only.

[a]Not available.

Table A.9.

Reserves and Profits of Fourteen Large Industrial
Companies in Egypt, 1926-1929

	Alexandria Pressing Company (£E150,000)		Associated Cotton Ginners of Egypt (£E263,250)		Kafr el-Zayat Cotton Company (£E312,000)	
	Reserves (£E)	Profits (%)	Reserves (£E)	Profits (%)	Reserves (£E)	Profits (%)
1926	6,561	0	64,961	8.3	136,611	10
1927	9,506	15	68,407	8.9	155,058	12.6
1928	18,445	17.5	55,914	0	144,539	11.3
1929	41,518	20	60,177	6.7	162,543	12.6

Société Générale de Pressage et de Depôts (£E431,395)		S.A. des Sucreries et de la Raffinerie d'Égypte (£E2,758,481)		Compagnie Frigorifique d'Égypte (£E230,240)		Egyptian Salt and Soda Company (£E516,157)	
Reserves (£E)	Profits (%)	Reserves (£E)	Profits (%)	Reserves (£E)	Profits (%)	Reserves (£E)	Profits (%)
224,721	43.7	120,408	3.0	58,850	11.3	155,680	5
207,054	31.3	97,098	18.4	60,636	12.5	154,045	6.3
221,237	40	76,173	10	61,301	12.5	167,229	10
230,461	50	73,727	0	57,851	12.5	176,298	12.5

Table A.9 (Continued)

Reserves and Profits of Fourteen Large Industrial
Companies in Egypt, 1926-1929

	S.A. des Bieres Bomonti et Pyramides (£E154,300)		United Egyptian Salt Company (£E146,250)		Clothing and Equipment Company of Egypt (£E150,000)	
	Reserves (£E)	Profits (%)	Reserves (£E)	Profits (%)	Reserves (£E)	Profits (%)
1926	24,667	4	54,416	5.5	0	0
1927	24,909	6	57,223	8	0	0
1928	26,532	6	17,431	16	0	0
1929	28,180	6	2,697	20	19,208	0

Filature Nationale d'Égypte (£E320,000)		S.A. des Huiles d'Égypte "Egolin" (£E267,883)		Société Misr de Filature et de Tissage (£E300,000)		S.A. Égyptienne de Ciment Portland-Tourah (£E300,000)	
Reserves (£E)	Profits (%)	Reserves (£E)	Profits (%)	Reserves (£E)	Profits (%)	Reserves (£E)	Profits (%)
70,296	8.8	0	0	a	a	a	a
71,091	5	0	0	0	0	0	0
61,629	0	0	0	0	0	0	0
61,629	0	in liquidation		0	0	0	0

SOURCE: Egypt, Ministry of Finance, Department of Statistics, *Statistique des Sociétés Anonymes par Actions.*

NOTES: Only companies with capitalization in excess of £E145,000 are included in this table; capitalization of each company is shown in parentheses beneath its name. Tobacco companies are not included because they did not report dividends.

Profits are calculated on the basis of the nominal value of ordinary shares only.

aNot available.

Table A.10.

Reserves and Profits of Fifteen Large Industrial
Companies in Egypt, 1930-1937

	Alexandria Pressing Company (£E225,000)		Associated Cotton Ginners of Egypt (£E210,600)		Kafr el-Zayat Cotton Company (£E312,000)	
	Reserves (£E)	Profits (%)	Reserves (£E)	Profits (%)	Reserves (£E)	Profits (%)
1930	49,806	20.0	66,903	8.3	164,250	12.5
1931	46,919	18.8	66,079	6.3	172,984	12.5
1932	49,475	16.3	64,884	0	169,389	11
1933	53,164	16.3	36,333	0	171,080	11
1934	60,824	18.8	42,257	0	203,685	12.5
1935	66,507	16.3	8,792	0	209,000	12.5
1936	73,427	17.5	10,899	4.6	203,529	11
1937	77,290	12.5	15,466	7.4	196,232	9

Société Générale de Pressage et de Depôts (£E400,000)		Société Générale des Sucreries et de la Raffinerie d'Égypte (£E2,605,729)		Société Anonyme de Ciment Portland de Helouan (£E300,000)		Société Égyptienne de Ciment Portland-Tourah (£E565,000)	
Reserves (£E)	Profits (%)	Reserves (£E)	Profits (%)	Reserves (£E)	Profits (%)	Reserves (£E)	Profits (%)
227,380	47.5	67,051	0	1,379	0	9,023	0
233,346	42.5	133,517	5.0	3,463	0	902	0
254,813	40.0	78,796	5.5	6,456	5.0	14,810	5.5
250,167	40.0	77,993	5.0	9,850	6.7	34,686	6.5
262,569	43.8	73,720	5.5	9,691	7.8	31,496	5.5
255,419	36.3	72,390	5.0	4,320	8	39,281	8.8
268,053	33.8	73,922	5.5	4,083	8	41,419	12.5
280,352	31.3	74,052	5.5	5,593	10	39,582	10.0

Table A.10 (Continued)

Reserves and Profits of Fifteen Large Industrial
Companies in Egypt, 1930-1937

	Compagnie Frigorifique d'Égypte (£E180,000)		Egyptian Salt and Soda Company (£E485,347)		Société Anonyme des Bières Bomonti et Pyramides (£E192,875)	
	Reserves (£E)	Profits (%)	Reserves (£E)	Profits (%)	Reserves (£E)	Profits (%)
1930	55,134	11.3	168,910	10	26,982	0
1931	53,641	8.3	167,014	7.5	18,041	0
1932	50,818	7.0	170,720	10	19,481	0
1933	52,114	7.0	172,350	10	19,639	4.5
1934	51,638	7.0	179,664	11.3	22,417	6.0
1935	52,243	7.0	180,327	11.3	1,527	6.0
1936	52,820	7.5	180,250	11.3	2,035	5.0
1937	53,607	20.5	179,191	11.3	4,645	6.0

Société Vinicole et Vinicolet d'Égypte (£E250,000)		Filature Nationale d'Égypte (£E487,500)		Société Égyptienne d'Électricité (£E400,000)		Société Égyptienne des Industries Textiles (£E240,000)	
Reserves (£E)	Profits (%)	Reserves (£E)	Profits (%)	Reserves (£E)	Profits (%)	Reserves (£E)	Profits (%)
a	a	61,629	0	a	a	a	a
a	a	92,474	0	1,248	0	a	a
a	a	61,548	0	9,650	0	a	a
a	a	61,864	6	19,807	0	a	a
a	a	87,760	7.7	31,504	0	a	a
a	a	97,650	7.7	51,667	5.0	198	0
a	a	135,998	8.2	72,090	5.0	415	7.0
12,626	0	153,403	9.2	104,948	5.0	6,507	7.5

Table A.10 (Continued)

Reserves and Profits of Fifteen Large Industrial
Companies in Egypt, 1930-1937

	Société Misr de Filature et de Tissage (£E1,964,400)	
	Reserves (£E)	Profits (%)
1930	17,643	0
1931	2,807	0
1932	16,709	5.0
1933	28,917	6.0
1934	99,065	6.0
1935	109,385	6.0
1936	158,995	6.0
1937	167,642	6.0

SOURCE: Egypt, Ministry of Finance, Department of Statistics, *Statistique des Sociétés Anonymes*, 1930-1937.

NOTES: Only companies with capitalization in excess of £E145,000 are included in this table; capitalization of each company is shown in parentheses beneath its name. Total capitalization of these fifteen companies in 1937 was £E8,818,456, or 68 percent of total capitalization in industrial joint stock companies. Tobacco companies are not included because they did not report dividends.

Profits are calculated on the basis of the nominal value of ordinary shares only.

Table A.11.

Egypt's Foreign Trade and Trade with Great Britain, 1909-1952

	Total Imports (£E)	Imports from Great Britain (£E)	Percentage	Total Exports (£E)	Exports to Great Britain (£E)	Percentage
1909	22,230,499	6,743,678	30	26,076,239	13,099,910	50
1910	23,552,826	7,311,218	31	28,944,461	14,343,381	50
1911	27,227,118	8,557,296	31	28,598,991	13,958,058	49
1912	25,908,000	7,991,000	31	34,574,000	16,022,000	46
1913	27,865,000	8,496,000	30	31,662,000	13,648,000	43
1919	47,409,717	21,840,957	46	75,888,321	40,222,821	53
1920	101,880,963	37,894,760	37	85,467,061	36,343,184	43
1921	55,507,984	16,937,815	31	36,356,062	17,045,830	47
1922	43,333,938	14,731,622	34	48,716,418	23,035,915	47
1923	45,276,963	14,771,677	33	58,387,327	28,354,293	49
1924	50,736,918	13,993,584	28	65,733,935	31,955,625	49
1925	58,224,895	14,660,664	25	59,198,662	26,167,972	44
1926	52,400,059	11,405,307	22	41,759,391	18,921,153	45
1927	48,685,785	12,482,606	26	48,340,503	19,138,089	40

Year						
1928	52,043,969	11,326,242	22	56,165,258	21,532,193	38
1929	56,089,512	11,895,512	21	51,751,984	17,958,982	35
1930	47,488,328			31,941,592		
1931	31,528,167	7,134,416	23	27,937,113	10,026,508	36
1932	27,425,691	6,586,724	24	26,987,417	10,373,014	38
1933	26,766,991	6,189,520	23	28,842,436	12,004,919	42
1934	29,303,723	6,486,611	22	31,055,759	9,947,871	32
1935	32,238,859	7,360,310	23	35,693,162	12,636,669	35
1936	31,515,555	7,526,926	24	32,978,400	12,491,478	38
1937	38,038,098	8,288,018	22	39,759,066	12,446,625	31
1938	36,934,373	8,496,512	23	29,342,486	9,863,701	34
1939	34,090,716	9,430,273	28	34,080,913	12,322,690	36
1945	60,475,769	10,955,431	18	41,629,998	11,408,030	27
1946	81,094,217	24,954,363	31	63,680,509	21,221,722	33
1947	100,246,974	21,601,771	22	85,716,069	23,781,700	28
1948	161,218,448	36,293,773	23	140,740,670	41,248,174	29
1949	167,519,216	37,984,924	23	135,671,053	23,594,048	17
1950	204,681,999	41,323,182	20	172,958,680	37,090,252	22
1951	235,840,586	41,926,742	18	200,639,051	38,571,673	19
1952	220,690,944	29,649,090	13	142,851,388	6,399,625	4

SOURCE: Egypt, Ministry of Finance, Statistical Department, *Annuaire Statistique*.

Table A.12.

British Trade with Egypt, 1913-1952

	British Exports to Egypt (£)	Percentage of Total British Exports	British Imports from Egypt (£)	Percentage of Total British Imports
1913	9,805,639	1.9	16,134,777	2.1
1919	19,405,263	2.4	53,972,906	3.3
1920	43,643,665	3.3	48,682,688	2.5
1921	18,884,073	2.7	23,457,908	2.2
1922	15,366,886	2.2	27,926,583	2.8
1923	15,073,468	2.0	29,747,472	2.7
1924	15,117,525	1.9	34,231,751	2.7
1925	16,424,231	2.1	28,094,217	2.1
1926	11,030,330	1.7	20,414,446	1.6
1927	12,564,387	1.8	20,823,833	1.7
1928	11,185,647	1.5	24,144,368	2.0
1929	12,576,232	1.7	21,540,261	1.8
1930	9,807,690	1.7	12,392,242	1.2
1931	6,650,427	1.7	10,202,114	1.2
1932	6,509,981	1.8	9,490,260	1.4
1933	6,260,049	1.7	11,550,939	1.7
1934	6,528,322	1.6	10,483,542	1.4
1935	7,631,373	1.8	11,677,567	1.5
1936	7,756,411	1.8	12,691,647	1.5
1937	7,878,890	1.5	13,374,165	1.3
1938	8,689,015	1.8	11,103,933	1.2
1939	9,670,053	2.2	11,522,322	1.3
1940	8,968,468	2.2	13,190,020	1.1
1941	9,018,048	2.5	8,970,198	.8
1942	8,901,901	2.3	15,643,591	1.3
1943	4,509,341	1.3	11,002,211	.6
1944	5,919,235	1.8	13,143,825	.6
1945	11,251,147	2.6	13,152,206	.9
1946	23,388,391	2.6	14,620,406	1.1
1947	21,969,636	1.9	13,240,351	.7

	British Exports to Egypt (£)	Percentage of Total British Exports	British Imports from Egypt (£)	Percentage of Total British Imports
1948	34,101,055	2.2	47,545,666	2.3
1949	35,980,906	2.0	28,915,472	1.3
1950	42,442,154	2.0	39,396,556	1.5
1951	40,586,453	1.6	47,320,926	1.2
1952	32,540,704	1.3	12,774,490	.5

SOURCE: Great Britain, Customs and Excise Department, *Trade with Foreign Countries and British Possessions,* 1913-1952.

Table A.13.
Main British Exports to Egypt, 1909-1939

	Coal		Textiles		Machinery and Metals	
	Value (£E)	Percentage of Total Egyptian Coal Imports	Value (£E)	Percentage of Total Egyptian Textile Imports	Value (£E)	Percentage of Total Egyptian Machinery and Metals Imports
1909	1,177,544	44	3,751,733	64	936,393	48
1910	1,233,472	44	4,068,115	61	1,138,709	48
1911	1,327,462	45	4,848,999	59	1,415,444	48
1912	1,483,314	48	4,196,002	61	1,311,111	45
1913	1,874,368	49	4,108,360	60	1,488,054	47
1919	2,665,497	68	13,207,183	70	2,553,100	68
1920	2,692,409	22	22,771,387	66	6,656,690	56
1921	1,359,070	22	9,291,385	63	3,309,760	45
1922	1,381,177	36	8,980,549	60	1,927,257	36
1923	1,663,265	42	8,776,996	53	1,944,498	36
1924	1,751,615	42	7,713,955	45	2,296,794	34

Year						
1925	1,841,180	38	7,544,024	42	2,935,316	35
1926	913,991	21	4,847,087	36	3,378,679	39
1927	1,915,544	45	5,130,549	37	3,253,392	39
1928	1,510,082	40	4,710,625	31	2,912,455	32
1929	1,702,581	39	4,715,250	29	3,003,431	31
1930						
1931	1,334,154	46	2,080,443	27	1,673,193	35
1932	1,171,438	37	2,240,879	29	1,320,930	35
1933	1,067,229	36	2,077,189	26	1,164,939	32
1934	1,147,446	37	1,922,659	23	1,404,454	32
1935	1,495,441	39	1,764,738	22	1,770,915	35
1936	981,438	32	2,369,491	31	1,752,651	34
1937	1,521,736	33	2,220,632	25	1,842,808	28
1938	1,672,111	36	1,693,602	24	1,919,432	29
1939	1,983,563	41	1,531,542	27	2,098,217	33

SOURCE: Egypt, Ministry of Finance, Statistical Department, *Annuaire Statistique*.

Table A.14.

British Overseas Investments, Selected Years from 1910 to 1952

	Total British Overseas Investments (£, Current Value in Year Indicated)	Total British Investments in Egypt (£, Current Value in Year Indicated)	Percentage of British Investments in Egypt
1910	3,191,836,000	43,753,000	1.37
1938	3,292,000,000	10,000,000	.30
1940	3,338,000,000	11,000,000	.33
1942	2,871,000,000	9,000,000	.31
1944	2,544,000,000	4,000,000	.16
1946	2,329,000,000	4,000,000	.17
1948	1,960,000,000	7,000,000	.36
1949	2,037,000,000	11,000,000	.54
1950	2,020,000,000	10,000,000	.50
1951	1,985,000,000	10,000,000	.50
1952	1,985,000,000	9,000,000	.45

SOURCES: 1910, George Paish, "Great Britain's Capital Investments in Individual Colonial and Foreign Countries," pp. 167-187. All other years, Bank of England, Statistics Office, *United Kingdom Overseas Investments, 1938 to 1948* (London, 1950) and *1948-1952* (London, 1954).

Table A.15.

Projected Expenditures in Egyptian Government Budgets, 1919-1920 to 1950-1951

	Total of Budget Estimates (£E)	Percentage of Budget Allocated to:				
		Education	Public Health	Public Works	Agriculture	War
1919-20	28,850,000	2.3	2.3	14.3	0.7	5.2
1920-21	64,522,658	a	a	a	a	a
1921-22	31,731,754	3.0	2.3	15.3	1.0	5.3
1922-23	28,058,791	4.2	2.7	13.7	1.1	6.7
1923-24	32,299,265	4.5	2.0	13.7	1.4	7.1
1924-25	34,275,483	5.0	2.3	14.5	2.7	5.9
1925-26	34,204,977	5.8	2.4	11.9	3.0	5.5
1926-27	38,973,340	6.0	2.4	11.5	2.8	5.5
1927-28	35,389,036	6.5	2.7	14.1	3.9	5.1
1928-29	40,170,052	6.9	2.8	17.1	3.8	4.9
1929-30	46,696,677	7.0	3.5	20.9	3.4	4.4
1930-31	41,222,580	7.0	3.5	a	3.2	4.5
1931-32	38,518,650	8.6	3.7	16.9	3.8	4.8
1932-33	37,309,639	8.5	3.7	17.6	1.7	4.9

1933-34	35,548,711b	8.6	3.7	16.8	2.0	4.9
1934-35	36,600,252b	8.8	4.0	17.0	2.3	4.9
1935-36	38,348,200	8.7	4.3	16.9	2.3	4.9
1936-37	40,549,107	8.9	7.1	17.0	2.3	5.1
1937-38	42,642,816	9.4	7.2	17.0	2.2	7.2
1938-39	47,234,450	9.5	6.9	17.0	2.1	13.2
1939-40	47,500,800	9.6	7.4	16.1	2.0	13.4
1940-41a						
1941-42	46,062,380	9.7	4.8	8.3	2.4	13.4
1942-43	56,553,450	8.5	4.2	8.1	2.4	10.5
1943-44	71,938,261	8.2	5.1	10.3	2.4	9.8
1944-45	82,097,005	8.7	5.1	7.9	2.8	8.8
1945-46	95,303,874	11.3	5.5	9.5	3.2	8.1
1946-47	102,192,123	10.9	5.8	9.5	2.7	7.7
1947-48	94,547,624	12.6	6.1	7.9	2.6	9.9
1948-49	157,694,643	10.3	4.8	6.3	2.0	21.3
1949-50	163,808,515	11.2	3.7	6.3	2.0	21.6
1950-51	190,183,808	11.5	3.8	7.7	1.8	16.2

SOURCE: Egypt, Ministry of Finance, Statistical Department, *Annuaire Statistique*.

aNot available.

bIn 1933-34 and 1934-35, the budget estimates did not include railway and telegraph expenditures. Since these were included in all other fiscal years, I added them in, estimating them at £E5,000,000 each year.

BIBLIOGRAPHY

ARCHIVES

Public Record Office, London. FO 371, 407, and 141.
United States National Archives, Washington, D.C. Materials on
    Egypt from the American Embassy, Cairo.
French Embassy Archives, located at the French Embassy, Cairo.
Egyptian Archives, Citadel, Cairo. Records of the Council of Min-
    isters and records of the Ministry of Commerce and Industry.

MANUSCRIPTS

Barker, Henry Michael. "Two Centuries in the Levant: The Bar-
    kers of Alexandria." (Typescript kindly lent by the author.)
Choremi, Argine. Typescript on Alexandria.
Khalifa, Ibrahim. "Historique de la Société Électro Cable Égypte."
    (Pastings lent by the author.)
Majlis al-Shuyukh, Majmuʿa Madabit, al-Jalsat al-Sirriya, vol. 1, 1936
    to 1944. (Volume housed in the building of the National
    Assembly.)
Manuscripts at the Middle East Studies Centre, St. Antony's Col-
    lege, Oxford, of which the papers of Bertram Hornsby proved
    the most valuable.
Memoir of Ladislas Pathy, Columbia Oral History Research Of-
    fice, Hungarian Project.
Note on Sir Victor Harari Pasha by his grandson, Paul Rolo.
Translation of the Tribunal of First Instance of Cairo, July 13,
    1966 (typescript lent by Solomon Green)
Yasin, Muhammad. "Nubda' Maqtadaba 'An Taʿrikh Haya wa
    Baʿd Aʿmal al-Sayyid Muhammad Sayyid Yasin."

PRINTED PRIMARY SOURCES

Journals in Western languages: L'Art Vivant, L'Aurore, La Bourse
    Égyptienne, Bulletin Commercial, Bulletin of the Greek Chamber of

Commerce at Alexandria (in Greek), *Bulletin Mensuel de la Chambre de Commerce Française d'Alexandrie, Bulletin de l'Union des Agriculteurs,* Chambre de Commerce Égyptienne d'Alexandrie *Rapport Annuel, L'Économiste Égyptien, L'Égypte Contemporaine, L'Égypte Industrielle, L'Informateur, Israel, Monthly Bulletin of the British Chamber of Commerce of Egypt,* National Bank of Egypt, *Economic Bulletin, The Near East Trader, La Revue du Caire, La Revue d'Égypte Économique et Financière, Times* (London), *La Tribune Juive.*

Journals in Arabic: *al-Ahram, al-Ahram al-Iqtasadi, al-Akhbar, al-Balagh, al-Basir, al-Fajr al-Jadid, al-Fallah al-Iqtisadi, al-Ishtirakiya, al-Jamahir, al-Kashkul, al-Katib, Majalla Ghurfa al-Iskandariya, Majalla Ghurfa al-Qahira, Majalla al-Ghurfa al-Tijariya al-Misriya, Misr al-Fatah, al-Misri, al-Muqattam, al-Muqtataf, Ruz al-Yusuf, Sahifa al-Tijara wa-l-Sinaʿa, Shams, Shubra, al-Taliʿa, al-Umdurman, Wafd al-Misri, Zamil al-Fallah.*

Yearbooks:

Annuaire de la Finance Égyptienne. Alexandria, 1907.

Annuaire desfosses: Valeurs Cotées au Parquet et en Banque à la Bourse de Paris. Paris, 1920+.

Annuaire des Juifs d'Égypte et du Proche Orient. Cairo, 1938+.

Annuaire Général de l'Industrie Égyptienne: Inventaire et Répertoire de la Production Industrielle de l'Égypte. Alexandria, 1939.

Compagnie des Agents de Change près la Bourse de Paris, Chambre Syndicale. *Annuaire des Valeurs Admisés à la Cote Officielle.* Paris, 1918–1921.

Handbook of Egyptian Securities, compiled by C. L. Mortera. Alexandria, 1922–1936.

Near East Directory. 1947+.

Papasian, Ed. *L'Égypte Économique et Financière.* Cairo, 1923 and 1926.

Papasian, Ed. *Annuaire de la Finance Égyptienne: Deuxième Année, 1910.* Alexandria, 1910.

Pilvachi, George, ed. *Egyptian Cotton Yearbook.* Cairo, 1931–32.

Politi, Elie I., ed. *Annuaire des Sociétés Égyptiennes par Actions.* Cairo, 1929, 1930, 1932, and 1937.

Recueil Financier, La. Brussels and Paris, 1919+.

Société Orientale de Publicité. *The Egyptian Directory, L'Annuaire Égyptien.* Cairo, 1915+.

Stock Exchange Yearbook of Egypt, The. Cairo, 1939 + .

Who's Who in Egypt and the Near East: The Leading Biographical Work in the Near East. Cairo, 1947 + .

Government Publications in Western Languages:

Belgique. *Recueil Consulaire Contenant les Rapports Commerciaux des Agents Belges à l'Étranger.* Brussels, 1890–1914.

Bowring, John. *Report on Egypt and Candia, House of Commons Sessional Papers,* 1840, vol. 21, no. 1.

Compte Rendu des Travaux de la Commission de la Dette Publique d'Égypte.

Egypt. *Annales de la Chambre des Députés.* 1924 + .

Egypt, Central Agency for Public Mobilization and Statistics. *Population and Development: A Study on the Population Increase and Its Challenge to Development in Egypt.* Cairo, 1978.

Egypt, Commission du Commerce et de l'Industrie. *Rapport.* Cairo, 1918.

Egypt, Ministry of Agriculture. *L'Égypte Agricole.* Cairo, 1937.

————. *Agricultural Census of Egypt, 1929.* Cairo, 1934.

————, Statistical Division. *Agricultural Yearbook, 1933* and *1934–35.*

————, Cotton Research Board. *Annual Report.* 1920 + .

Egypt, Ministry of Commerce and Industry. *Opportunities for Industrial Development in Egypt.* Cairo, 1955.

————, Mines and Quarries Department. *The Geology of Iron-Ore Deposits in Egypt,* by M. I. Attia. Cairo, 1950.

Egypt, Ministry of Education. *Rapport Final de la Commission de l'Université.* Cairo, 1921.

————. *La Renaissance de l'Enseignement en Égypte de 1917 à 1923.* Cairo, 192?.

Egypt, Ministry of Finance. *A Brief Note on the Phosphate Deposits of Egypt,* by John Ball (*Survey Paper no. 30*). Cairo, 1913.

————. *Egypt in the Post-War Economy,* by J. I. Craig. Cairo, 1945.

————. Mines and Quarries Department. *Report on Boring for Oil in Egypt,* 3 parts in 1, by T. Sutton Bowman. Cairo, 1925–1931.

————. *Report on the Mineral Industry of Egypt.* Cairo, 1922.

Egypt, Ministry of Finance. *Note on the Programme and Policy of the Government with Regard to the Investigation and Development of the Petroleum Resources of Egypt,* by E. M. Dowson. Cairo, 1921.

————. *Recueil des Documents Relatifs à la Guerre, Publiés au Journal Officiel,* 2 vols. Cairo, 1914 and 1915.

————, Statistical Department. *Annuaire Statistique.* 1906+.

————. *Annual Statement of the Foreign Trade of Egypt.* 1919+.

————. *Census of Industrial Production, 1944.* Cairo, 1947.

————. *Final Account for the Financial Year. . . .* Cairo, 1917+.

————. *Joint Stock Companies Operating Chiefly in Egypt, Part II, Situation on December 31, 1907.* Cairo, 1909.

————. *Statistique des Sociétés Anonymes par Actions.* 1925+.

————, Statistical and Census Department. *Industrial and Commercial Census, 1927.* Cairo, 1931.

————. *Population Census of Egypt* for the years 1882, 1897, 1907, 1917, 1927, 1937, 1947, and 1960. (Title varies.)

————, Statistical Department. *Statistics of Wages and Working Hours in Egypt, July, 1945.* Cairo, 1946.

————, Department of Statistics. *Statistique des Sociétés Anonymes par Action Travaillant Principalement en Égypte,* 1913, 1925–1926+.

————, Survey Department. *The Distribution of Iron Ores in Egypt,* by W. F. Hume. Cairo, 1909.

————, Survey of Egypt. *The Phosphate Deposits in Egypt,* no. 41, by W. F. Hume. Cairo, 1927.

Egypt, Ministry of Finance and Economy, Statistical Department. *Industrial and Commercial Census, 1947.* Cairo, 1955.

————, Statistical and Census Department. *National Income of Egypt for 1953.* Cairo, 1955.

Egypt, Ministry of Industry. *Industry after the Revolution and the Five-Year Plan.* Cairo, 1957.

Egypt, Ministry of the Interior. *Report on Labour Conditions in Egypt with Suggestions for Future Social Legislation,* by H. B. Butler. Cairo, 1932.

Egypt, Ministry of National Economy, Statistical Department. *Census of Industrial Production, 1947.* Cairo, 1952.

Egypt, Nile Projects Commission. *Report of the Nile Projects Commission.* London, 1920.

Egypt, Ministry of Public Works. *Annual Reports.* 1912–1913+.

————. *Report of the Mission to Lake Tana, 1920–1921,* by G. W. Grabham and R. P. Black. Cairo, 1925.

Egypt, Ministry of Public Works. *Nile Control,* by Sir Murdoch MacDonald, 2 vols. Cairo, 1920.

————. *Nile Control Works: Note on a Series of Control Works to Reg-*

ulate the Irrigation Water Supply of the Nile Valley by Murdoch MacDonald. Cairo, 1919, 1920.

————. *Upper White Nile Mission, 1923, Interim Report*, by P. M. Tottenham. Cairo, 1926.

Great Britain, Board of Trade. *Report of the British Goodwill Trade Mission to Egypt, November-December, 1945*. London, 1946.

————. *United Kingdom Trade Mission to Egypt*. London, 1931.

————, Overseas Economic Surveys. *Egypt: Economic and Commercial Conditions in Egypt, 1947*, by J. W. Taylor. London, 1948.

————. *Egypt, 1951*, by A. N. Cumberbatch. London, 1952.

Great Britain, Department of Overseas Trade. *Report on the Economic and Financial Conditions in Egypt for 1919, 1921, 1922, 1928*, and *1935*. London, 1920 +. (Title varies.)

Great Britain, Department of Trade, *Report on the Economic and Commercial Conditions in Egypt*, by G. H. Selous, London, 1937.

United States, Department of State. *Foreign Relations of the United States*. Washington, 1919 +.

Government Publications in Arabic:

Misr, Majlis al-Shuyukh. *Majmu'a Madabit*. Cairo, 1924 +.

Misr, al-Wizara al-Maliya. *al-Hisab al-Khitami*. Cairo, 1947–1948.

Misr, Wizara al-Maliya. *Mizaniya al-Dawla al-Misriya*. Cairo, 1918–1952.

Misr, Wizara al-Tijara wa-l-Sina'a. *Taqrir lajna al-Sina'at*. Cairo, 1948.

Other Primary Works in Western Languages:

Barker, Edward B. B., ed. *Syria and Egypt under the Last Five Sultans*. London, 1876.

Bosch, Baron Firman van den. *Vingt Années d'Égypte*. Paris, 1932.

Boulad, Gabriel Selim. *Notice Historique sur la Famille Boulad*. N. p., 1957.

Boutigny, Henri. *L'Homme Propose*. Cairo, 1950.

Bulletin du Parti National Égyptien. Stockholm, 1917.

Calligrammes: Art-Science-Littérature (November 1936).

Catalogue des Collections de Madame Lina Gabriel Aghion. Alexandria, 1959.

Committee of Egyptian Engineers. *English Version of the Despatch Submitted to Adly Yeghen Pasha*. Cairo, 1921.

Egyptian Delegation to the Peace Conference. *Collection of Official Correspondence from November 11, 1918 to July 14, 1919.* Paris, 1919.

Eid, Alfred. *La Fortune Immobilière de l'Égypte et sa Dette hypothécaire.* Paris, 1907.

Elgood, P. G. *Egypt and the Army.* Oxford, 1924.

Eman, André. *L'Industrie du Coton en Égypte: Étude d'Économie Politique.* Cairo, 1943.

Fargeon, Raoul. *Silhouettes d'Égypte.* Cairo, 1931.

Forster, E. M. *Alexandria: A History and a Guide.* Alexandria, 1922 and 1938.

International Federation of Master Cotton Spinners and Manufacturers Associations. *Official Report of the International Cotton Congress Held in Egypt.* Cairo, 1927.

Killearn, Baron Miles Lampson. *The Killearn Diaries, 1934–1946: The Diplomatic and Personal Record of Lord Killearn (Sir Miles Lampson), High Commissioner and Ambassador, Egypt.* London, 1972.

Klat, Jules. *Les Opérations de Bourse en Égypte.* Alexandria, 1933.

Kotb, Sayed. *Social Justice in Islam.* Translated by John B. Hardie. Washington, 1953.

Lane, Edward W. *The Manners and Customs of the Modern Egyptians.* London, 1936.

Le Livre d'Or du Journal la Réforme, 1895–1945: 50 Ans de Vie d'Égypte à Travers la Réforme. Alexandria, 1945.

Lloyd, George Ambrose. *Egypt since Cromer.* 2 vols. London, 1933.

Member of the Egyptian Delegation, A. *The Independence of Egypt.* London, 1921.

Memorandum Presented to the Peace Conference by the Egyptian Delegation Charged with the Defence of Egyptian Independence, Egyptian National Claims, A. N. p., 1919.

Mizrahi, Maurice. *L'Égypte et Ses Juifs: Le Temps Révolu.* Lausanne, 1978.

Nasser, Gamal Abdal. *Egypt's Liberation.* Washington, 1955.

Part du Sable, La. *Cahier de Littérature Appliquée* (April 1950).

Politi, E. I. *L'Égypte de 1914 à Suez.* Paris, 1965.

Rowlatt, Mary. *A Family in Egypt.* London, 1956.

Sadat, Anwar al-. *Revolt on the Nile.* London, 1957.

Saint-Omer, Henry de. *Les Entreprises Belges en Égypte: Rapport sur la Situation Économique des Sociétés Belges et Belgo-Égyptiennes Fonctionnant en Égypte.* Brussels, 1907.

Samuel, Sydney Montagu. *Jewish Life in the East*. London, 1881.

Schanz, Moritz. *Cotton in Egypt and the Anglo-Egyptian Sudan*. Manchester, 1913.

Simou, Kosta. *Parikiako Lefkoma*. Cairo, 1961.

Todd, John A. *The Cotton World: A Survey of the World's Cotton Supplies and Consumption*. London, 1927.

Willcocks, William. *The Nile Projects*. Cairo, 1919.

————. *The Sudd Reservoir or Nature's Provision of Perennial Irrigation and Flood Protection for the Whole of the Nile Valley*. Cairo, 1919.

Wilson, Florence. *Near East Educational Survey: Report of a Survey Made during the Months of April, May, and June, 1927*. Edinburg, 1927.

Other Primary Works in Arabic:

Abazah, Fikri. *al-Dahik al-Baki*. Cairo, 1973.

————. *Majmu'a Maqalat*. 3 vols. Cairo n.d.

Abu al-Fath, Mahmud. *al-Mas'la al-Misriya wa-l-Wafd*. Cairo, 1921.

'Allubah, 'Ali. *Mabadi fi-l-Siyasa al-Misriya*. Cairo, 1942.

Bank Misr. *Insha' al-Sina'at al-Ahliya*. Cairo, 1929.

————. *Taqrir*. 1921 +.

————. *al-Yubil al-Dhahabi, 1920–1970*. Cairo, 197?.

Barakat, Muhammad Bahi al-Din. *Safahat min al-Ta'rikh*. Cairo, 1961.

Bibawi, Ya'qub. *Haya 'Isami*. Cairo, 1965.

Fahmi, 'Abd al-'Aziz. *Hadhihi Hayati*. Cairo, 1963.

Fahmi, Qallini. *Mudhakkirat*. 2 vols. Cairo, 1934.

Fahmi, Zaki. *Safwa al-'Asr fi Ta'rikh wa Rusum Mashahir Rijal Misr*. Cairo, 1926.

Fu'ad, Faraj Sulayman. *al-Kanz al-Thamin li-'Uzama' al-Misriyin*. Cairo, 1917.

Ghali, Marit. *al-Islah al-Zira'i*. Cairo, 1945.

————. *al-Islah al-Zira'i*. Cairo, 1948.

Ghazzali, Muhammad al-. *al-Islam al-Muftara 'alayh bayn al-Shuyu'iyin wa-l-Ra'smaliyin*. Cairo, 1951.

————. *al-Islam w-al-Manahij al-Ishtirakiya*. Cairo, n.d.

Ghazzali, Sayf al-Din al-. *al-Wafd wa-l-Ishtirakiya*. Cairo, 1977.

Ghurfa al-Iskandariya al-Tijariya al-Misriya. *Nahda Misr*. Alexandria, 1950.

Hamzah, 'Abd al-Latif. *Adab al-Maqala al-Sahafiya fi Misr*, vol. 7, *Amin al-Rafi'i*. Cairo, 1959.

Harb, Muhammad Tal'at. *'Ilaj Misr al-Iqtisadi wa Mashru' Bank al-Misriyin aw Bank al-Umma*. Cairo, 1911.

————. *Majmu'a Khutab Muhammad Tal'at Harb*. 3 vols. Cairo, 1927+.

————. *Qana al-Suwis*. Cairo, 1910.

————. *Tarbiya al-Mar'a wa-l-Hijab*. Cairo, 1899.

Haykal, Muhammad Husayn. *Mudhakkirat fi-l-Siyasa al-Misriya*. 3 vols. Cairo, 1953.

————. *al-Siyasa al-Misriya wa-l-Inqilab al-Dusturi* Cairo, 1931.

Husayn, Ahmad. *Imani*. Cairo, 1936.

————. *al-Ishtirakiya Allati Nad'u Illayha*. Cairo, 1950.

————. Kayfa 'Araftu 'Abd al-Nasir wa 'Ishtu Ayyam Hukmih. Cairo, 1970.

'Id Bank Misr. Cairo, 1935.

'Inayat, 'Abd al-Fattah. *Qissa Kifah*. Cairo, n.d.

Islam, 'Ali. *Khawatir*. 2 parts. Cairo, 1957.

————. *Muhadara fi Shirikat al-Ta'awun*. Beni Suef, 1922.

————. *Wasa'il al-Nuhud b-il-'Amil*. Cairo, 1939.

————. *Wasa'il Tahsin Hala al-Fallah al-Iqtisadiyan*. Cairo, 1937.

Ittihad al-Sina'at al-Misriya. *al-Kitab al-Dhahabi*. Cairo, 1972.

Jaziri, Muhammad Ibrahim al-. *Athar al-Za'im Sa'd Zaghlul*. Cairo, 1927.

Judah, Ahmad Qasim, ed. *al-Makramiyat*. Cairo, n.d.

Khanki, 'Aziz. *Shu'un Misriya*. Cairo, 1940.

Kulliya al-Tijara. *al-Yubil al-Fiddi*. Cairo, 1937.

Mahmud, Muhammad. *al-Yad al-Qawi*. Alexandria, ca. 1929.

Mu'atamar al-Iqtisadi al-Awwal, al-. *Majmu'a A'mal al-Mu'atamar*. Cairo, 1947.

Mubarak, 'Ali. *'Alam al-Din*. 4 vols. Cairo, 1882.

————. *al-Khitat al-Tawfiqiya al-Jadida*. 20 vols. Cairo, 1887.

Nahhas, Yusuf. *Juhud al-Niqaba al-Zira'iya al-Misriya al-'Amma fi Thalathin 'Am*. Cairo, 1952.

————. *al-Qutn fi Khamsin 'Am*. Cairo, 1954.

Qarali, al-Khuri Bulus. *al-Surriyun fi Misr*. Cairo, 1928.

Qutb, Sayyid. *Ma'araka al-Islam wa-l-Ra'smaliya*. Cairo, 1952.

Rifa'i, Husayn 'Ali al-. *al-Sina'a fi Misr*. Cairo, 1935.

Sabam, Isma'il Hasan. *Bank Misr*. Cairo, n.d.

Sa'd, Ahmad Sadiq. *Safahat min al-Yasar al-Misri fi A'qab al-Harb al-'Alamiya al-Thaniya, 1945–1946*. Cairo, 1976.

Sadiq, Hasan. *Nazrat Ta'rikhiya wa Suturiya*, Cairo, 1936.
Sami, Salib. *Dhikrayat, 1891–1952*. Cairo, n.d.
Sayyid, Ahmad Lutfi al-. *Qissa Hayati*. Cairo, 1962.
Shafiq, Ahmad. *Hawliyat Misr al-Siyasiya*. Cairo, 1926+.
Shahid, Salah al-. *Dhikrayati fi 'Ahdayn*. Cairo, 1976.
Shati', Bint al-. *Qadiya al-Fallah*. Cairo, n.d.
Shirikat Bank Misr. *Taqrir*. Cairo, 1923+.
Sidqi, Isma'il. *Mudhakkirati*. Cairo, 1950.
Tusun, 'Umar. *Kalimat fi Sabil Misr*. Cairo, 1928.
———. *Mudhakkira bi ma Sadara 'Anna Mundhu Fajr al-Haraka al-Wataniya al-Misriya min Sana 1918 ila Sana 1928*. Cairo, 1942.
'Uthman, Taha Sa'd. "Mudhakkirat wa Watha'iq fi Ta'rikh al-Tabaqa al-'Amila al-Misriya." *al-Katib*, 13 (January 1972), 136–145, (February 1972), 39–52, (March 1972), 140–148, and (April 1972), 138–150.
———. "Mudhakkirat wa Watha'iq min Ta'rikh al-Tabaqa al-'Amma." *al-Katib*, 11 (July 1971), 170–188, (August 1971), 176–191, (September 1971), 172–190, and (November 1971), 111–126.
Wahidah, Subhi. *Fi Usul al-Mas'ala al-Misriya*. Cairo, 1950.

SECONDARY WORKS

Works in Western Languages

Abdel-Fadil, Mahmoud. *Development, Income Distribution, and Social Change in Rural Egypt, 1952–1970: A Study in the Political Economy of Agrarian Transition*. Cambridge, 1975.
Abdel-Malek, Anour. *Idéologie et Renaissance Nationale: L'Égypte Moderne*. Paris, 1969.
———. *Egypt: Military Society: The Army Regime, the Left, and Social Change under Nasser*. Translated by Charles Lam Markman. New York, 1968.
Abdel-Moneim Abul-Fadl, Mona Mohamed. "The Sidqi Regime in Egypt, 1930–1935: New Perspectives," Ph.D. dissertation, London School of Oriental and African Studies, 1975.
Abd el-Motaal, M. Zaki. *Les Bourses en Égypte; Historique, État-Actuel, Reorganization*. Paris, 1930.
Abu-Lughod, Janet. *Cairo: 1001 Years of the City Victorious*. Princeton, 1971.

Amin, Galal A. *Food Supply and Economic Development with Special Reference to Egypt.* London, 1966.

Amin, Samir. *Accumulation on a World Scale: A Critique of the Theory of Underdevelopment.* 2 vols. Translated by Brian Pearce, New York, 1974.

Ammar, Abbas M. *The People of Sharqiya, Their Racial History, Serology, Physical Characters, Demography, and Conditions of Life.* 2 vols. Cairo, 1944.

Ammar, H. M. "An Enquiry into Inequalities of Educational Opportunities in Egypt." Master's thesis, University of London, 1929.

Ammar, Hamed. *Growing up in an Egyptian Village: Silwa, Province of Aswan.* London, 1954.

Anderson, John. "The Egyptian Rural Middle Class and Party Politics under the Constitutional Monarchy." Master's thesis, University of Chicago, 1976.

Anis, Mahmoud Amin. *A Study of the National Income in Egypt.* Cairo, 1950.

Antonini, Emile. *Le Crédit et la Banque en Égypte.* Lausanne, 1927.

Argenti, Philip P. *Bibliography of Chios from Classical Times to 1936.* Oxford, 1936.

Arminjon, Pierre. *La Situation Économique et Financière de l'Égypte.* Paris, 1911.

Assaad, Fawzia. *L'Égyptienne: Roman.* Paris, 1975.

Assabghy, A. *Les Questions de Nationalité en Égypte* Cairo, 1926.

Ayoub, Christian. "Une Famille Levantine avant 1850." *Cahiers d'Alexandrie*, 1964, pp. 19–30.

———. "Levant." Phillippe Jullian, ed., in *Dictionnaire du Snobisme.* Paris, 1958.

Badaoui, Zaki. *Les Problèmes du Travail et les Organisations Ouvrières en Égypte.* Alexandria, 1948.

Baer, Gabriel. *Studies in the Social History of Modern Egypt.* Chicago, 1969.

———. *A History of Landownership in Modern Egypt, 1800–1950.* New York, 1962.

Balboni, L. A. *Gli Italiani nella Civiltà Egiziana del Secolo XIX.* 3 vols. Alexandria, 1906.

Banque Belge et Internationale en Égypte, Recueil des Statistiques. 25 Ans au Service de l'Économie Égyptienne, 1929–1954.

Baster, A.S.J. *The International Banks.* London, 1935.

Berger, Morroe. *Bureaucracy and Society in Modern Egypt: A Study of the Higher Civil Service*. Princeton, 1957.

Berque, Jacques. *L'Égypte: Impérialisme et Révolution*. Paris, 1967.

———. "The Establishment of the Colonial Economy." In William R. Polk and Richard Chambers, eds., *Beginnings of Modernization in the Middle East: The Nineteenth Century*, pp. 233–243. Chicago, 1968.

Binder, Leonard. *In a Moment of Enthusiasm: Political Power and the Second Stratum in Egypt*. Chicago, 1978.

Bishry, Tareq al-. "Aperçu Politique et Social." In Ibrahim Douek, ed., *La Voie Égyptienne vers le Socialisme*, pp. 11–71. Cairo, 1966.

Cantori, Louis Joseph. "The Organizational Basis of an Elite Political Party: The Egyptian Wafd." Ph.D. dissertation, University of Chicago, 1966.

Carnoy, Norbert. *La Colonie Française du Caire*. Paris, 1928.

Carr, David William. *Foreign Investment and Development in Egypt*. New York, 1979.

Carson, William Norris. *The Mehalla Report*. Cairo, 1953.

Charles-Roux, François. *La Production du Coton en Égypte*. Paris, 1908.

Chenery, Hollis, and Moises Syrquin. *Patterns of Development, 1950–1970*. London, 1975.

Christophe, Leon-Roger. *L'Égypte et le Régime des Capitulations: La Conférence de Montreux*. Paris, 1938.

Clement, R. *Les Français d'Égypte aux XVIIe et XVIIIe Siècles*. Cairo, 1960.

Clerget, Marcel. *Le Caire: Étude de Géographie Urbaine et d'Histoire Économique*. 2 vols. Cairo, 1934.

Cohen, Hayyim J. *The Jews of the Middle East, 1860–1972*. New York, 1973.

Colombe, Marcel. *L'Évolution de l'Égypte, 1921–50*. Paris, 1951.

Conrardy, Joseph. *Firman van den Bosch: Ce Diable d'Homme*. Brussels, 1948.

Cook, M. A., ed. *Studies in the Economic History of the Middle East from the Rise of Islam to the Present Day*. London, 1970.

Cook, P. Lesley. *Effects of Mergers: Six Studies*. London, 1958.

Crédit Foncier Égyptien, 1880–1930. [Cairo, 1930.]

Crouchley, A. E. *The Economic Development of Modern Egypt*. New York, 1938.

———. *The Investment of Foreign Capital in Egyptian Companies and Public Debt*. Cairo, 1936.

Davis, Eric. *Challenging Colonialism: Bank Misr and Egyptian Industrialization, 1920–1941*. Princeton, 1982.

Davison, Roderic H. *Reform in the Ottoman Empire, 1856–1876*. Princeton, 1963.

Deeb, Marius. "The Socioeconomic Role of the Local Foreign Minorities in Modern Egypt, 1805–1961." *International Journal of Middle East Studies*, 9 (1978), 11–22.

———. *Party Politics in Egypt: The Wafd and its Rivals, 1919–1939*. London, 1979.

———. "Bank Misr and the Emergence of the Local Bourgeoisie in Egypt." *Middle Eastern Studies*, 12 (1976), 69–86.

Delpuget, David. *Les Juifs d'Alexandre, de Jaffa, et de Jerusalem*. Bordeaux, 1866.

Douek, Ibrahim, ed. *La Voie Égyptienne vers le Socialisme*. Cairo, 1966.

Duchesne, Albert. "Héliopolis, Création d'Edouard Empain en Plein Désert: Une Page de la Présence Belge en Égypte." *Africa-Tervuen*, 22 (1976), 113–120.

Ducruet, Jean. *Les Capitaux Européens au Proche-Orient*. Paris, 1964.

Dudgean, Gerald C. "The Boll Worm in Egypt." *Transactions of the Third International Congress of Tropical Agriculture*, 1916.

Dumont, Georges H. *La Vie Quotidienne en Belgique sous le Règne de Léopold II, 1865-1909*. Paris, 1974.

Fahmy, Fawzi R. "Growth Pattern of Manufacturing Sector in Egypt, 1950–1970." United Arab Republic, Institute of National Planning, *Memo No. 386* (January 8, 1964).

Fargeon, Maurice. *Les Juifs en Égypte depuis les Origines jusqu'à Ce Jour*. Cairo, 1938.

Farhi, Elie C. *Egyptian Income Tax Legislation*. Alexandria, 1946.

Farnie, D. A. *East and West of Suez: The Suez Canal in History, 1854–1956*. Oxford, 1969.

Forte, Albert. *Les Banques en Égypte*. Paris, 1938.

Franco, M. *Essai sur l'Histoire des Israélites de l'Empire Ottoman depuis les Origines jusqu'à Nos Jours*. Paris, 1897.

Gallissot, Rene. "Le Socialisme dans le Domaine Arabe: Syrie, Liban, Irak, Palestine, Égypte, Maghreb." In Jacques Droz, ed., *Histoire Générale du Socialisme*, vol. 3, pp. 545–606. Paris, 1977.

Garbati, Romolo. *Nous et les Égyptiens*. Alexandria, 1925.

Gendziher, Irene L. *The Practical Visions of Ya'qub Sanu'* Cambridge, Mass., 1966.

Georges-Picot, Jacques. *The Real Suez Crisis: The End of a Great Nineteenth Century Work.* Translated by W. G. Rogers. New York, 1978.

Ghali, Ibrahim Amin. *L'Égypte Nationale et Libérale de Moustapha Kamel à Saad Zaghloul, 1892–1927.* The Hague, 1969.

Graetz, H. *History of the Jews,* vol. 5. Philadelphia, 1895.

Grafftey-Smith, Laurence. *Bright Levant.* London, 1970.

Gresh, Marie-Dominique. "Le P.C.F. et l'Égypte, 1950–1956." Maitrise Présentée, Université de Paris, I, 1976–1977.

Gritly, A.A.I. el-. "The Structure of Modern Industry in Egypt." *L'Égypte Contemporaine,* nos. 241–242. (November-December 1947) (entire issue).

Groupe d'Études de l'Islam, Le. *L'Égypte Indépendante.* Paris, 1938.

Guemard, Gabriel. *Le Régime Hypothécaire Égyptien.* Aix, 1914.

Haddad, Robert M. *Syrian Christians in Muslim Society: An Interpretation.* Princeton, 1970.

Hansen, Bent. "The Distributive Shares in Egyptian Agriculture, 1897–1961." *International Economic Review,* 9 (1968), 175–194.

———. "The Growth of National Income in the UAR (Egypt), 1939–1962." Institute of National Planning, *Memo No. 343* (June 17, 1963).

———. "Income and Consumption in Egypt, 1886/87 to 1937." *International Journal of Middle East Studies,* 10 (1979), 27–47.

———. "Marginal Productivity, Wage Theory, and Subsistence Wage Theory in Egyptian Agriculture." United Arab Republic, Institute of National Planning, *Memo No. 547* (March 1965).

———. "The National Outlay of the UAR (Egypt), 1937–39 and 1945–1962/63." United Arab Republic, Institute of National Planning, *Memo No. 377* (December 8, 1962).

———. "Preliminary Report on an Attempt to Estimate National Product and Income for Egypt, ca 1880–1912." Typescript, 1974.

———. "Savings and Investments, Flow of Funds: Egypt, 1884–1914." *Working Paper,* no. 135, Department of Economics, University of California at Berkeley (October 1979).

———. "Savings in the UAR (Egypt), 1938/39 and 1945/46–62/63." United Arab Republic, Institute of National Planning, *Memo No. 551* (March 1965).

Hansen, Bent, and Edward Lucas. "A New Set of Foreign Trade Indices for Egypt." Paper presented at the Annual meeting of the Middle East Studies Association, November 1976.

Hansen, Bent, and Girgis A. Marzouk. *Development and Economic Policy in the UAR (Egypt).* Amsterdam, 1965.

Hansen, Bent, and Donald Mead. "The National Income of the UAR (Egypt)." United Arab Republic, Institute of National Planning, *Memo No. 355* (July 21, 1963).

Hansen, Bent, and Karim Nashashibi. *Foreign Trade Regimes and Economic Development: Egypt.* New York, 1975.

Hansen, Bent, and Khairy Tourk. "The Profitability of the Suez Canal as a Private Enterprise, 1859–1956." Working Papers in Economics. Institute of International Studies, University of California at Berkeley, October 1976.

Hansen, Bent, and Michael Wattleworth. "Agricultural Output and Consumption of Basic Foods, 1886/87–1967/68." *International Journal of Middle East Studies,* 9 (1978), 449–469.

Harris, Christina Phelps. *Nationalism and Revolution in Egypt: The Role of the Muslim Brotherhood.* London, 1964.

Harschler, G. "Zionism in Egypt." In Raphael Patai, ed., *Encyclopedia of Zionism and Israel,* vol. 1, pp. 278–280. New York, 1971.

Hassan, Mostafa Fahmi. "The Role of the Government in the Economic Development of Egypt." Ph.D. dissertation, University of Wisconsin, 1957.

Heyworth-Dunne, J. *Religious and Political Trends in Modern Egypt.* Washington, 1950.

Hirschberg, H. A. "The Oriental Jewish Communities." In A. J. Arberry, ed., *Religion in the Middle East: Three Religions in Concord and Conflict,* vol. 1, pp. 119–226. Cambridge, 1969.

Holt, P. M., ed. *Political and Social Change in Modern Egypt: Historical Studies from the Ottoman Conquest to the United Arab Republic.* London, 1968.

Hourani, A. H. *Minorities in the Arab World.* New York, 1947.

Hourani, Albert. "The Syrians in Egypt in the Eighteenth and Nineteenth Centuries." In *Colloque Internatinal sur l'Histoire du Caire,* pp. 221–233. Cairo, 1969.

Husaini, Ishak Musa. *The Moslem Brethren.* Beirut, 1956.

Ibrahim, Abdel Kader. "The Labor Problem in Industrialization in Egypt." Ph.D. dissertation, Princeton University, 1957.

Imam, M. M. el-. "A Production Function for Egyptian Agriculture, 1913–1955." United Arab Republic, Institute of National Planning, *Memo No. 259* (December 31, 1962).

———. "Some Remarks on the Labour-Force in the Egyptian Region, UAR." United Arab Republic, Institute of National Planning, *Memo No. 68* (October 21, 1961).

International Institute of Agriculture. *World Cotton Production and Trade.* Rome, 1936.

Issa, Hossam M. *Capitalisme et Sociétés Anonymes en Égypte: Essai sur la Rapport entre Structure Sociale et Droit.* Paris, 1970.

Issawi, Charles. "Asymmetrical Development and Transport in Egypt, 1800–1914." In William R. Polk and Richard L. Chambers, eds., *Beginnings of Modernization in the Middle East: The Nineteenth Century,* pp. 383–400. Chicago, 1968.

———. *Egypt: An Economic and Social Analysis.* New York, 1947.

———. *Egypt at Mid-Century: An Economic Survey.* New York, 1954.

———. "Egypt since 1800: A Study in Lopsided Development." *Journal of Economic History,* 21 (1961), 1–25.

Istiphan, Isis. *Directory of Social Agencies in Cairo.* Cairo, 1956.

Jankowski, James. "Egyptian Responses to the Palestine Problem in the Inter-war Period." *International Journal of Middle East Studies,* 12 (1980), 1–38.

Jankowski, James P. *Egypt's Young Rebels: "Young Egypt," 1933–1952.* Stanford, Cal., 1975.

Kedourie, Elie. *The Chatham House Version and Other Middle Eastern Studies.* London, 1970.

———. *Arabic Political Memoirs and Other Studies.* London, 1974.

Keeley, Edmund. *Cavafy's Alexandria: A Study of a Myth in Progress.* Cambridge, Mass., 1976.

Khallaf, Hussein. "Financing Economic Development in Egypt." *Middle East Economic Papers* (1955), 27–46.

Kilpatrick, Hilary. *The Modern Egyptian Novel: A Study in Social Criticism.* London, 1974.

Kindleberger, Charles P. *The World in Depression, 1929–1939.* London, 1973.

Kirk, George. *The Middle East in the War.* New York, 1953.

———. *The Middle East, 1945–1950.* New York, 1954.

Kurgan-Van Hentenryk, G. *Léopold II et les Groupes Financiers Belges en Chine: La Politique Royale et Ses Prolongements, 1895–1914.* Brussels, 1972.

Lacouture, Jean, and Simone Lacouture. *Egypt in Transition.* New York, 1958.

Lambelin, Roger. *L'Égypte et l'Angelterre vers l'Indépendance.* Paris, 1922.

Landau, J. M. "Language Problems of the Jews in Egypt." *Orientalia Hispanica,* 1 (1970), 439–443.

Landau, Jacob M. *Parliaments and Parties in Egypt.* Tel Aviv, 1953.

———. *Jews in Nineteenth Century Egypt.* New York, 1969.

Landes, David S. *Bankers and Pashas: International Finance and Economic Imperialism in Egypt.* Cambridge, Mass., 1958.

Landshut, S. *Jewish Communities in the Muslim Countries of the Middle East: A Survey.* London, 1950.

Laqueur, Walter. *Communism and Nationalism in the Middle East.* New York, 1956.

Leven, N. *Cinquante Ans d'Histoire: L'Alliance Israélite Universelle, 1860–1910.* 2 vols. Paris, 1911, 1920.

Liddell, Robert. *Cavafy: A Critical Biography.* London, 1974.

Luthi, Jean-Jacques. *Introduction à la Littérature d'Expression Française en Égypte, 1798–1945.* Paris, 1974.

Mabro, Robert. "Industrial Growth, Agricultural Under-Employment, and the Lewis Model: The Egyptian Case, 1937–1965." *Journal of Development Studies,* 3 (1967), 322–351.

———. *The Egyptian Economy, 1952–1972.* Oxford, 1974.

Mabro, Robert, and Patrick O'Brien. "Structural Changes in the Egyptian Economy." In M. A. Cook, ed., *Studies in the Economic History of the Middle East from the Rise of Islam to the Present Day.* London, 1970.

Mabro, Robert, and Samir Radwan. *The Industrialization of Egypt, 1939–1973: Policy and Performance.* Oxford, 1976.

McCarthy, Justin A. "Nineteenth Century Egyptian Population." *Middle East Studies,* 12 (1976), 1–40.

Mahfouz, el Kosheri. *Socialisme et Pouvoir en Égypte.* Paris, 1972.

Mallakah, Ragaei W. el-. "The Effects of the Second World War on the Economic Development of Egypt." Ph.D. dissertation, Rutgers University, 1955.

Mansour, Fawzi. "Development of the Financial System in the UAR." Typescript.

Masriya, Yahudiya. *Les Juifs en Égypte.* N. p., n.d.

Mazuel, Jean, *Le Sucre et Égypte: Étude de Géographie Historique et Économique.* Cairo, 1937.

Mead, Donald C. *Growth and Structural Change in the Egyptian Economy.* Homewood, Ill., 1967.

Mitchell, Richard P. *The Society of the Muslim Brothers*. London, 1969.

Mohie-eldin, Mar Mohie-eldin Mohammad Amin. "Agricultural Investment and Employment in Egypt since 1935." Ph.D. dissertation, London School of Economics, 1966.

Moscatelli, Jean, ed. *Poètes en Égypte*. N. p., n.d.

Najjar, Said el-. *Industrialization and Income with Special Reference to Egypt*. Cairo, 1952.

Nassef, Abdel-Fattah. *The Egyptian Labor Force: Its Dimensions and Changing Structure, 1907–1960*. Philadelphia, 1970.

National Bank of Egypt, 1898–1948. Cairo, 1948.

O'Brien, Patrick. "The Long-Term Growth of Agricultural Productivity in Egypt, 1821–1962." In P. M. Holt, ed., *Political and Social Change in Modern Egypt*. London, 1968.

Owen, E.R.J. "The Cairo Building Industry and the Building Boom of 1897 to 1907." In *Coloque International sur l'Histoire du Caire*, pp. 337-350. Cairo, 1969.

———. *Cotton and the Egyptian Economy, 1820–1914*. Oxford, 1969.

———. "Lord Cromer and the Development of Egyptian Industry, 1883–1907." *Middle Eastern Studies*, 2 (1966), 282–301.

Owen, E.R.J., and Frank Dux. "A List of the Location of Records Belonging to the British Firms and to British Businessmen Active in the Middle East, 1800-1950." Typescript.

Paish, George. "Great Britain's Capital Investment in Individual Colonial and Foreign Countries." *Journal of the Royal Statistical Society*, 74 (1911), 167–200.

Parvin, Manoucher, and Louis Pullerman. "Population and Food Dynamics: A Caloric Measurement in Egypt." *International Journal of Middle East Studies*, 12 (1980), 81–100.

Payne, P. L. "The Emergence of the Large-Scale Company in Great Britain, 1870–1914." *Economic History Review*, 20 (1967). 519–542.

Peretz, Don. *Egyptian Jews Today*. New York, 1956.

Petropulos, John Anthony. *Politics and Statecraft in the Kingdom of Greece, 1833–1843*. Princeton, 1968.

Pinchin, Jane Lagoudis. *Alexandria Still: Forster, Durrell, and Cavafy*. Princeton, 1977.

Politis, Athanase G. *L'Hellénisme et l'Égypte Moderne*. 2 vols. Paris, 1929.

Radwan, Samir. *Capital Formation in Egyptian Industry and Agriculture, 1882–1967*. London, 1974.

———. "The Impact of Agrarian Reform on Rural Egypt, 1952–75." International Labour Office, World Employment Programme Research, *Working Papers*, 1977.

Raymond, André. *Artisans et Comerçants au Caire au XVIIIe Siècle*. Damascus, 1973.

Reid, Donald M. "Educational Career Choices of Egyptian Students." *International Journal of Middle East Studies*, 8 (1977), 349–378.

———. "Farah Antun: The Life and Times of a Syrian Christian Journalist in Egypt." Ph.D dissertation, Princeton University, 1968.

———. "The Rise of Professions and Professional Organizations in Modern Egypt." *Comparative Studies in Society and History*, 16 (1974), 24–57.

Riad, Hassan. *L'Égypte Nassérienne*. Paris, 1964.

Richards, Alan. "Accumulation, Distribution, and Technical Change in Egyptian Agriculture, 1800–1940." Ph.D. dissertation, University of Wisconsin, 1975.

———. "Agricultural Technology and Rural Social Classes in Egypt, 1920–1939." *Middle East Studies*, 16 (1980), 56–83.

———. *Egypt's Agricultural Development, 1800–1980: Technical and Social Change*. Boulder, Col., 1982.

———. "Land and Labor on Egyptian Cotton Farms, 1882–1940." Manuscript kindly lent by the author.

Rifaat, Mohammed Ali. *The Monetary System of Egypt: An Enquiry into Its History and Present Working*. London, 1935.

Rodinson, Maxime. *Islam et Capitalisme*. Paris, 1966.

Royal Institute of International Affairs, Information Department. *Great Britain and Egypt, 1914–1951*. London, 1952.

Saab, Gabriel S. *The Egyptian Agrarian Reform, 1952–1962*. New York, 1967.

Safran, Nadav. *Egypt in Search of Political Community: An Analysis of the Intellectual and Political Evolution of Egypt, 1804–1952*. Cambridge, Mass., 1961.

Sakkut, Hamdi. *The Egyptian Novel and Its Main Trends from 1913 to 1952*. Cairo, 1971.

Sammarco, Angelo. *Gli Italiani in Egitto*. Alexandria, 1937.

Sarki, Mohamed Youssel el-. *La Monoculture du Coton en Égypte et le Développement Économique*. Paris, 1964.

Sayyid-Marsot, Afaf Lutfi al-. *Egypt's Liberal Experiment: 1922–1936*. Los Angeles, 1977.

Schölch, Alexander. *Ägypten den Ägyptern, Die Politische und Gesellschaftliche Krise der Jähre 1878–1822 in Ägypten*. Freiburg, 1972.

Shaw, Stanford J. *History of the Ottoman Empire and Modern Turkey*, vol. 1, *Empire of the Gazis*. Cambridge, 1976.

Somekh, Sasson. *The Changing Rhythm: A Study of Najib Mahfuz's Novels*. Leiden, 1973.

Springbork, Robert. "Sayed Bey Marei and the Changing Nature of Political Clientelism in Egypt." Typescript lent by the author.

Stillman, Norman A. *The Jews of Arab Lands: A History and Source Book*. Philadelphia, 1979.

Sultan, Fouad. *La Monnaie Égyptienne*. Paris, 1914.

Tadros, Henry. "Recent Developments of Egypt's Balance of Payments." *Middle East Economic Paper*, 1957, pp. 111–145.

Taragon, Benison. *Les Communautés Israélites d'Alexandrie*. Alexandria, 1932.

Thobie, Jacques. *Intérêts et Impérialisme Français dans l'Empire Ottoman, 1894–1914*. Paris, 1977.

Tomiche, F. J. *Syndicalisme et Certains Aspects du Travail en République Arabe Unie (Égypte), 1900–1967*. Paris, 1974.

Tsakona, Taki. *Ena Taxidi Giro Sto Kairo*. Cairo, 1941.

Tsirka, Strati. *O Kavafis Ke H Epochi Tou*. Athens, 1958.

United Nations, Department of Economic and Social Affairs. *The Development of Manufacturing Industry in Egypt, Israel, and Turkey*. New York, 1958.

Vallet, Jean. *Contribution à l'Étude de la Condition des Ouvriers de la Grande Industrie au Caire*. Valencia, 1911.

Vatikiotis, P. J. *The Egyptian Army in Politics*. Bloomington, 1961.

———. *The Modern History of Egypt*. Baltimore, 1980.

Vincenot, Marcel. *Capitaux Étrangers en Égypte*. Alexandria, 1938.

Wakin, Edward. *A Lonely Minority: The Modern Story of Egypt's Copts*. New York, 1963.

Wavell, Viscount. *Allenby, Soldier and Statesman*. London, 1946.

Willis, H. Parker, and B. H. Beckhart, eds. *Foreign Banking Systems*. New York, 1929.

Wilmington, Martin W. *The Middle East Supply Center*. Albany, N.Y., 1971.

Wright, Arnold, ed. *Twentieth Century Impressions of Egypt: Its History, People, Commerce, Industries, and Resources*. London, 1909.

Yeghen, Foulad. *L'Égypte sous le Règne de Fouad I*. Cairo, 1929.

Zaghloul, Fathia. "A Cost of Living Index for Rural Laborers, 1913–1961." United Arab Republic, Institute of National Planning, *Memo No. 557* (April 1965).

Ziadeh, Farhat J. *Lawyers, the Rule of Law, and Liberalism in Modern Egypt.* Stanford, Cal., 1968.

Works in Hebrew (translated for me by Mrs. Vera Moreen, whose help I gratefully acknowledge)

Almaliyah, A. "Jews of Egypt and North Africa in 1945." *Hed Hamizrach*, September 14, 1945, p. 4.

Ben-Yisrael, Sh. "After the Riots in Egypt." *Hed Hamizrach*, November 16, 1945, p. 4.

Benah, Baroch. "On the Jews of Egypt." In *Mirah u-Ma'arav*, 1 (1919), 61–66.

"The Jews of Egypt and Their Emigration to Israel." *Iggeret le-Shelichum*, March 19, 1950, pp. 5–7.

Landau, Jacob. "On the Use of Languages in Jewish Education in Modern Egypt." *Annual of Bar-Ilan University*, pp. 220–229. Jerusalem, 1967.

Setton, David. *Kehelot Yehude Sefarad ve-ha-Mezrah ba-'Ulam ba-Yameno*, pp. 80–87. Jerusalem, 1974.

Works in Arabic

'Abd al-Fattah, Fathi. *al-Qarya al-Misriya: Dirasa fi-la-Milkiya wa 'Alaqat al-Intaj.* Cairo, 1973.

———. *al-Qarya al-Mu'asira bayn al-Islah wa-l-Thawra.* Cairo, 1974.

'Abd al-Karim, Ahmad 'Uzzat. *Thawra, 1919.* Cairo, 1969.

'Abduh, 'Ali Ibrahim. *Yahud al-Bilad al-'Arabiya.* Beirut, 1971.

'Abduh, Ibrahim, and 'Ali 'Abd al-'Azim, eds. *Tadhkar Muhammad Tal'at Harb.* Cairo, 1945.

Abu Kaf, Ahmad, and Ahmad Ghunaym. "al-Haya al-Yahudiya wa-l-Haraka al-Sahyuniya fi Misr." *al-Musawwar*, February 7, 14, and 21, 1969.

Amin, Mustafa. *al-Kitab al-Mamnu'.* 2 vols. Cairo, 197?.

'Amir, Ibrahim. *al-Ard wa-l-Fallah.* Cairo, 1958.

Anis, Muhammad. *Arba'a Fabrayir, 1942 fi Ta'rikh Misr al-Siyasi.* Beirut, 1972.

———. *Hariq al-Qahira.* Cairo, 1972.

———. *Dirasat fi Watha'iq Thawra 1919.* Cairo, 1963.

Anis, Muhammad. *Thawra 23 Yulyu 1952 wa-Usuluha al-Ta'rikhiya.* Cairo, 1969.

'Aqqad, 'Abbas Mahmud al-. "al-Marhum al-Ustadh Hayim Nahum." In *Majalla Majma' lilugha al-'Arabiya*, vol. 15, pp. 135–139. Cairo, 1963.

———. *Sa'd Zaghlul: Sura wa Tahiya.* Cairo, n.d.

Barakat, 'Ali. *al-Milkiya al-Zira'iya bayn Thawratayn.* Cairo, 1978.

———. *Tatawwur al-Milkiya al-Zira'iya fi Misr, 1813–1914.* Cairo, 1977.

Barrawi, Rashid al-. *Haqiqa al-Inqilab al-Akhir fi Misr.* Cairo, 1952.

———. *al-Tatawwur al-Iqtisadi fi Misr fi-l-'Asr al-Hadith.* Cairo, 1954.

Bishri, Tariq al-. "Dustur 1923, Sira' Hawla al-Sulta." *al-Tali'a*, 8 (1972), 49–59.

———. *al-Haraka al-Siyasiya fi Misr 1945–1952.* Cairo, 1972.

———. "Qanun al-Islah al-Zira'i bayn al-Thawra wa Kibar al-Mullak." *al-Tali'a*, 2 (1966), 70–83.

———. "Sa'd Zaghlul wa Fikruh al-Siyasi." *al-Tali'a*, 5 (1969), 38–61.

———. *Sa'd Zaghlul: Yufawid al-Isti'mar.* Cairo, 1977.

Din, Amin 'Izz al-. *Ta'rikh al-Tabaqa al-'Amila al-Misriya, 1919–1929.* Cairo, 1969.

———. *Ta'rikh al-Tabaqa al-'Amila al-Misriya mundh Nasha'tiha hatta Thawra 1919.* Cairo, 196?.

Disuqi, 'Asim Ahmad al-. *Misr fi-l-Harb al-'Alamiya al-Thaniya.* Cairo, 1976.

Disuqi, 'Asim al-. *Misr al-Mu'asira fi Dirasat al-Mu'arrikhin al-Misriyin.* Cairo, 1978.

———. *Kibar Mullak al-Aradi al-Zira'iya.* Cairo, 1975.

Ghurbal, Muhammad Shafiq. *Ta'rikh al-Mufawadat al-Misriya al-Britaniya.* Cairo, 1952.

Hafiz, 'Abbas. *Mustafa al-Nahhas aw al-Zu'ami' wa-l-Za'im.* Cairo, 1936.

Hamid, Ra'uf 'Abbas. *al-Haraka al-'Ummaliya fi Misr, 1899–1952.* Cairo, 1967.

———. "Hizb al-Fallah al-Ishtiraki, 1938–1952." *Majalla al-Ta'rikhiya al-Misriya*, 19 (1972), 169–214.

———. "Istiqrar al-Milkiya al-Fardiya lil-Ard al-Zira'iya." In al-Jam'iya al-Misriya lil-Dirasat al-Ta'rikhiya, *al-Ard wa-l-Fallah fi Misr 'Ali Marr al-Usur*, pp. 275–294. Cairo, 1974.

———. *al-Nizam al-Ijtima'i fi Misr fi Zill al-Milkiyat al-Zira'iya al-Kabira, 1837–1914.* Cairo, 1973.

Hittah, Ahmad Ahmad al-. *Ta'rikh Misr al-Iqtisadi fi-l-Qarn al-Tasi' 'Ashar.* Cairo, 1967.

Jam'iya al-Misriya lil-Dirasat al-Ta'rikhiya, al-. *al-Ard wa-l-fallah fi Misr 'Ali Marr al-Usur.* Cairo, 1974.

Jam'iya al-Misriya lil-Iqtisad al-Siyasi wa-l-Ihsa' wa-l-Tashri'. *Buhuth al-'Id al-Khamsini, 1909-1959.* Cairo, 1960.

Jiritli, 'Ali al-. *Khamsa wa 'Ishrun 'Am: Dirasa Tahliliya lil-siyasat al-Iqtisadiya fi Misr, 1952–1977.* Cairo, 1977.

———. "Tatawwur al-Nizam al-Masrifi fi Misr." In al-Jama'iya al-Misriya lil-Iqtisad al-Siyasi wa-l-Tashri', *Buhuth al-'Id al-Khamsini, 1909–1959*, pp. 197–302. Cairo, 1960.

Karam, Fu'ad. *al-Nizarat wa-l-Wizarat al-Misriya.* Cairo, 1969.

Khallaf, Husyn. *Tatawwur al-Iradat al-'Amma fi Misr al-Haditha.* Cairo, 1966.

Kilani, Muhammad Sayyid. *al-Sultan Husayn Kamil: Fatra Muzlima fi Ta'rikh Misr, 1914–1917.* Cairo, 1963.

Lashin, 'Abd al-Khaliq Muhammad. *Sa'd Zaghlul: Dawruh fi-l-Siyasa al-Misriya hatta Sana 1914.* Cairo, 1971.

———. *Sa'd Zaghlul: Dawruh fi-l-Siyasa al-Misriya min 1914 hatta 1927.* Cairo, 1977.

Luhaytah, Muhammad Fahmi. *Ta'rikh Fu'ad al-Awwal al-Iqtisadi.* Cairo, 1945.

Mahumd, Hafiz, Mustafa Kamil al-Falaki, and Mahmud Fathi 'Umar. *Tal'at Harb.* Cairo, 1936.

Makaryus, Shahin. *Ta'rikh al-Isra'iliyin.* Cairo, 1904.

"Mandur fi Turathna al-Qawmi." *al-Tali'a* 2 (1966), 130–152.

Mar'i, Sayyid. *Awraq Siyasiya.* 3 vols. Cairo, 1979.

———. "al-Islah al-Zira'i fi Misr." In al-Jam'iya al-Misriya lil-Dirasat al-Ta'rikhiya, *al-Ard wa-l-Fallah fi Misr 'ala Marr al-'Usur*, pp. 295–312. Cairo, 1974.

———. *al-Islah al-Zira'i wa Mushkila al-Sukkan fi-l-Qutr al-Misri.* Cairo, 196?.

Mujahid, Zaki Muhammad. *al-A'lam al-Sharqiya.* 4 vols. Cairo, n.d.

Murad, Mahmud. *Man Kana Yahkum Misr.* Cairo, 1975.

Mursi, Fu'ad. *al-Niqud wa-l-Bunuk fi-l-Bilad al-'Arabiya*, vol. 1, *Misr wa-l-Sudan.* Cairo, 1955.

———. *Qanun al-Daman al-Ijtima'i.* Cairo, 1952.

Mutawalli, 'Issa. *Nahdatuna al-Iqtisadiya.* Cairo, 195?.

Mutawalli, Mahmud. "Shakhsiyat Ra'smaliya fi-l-Ta'rikh al-Iqtisadi al-Misri." *al-Katib* 13 (1973), 26–43 and 60–97.

Mutawalli, Mahmud. "Thawra 23 Yulyu wa-l-Ra'smaliya al-Misriya hatta Sana 1961." *al-Katib*, 12 (1972), 13-24.

————. *al-Usul al-Ta'rikhiya lil-Ra'smaliya al-Misriya wa Tatawwuriha*. Cairo, 1974.

————. "Watha'iq Britaniya 'An al-Haraka al-Shuyu'iya fi Misr Athna'a al-Harb al-'Alamiya al-Thaniya." Paper prepared for seminar on contemporary history at 'Ain Shams University, May 1977.

Nahhas, Yusuf. *Dhikrayat: Sa'd, 'Abd al-'Aziz, Mahir, wa Rifaquh fi Thawra Sana 1919*. Cairo, 1952.

Nukhayli, Sulayman Muhammad al-. *al-Haraka al-'Ummaliya fi Misr*. Cairo, 1967.

————. *Ta'rikh al-Haraka al-'Ummaliya fi Misr*. Cairo, 1963.

Nussar, Siham 'Abd al-Raziq 'Ashri. "Sihafa al-Yahud al-'Arabiya fi Misr." Master's thesis, Cairo University, 1978.

Qurra'a, Saniya. *Nimr al-Siyasa al-Misriya*. Cairo, 1952.

Radwan, Fathi. *Tal'at Harb*. Cairo, 1970.

Rafi'i, 'Abd al-Rahman al-. *Fi A'qab al-Thawra al-Misriya*. 2 vols. Cairo, 1959.

————. *Niqabat al-Ta'awun al-Zira'iya*. Cairo, 1914.

————. *Thawra Sana 1919*. 2 vols. Cairo, 1956.

————. *Thawra 23 Yulya 1952*. Cairo, 1959.

Rahim, 'Abd al-Rahim 'Abd al-Rahman 'Abd al-. *al-Rif al-Misri fi-l-Qarn al-Thamin 'Ashar*. Cairo, 1974.

Ramadan, 'Abd al-'Azim. "al-Burjwaziya al-Misriya Qabla Thawra 23 Yulyu." *al-Katib*, 11 (1971), 91–102.

————. "al-Haraka al-Dayalaktikiya lil-Burjwaziya al-Misriya Qabla Thawra 23 Yulya." *al-Katib* 11 (1971), 80–98.

————. "Hizb al-Wafd bayn al-Yamin wa-l-Yasar." *al-Katib*, 13 (1973), 56–65.

————. "Maghib al-Ahzab al-Libraliya fi Misr." *al-Katib*, 11 (1971), 25–39.

————. "Nisf Qarn min Kifah al-Burjwaziya al-Misriya lil-Insha' Bank Misr." *al-Katib*, 11 (1971), 170–84.

————. *al-Sira' al-Ijtima'i wa-l-Siyasi fi Misr*. Cairo, 1975.

————. *Sira' al-Tabaqat fi Misr, 1937–1952*. Beirut, 1978.

————. *Tatawwur al-Haraka al-Wataniya fi Misr*. 2 vols. Beirut, 1974.

————. "al-Thawra wa-l-Islah al-Zira'i al-Awwal." *al-Katib*, 11 (1971), 20–35.

Rifa'i, 'Abd al-'Aziz. *Thawra Misriya*. Cairo, 1969.

Rizq, Yunan Labib. "Ashab al-Qumsan al-Mulawwana fi Misr, 1933–1937." *Majalla al-Ta'rikhiya al-Misriya*, 21 (1974), 195–252.

———. *al-Ahzab al-Misriya Qabla Thawra 1952*. Cairo, 1977.

Rushdi, Muhammad. *al-Tatawwur al-Iqtisadi fi Misr*. 2 vols. Cairo, 1972.

Sabri, Musa. *Qissa Malik wa Arba'a Wizarat*. Cairo, n.d.

Sabrut, 'Abd al-'Aziz al-. "Tal'at Harb wa Ra'smaliya al-Misriya." *al-Katib*, 13 (1972), 149–156.

Sa'id, Jamal al-Din Muhammad. *Iqtisadiyat Misr*. Cairo, 1951.

Sa'id, Jamal al-Din. *al-Tatawwur al-Iqtisadi fi Misr mundhu al-Kasad al-'Alami al-Kabir*. Cairo, 1955.

Sa'id, Rif'at al-. "'Adat al-Libraliya." *al-Tali'a*, 8 (1972), 36–47.

———. *al-Asas al-Ijtima'i lil-Thawra al-'Urabiya*. Cairo, 1966.

———. *Hasan al-Banna: Mata, Kayfa, wa-l-Madha*. Cairo, 1977.

———. *al-Sihafa al-Yasariya fi Misr, 1925–1948*. Beirut, 1974.

———. *Ta'rikh al-Munazzamat al-Yasariya al-Misriya, 1940–1950*. Cairo, 1976.

———. "Thawra 1919: al-Muqaddimat wa-l-Muwaqif al-Tabaqiya al-Mukhtalifa." *al-Tali'a*, 5 (1969), 16–37.

Salama, Jirjis. *Athar al-Ihtilal al-Britani fi-l-Ta'lim al-Qawmi fi Misr, 1882–1922*. Cairo, 1966.

Salih, Zaki, and al-Sayyid Hasan. *'Id Lamahat min Ta'rikh Wizara al-Tarbiya wa-l-Ta'lim*. Cairo, 1959.

Sami, Amin. *al-Ta'lim fi Misr*. 3 vols. in 1. Cairo, 1917.

Subhi, Muhammad Khalil. *Ta'rikh al-Haya al-Niyabiya fi Misr*. 6 vols. and supplement. Cairo, 1939.

Wahbi, 'Azzah. "Tajarib al-Dimuqratiya al-Libraliya fi Misr." Master's thesis, Cairo University, 1978.

Zakhkhura, Ilyas. *al-Suriyun fi Misr*. Cairo, 1927.

———. *Mira' al-'Asr fi Ta'rikh wa Rusum Akabir Rijal bi Misr*. Cairo, 1916.

Zaydan, Jurji. *Tarajim Mashahir al-Sharq fi-l-Qarn al-Tasi' 'Ashar*. 2 vols. Cairo, 1922.

INTERVIEWS

I conducted interviews with the following people. Wherever it was possible, I taped the interview; these tapes remain in my possession: Paul Aghion, Abdel Maqsud Ahmad, Muhammad Amin Ahmad, S. Akerib, Christian Ayoub, Ala al-Din Badrawi, Hosam

al-Din Badrawi, J. B. Bailey, Henry Michael Barker, Albert Bay-
occhi, Vera Bayocchi, John Brinton, Guido Castro, Argine Cho-
remi, Cesar Douek, Father Eid, Ibrahim Faraj, Ibrahim Ghali,
Mirrit Boutros Ghali, Solomon Green, Kamal Fahmi Hanna, Max
Harari, Mahmoud Hassan, Mona Abbud Husayn, Muhammad
Ali Husayn, Ali Islam, Ali Ismail, Mary Keeley, Ibrahim Khalifa,
Henry Krischewsky, Ahmad al-Lawzi, Joseph Mallez, Sayyid Mar'i,
Julia Melas, Leonie Menasche, Joseph Nahum, Andreas Nomikos,
Corinna Nomikos, Ladislas Pathy, Guido Riso-Levi, Charles Roger-
Marchart, Charles Rolo, Ahmad Sa'd Sa'd, Samir Sami, Victor
Sanua, Louis van Damme, Jacques Vincenot, Magda Wahba, al-
Sayyid Yassin, Hassan Youssef, H. M. el-Zeini, George Zezos, Ezra
Zilkha, Ion Zottos.

INDEX

Library of Congress Cataloging in Publication Data

Tignor, Robert L.
State, private enterprise, and economic change
in Egypt, 1918-1952.

(Princeton studies on the Near East)
Bibliography: p.   Includes index.
1. Egypt—Economic conditions—1918-
2. Egypt—Industries—Finance—History—20th century.
3. Investments—Egypt—History—20th century.
4. Middle classes—Egypt—History—20th century.
I. Title. II. Series.
HC830.T54   1984   338.962   83-43097
ISBN 0-691-05416-9

9 780691 612652